# HARDWARE
# SOFTWARE
# HEARTWARE:

## DIGITAL TWINNING FOR MORE SUSTAINABLE BUILT ENVIRONMENTS

This richly illustrated book examines the full potential of Digital Twins (DTs) as a means of creating more sustainable urban habitats. It reveals how, in this digitally-enabled age, DTs are increasingly being adopted by cities as a tool for urban governance, with the hope of increasing operational efficiencies and enhancing citizens' lives.

While the study and implementation of DTs has been critically explored as virtual, dynamic 3D replicas of physical entities across different disciplines and industries, this book establishes a strategy that recognises the need for the 'software' behind virtual DT platforms to not only represent the 'hardware' of our physical cities but also to reflect the 'heartware' of socio-economic and cultural practices. Knowledge gaps and challenges in existing DTs are identified and insights into rethinking their purpose are provided to propose a new DT paradigm for city-wide application. With multiple case studies illustrating the different concepts of DTs being applied in cities from Europe, North America, The Middle East, Asia and Oceania, the book highlights the reasons why and how DTs can play an integral role in the sustainability of our urban habitats.

Beautifully designed and illustrated in full colour throughout, this book combines academic theory with practical application and will be a useful reference for professionals, students, academics and policymakers, working in the fields of smart cities, sustainable urbanism, and the digitisation, digitalisation and digital transformation of the built environment industry.

# HARDWARE SOFTWARE HEARTWARE:

## DIGITAL TWINNING FOR MORE SUSTAINABLE BUILT ENVIRONMENTS

Jason Pomeroy

Routledge
Taylor & Francis Group

LONDON AND NEW YORK

Cover designed image: GarryKillian on Freepik

First published 2024
by Routledge
4 Park Square, Milton Park, Abingdon, Oxon OX14 4RN

and by Routledge
605 Third Avenue, New York, NY 10158

*Routledge is an imprint of the Taylor & Francis Group, an informa business*

*British Library Cataloguing-in-Publication Data*
A catalogue record for this book is available from the British Library

ISBN: 978-1-032-56939-0 (hbk)
ISBN: 978-1-032-56938-3 (pbk)
ISBN: 978-1-003-43776-5 (ebk)

DOI: 10.4324/9781003437765

Typeset in Catriel, Gotham, and Bebas Neue

Printed in Great Britain by Bell Bain Ltd, Glasgow

This book has been prepared from camera-ready copy provided by Pomeroy Academy

**POMEROY
ACADEMY**

For Yasmin and Ethan

# CONTENTS

# ABOUT THE AUTHOR

**Jason Pomeroy** is an award-winning architect, academic, author and TV presenter, regarded as one of the world's thought leaders in sustainable design. He is the Founder of interdisciplinary sustainable design and research firm Pomeroy Studio and sustainable education provider, Pomeroy Academy. His career has included critically-acclaimed green cities, buildings and landscapes: from the microscale of the first zero-carbon house in Asia, to the macroscale of Indonesia's 'Silicon Valley'. Pomeroy authored *Cities of Opportunities: connecting culture and innovation* (2020), *Pod Off-Grid: explorations into low energy waterborne communities* (2016), *The Skycourt and Skygarden: greening the urban habitat* (2014) and *Idea House: future tropical living today* (2011). He holds a professorship at the University of Nottingham and leads a sustainable urbanism module at the University of Cambridge. He continues to raise cultural awareness of cities through his TV series *Smart Cities 2.0, City Time Traveller, Futuropolis* and *City Redesign*. He gained Bachelor and Master degrees from the Canterbury School of Architecture and the University of Cambridge; and a PhD from the University of Westminster. He is a Fellow of the University of Cambridge Institute for Sustainability Leadership.

# ACKNOWLEDGEMENTS

To Martin Hypký and Štefan Holý: thank you for recognising how this book could potentially benefit policymakers, academics, captains of industry and citizens' lives beyond Slovakia. Your pursuit of digital transformation and the sharing of your journey will be an inspiration to others.

To all the cities featured in this book, and those individuals behind the digital twins that have helped shape positive outcomes in their respective cities: thank you for openly and generously sharing information with us. It was enlightening and humbling.

To Alexandra Bolton, the Centre for Digital Built Britain and the Cambridge Institute for Sustainability Leadership: thank you for laying the inspirational groundwork that was a critical platform from which to embark on this research journey.

To Amrita Chatterjee and Denise Lim: thank you both for your tireless dedication to the research that went above and beyond finding and researching case studies from around the world, to also helping with the development of the digital twin for Slovakia.

To Rosie Anderson, Matthew Shobbrook and the Routledge team: thank you all for your guidance and support. Despite having taken this journey before, your inputs were critical and your fresh pairs of eyes have enriched the end result.

To Mia Aveline: thank you for bringing your creative flair to the book and in being able to convey my thoughts into graphic representations with such apparent ease, and for never giving up until all options had been exhausted.

Last and by no means least, a very special thank you to Summer Ha. Simply put, this book could not have been written without your subject matter knowledge, research tenacity, ability to be a counterpoint in discussions and tireless work ethic that were constant sources of inspiration and empowerment.

# FOREWORD

*By: Štefan Holý, Deputy Prime Minister, Republic of Slovakia*

The fourth industrial revolution has fundamentally transformed our lives: our shift from the analogue world to the digital world has given life to new technologies and their revenues that, despite a nascent existence, far exceed the value of the previous industrial revolution. The digital transformation not only bridges the gap between the two worlds but, with time, will become common place in the way we live, work, play, and learn. But for such a positive transformation to take place, principles of good governance and social responsibility require the collaboration between regulatory authorities, captains of industry, civil society groups and academia. A new approach to the creation of legislation, which introduces clear and transparent procedures and is based on objective digital data known to every participant from the beginning, should ensure the elimination of wilful actions and the eradication of corrupt practices.

This process in itself necessitates an overhaul of the bureaucratic apparatus of yesteryear and instead engenders 'smart' practices that can foster greater open dialogue amongst all stakeholders. This should yield optimised decision-making and consequently more positive outcomes for both people and nation. With the shift from the analogue to the digital, we similarly have the potential to shift from the unpredictable and chaotic, to the predictable and organised. Bureaucracy (i.e., a system of governance in which decisions are taken by state officials as opposed to elected representatives) has the potential to take on a new 'democratised' complexion: the curation and maintenance of big data from multiple stakeholders, drawn from civil society, academia, industry and state, to create a digital ecosystem that can evaluate the fulfilment of conditions needed for specific decision taking in the public domain.

Herein lay the challenge. When I was elected as deputy prime minister of Slovakia for legislation and strategic planning back in 2020, the country had construction legislation that was first adopted in 1976. It had been amended more than forty times and followed the principles of a communist, centrally planned economy. Before my term, there had been 18 attempts to replace the legislation, but all of them failed: the bureaucratic adjustments did not include any significant change in the concept of the law that a modern society would either understand or appreciate. To affect change, I asked colleagues to convert the planning and building codes into diagrams depicting all the systems and processes. Once this task was accomplished, we were able to identify the conflicts, eliminate the duplicities in the old legal framework, and integrate many processes into a more resilient and sustainable systems map.

At the same time I invited ICT analysts and smart city specialists to work alongside our legislative teams to help identify the components of our legal and policy ecosystem that would be suitable for digitalization and to determine the appropriate digital environment. As the legislation had to introduce clear and transparent procedures based on objective (digital) data known to every stakeholder from the beginning, we came to the conclusion that a digital twin of the entire country, which would include the planning and building code procedures and, over time, incorporate other sources of digital data, could hopefully transcend departmental silos. This conceptual vision led to a series of exciting conversations with world-leading academic institutions, captains of industry, civil society groups and academia to help evaluate, shape and hone what we hope will be an inclusive digital (twin) platform.

The research and development cooperation with Prof. Jason Pomeroy and his eponymous academy has allowed us to fully understand not only the complexities of a digital transformation but also the benefits of a digital twin for the country. Initially sceptical stakeholders have become digital twin believers who finally understand the benefits of a digitally transformed ecosystem that will allow the testing and shaping of ideas and innovations in a safe (virtual) environment before they become (physical) reality. The results of this journey is a case study in this book and I am delighted to see how its contents will act as a prompt for thinking for policymakers and professionals alike.

# FOREWORD

*By: Alexandra Bolton, Founding Executive Director of the Centre for Digital Built Britain (CDBB)*

Decision-making has never been more important. The choices we make now will affect the future of humanity and of our planet for millennia. We know that earth is in peril from the triple planetary crisis and that we have very little time left to act. For the first time, the weight of what we have built exceeds the weight of everything living on our planet. The decisions that we make about our built environment are crucial. In 2021, a group of industry leaders came together to create *Our Vision for the Built Environment*, a vision of a built environment created and run with the explicit purpose of enabling people and nature to flourish together for generations.

We must make the right decisions, deliberately and purposefully, if we are to create that future for people and the planet. We need tools to help us make sense of this interconnected complexity, avoiding unintended consequences, to produce the outcomes that we want. The great challenges facing humanity are systems-level and require systems-based solutions. Cities and the wider built environment are complex and interconnected systems of systems, far beyond that which can be understood by a single human mind. We have to consider our economic infrastructure – transport, energy, water, communications, waste management; our social infrastructure – hospitals, schools, housing, recreational buildings; and the natural environment. We must also think about the services provided by the built environment, and, importantly, the people who live, work, and play within it.

Connected digital twins are powerful tools, allowing us to gain insights and make sure those all-important decisions are correct. They work across sectoral and organisational boundaries, breaking down silos, taking account of interdependencies, and giving insights into what must be done to produce the outcomes that we require. They look at what already exists, what is under construction, and what might be built, bringing together the existing and the novel to consider the whole. Yet technology alone is not enough. Any ecosystem of connected digital twins is a combination of the human and the technological. However, like all tools, it is not what we have but how we use it that will make the difference. A national digital twin should follow the blueprint of the Gemini Papers and be founded on the Gemini Principles. We need to keep people and nature at the forefront of our decisions. We must put in place appropriate ethics, privacy, skills and training, ways of working, and contracts to enable connected digital twins. We need to involve citizens, as well as governments and corporations, to ensure that a national digital twin works for all. And we must embed protection and stewardship of nature and the planet.

But we need more than that; we need the right people to come together to make this happen. Secretary-General of the United Nations, António Guterres, gave the stark message 'collaborate or perish'. We need visionary, boundary-spanning leadership to bring people and organisations together to collaborate on connecting digital twins at local, city, national, and global levels. We need this servant leadership to connect, coordinate, and convene, to rally the many individual leaders, experts, and projects. Collaboration is vital if we are to realise the potential of national digital twins and, further, of connecting them to produce a planetary digital twin.

This book envisages an ecosystem of connected digital twins that is people-led and technology-enabled; that puts people – 'heartware' – at the core of that ecosystem; that uses data for the public good. It challenges leaders from industry, academia, government, and society to work together to unlock the significant benefits of sharing data to make better decisions. It is inspiring to see Slovakia seek to seize the opportunity to use this socio-technology to produce better outcomes for its citizens. By joining the group of nations building on their digital foundations to develop national digital twins, the promise of a better quality of life for all can become reality. We have a one-time opportunity. We can use connected digital twins to help us make the correct decisions and tackle the immense challenges that we face. But only if we collaborate; only if we take a systems-led, nature-centric approach that puts people at its heart. We have the opportunity to use digital twins to do something truly amazing; to create a future in which people and nature flourish together for generations.

# INTRODUCTION

Skyscrapers Skyline City 2019 © Photo by Tumisu on Pixabay

# FROM ANALOGUE TO DIGITAL CITY

## THE REPRESENTATION OF THE CITY

The four Industrial Revolutions that reflect agricultural, industrial, technological and digital advances have each influenced the way in which we conceive and plan cities. Labour-intensive farming processes, and traditional hierarchical systems of landlords and tenant farmers, were soon replaced in the eighteenth century by manufacturing processes in the hands of prominent industrialists to give us the world's first Industrial Revolution. By the nineteenth century, electrification and streamlining methods of production would come to characterise a second Industrial Revolution. Subsequent technological advances, built upon business outputs heightened by computerised technology and automation, came to characterise a third revolution in the latter part of the twentieth century. Today, we are witnessing the shift from 'the analogue' to 'the digital' in a fourth Industrial Revolution that is characterised by big data and the integration of information across all sectors and systems (Schwab, 2017).

'Digital' has become a ubiquitous term in everyday life and is often used with the promise of enhancing the quality of our lives. Unlike its forebears, the digital revolution has taken place in a shockingly shorter period of time. Between 1990 and 2010, the internet saw the digital economy valued at more than US$3 trillion (Delices, 2010). The twenty-first-century digital phenomena has enabled networks of cities to go beyond their spatial confines to embrace technological ingenuity, digital innovation and global initiatives as a means of spurring local and global economic growth, whilst addressing the pressing challenges of climate change, transmigration and geo-political instability. Technological and digital innovations have ameliorated the boundaries of time zone and geographic location, increased the speed in which people can connect and have offered unprecedented social and economic benefits to cities and its citizens (Sassen, 2018).

The way cities are represented and understood has similarly evolved significantly. The Renaissance period established similarities between objects through analogies (for instance, a city to a set of houses, a house to a set of rooms) (Agrest, 1980; Foucault, 1970; Panofsky, 1939, 1955). By the seventeenth century, relationships were drawn between objects and their hidden meanings of terrestrial life. By the late eighteenth century, there was a departure from the prevailing theories to instead perceive the city as a social production towards a utopia (Agrest, 1980).

The technologies brought forth by the first Industrial Revolution and the fourth Industrial Revolution have been reshaping human experiences at an individual level (Sacasas, 2020, p. 4), and the way cities and urban infrastructure operate. As cities have become smarter, the advent of new technologies in the past century has influenced city planning and design, particularly in the representation of cities. This has manifested in the hand drawings of the (analogue) city to the programmable software products in the (digital) city. It has further enabled different entities in the cities to behave in intelligent, coordinated ways (Metropolis Magazine, 2006; Moore, 2015, p. 11).

Yet about half a century ago, hand drawings were still widely recognised as the dominant means for planning, designing and representing cities, buildings, and their infrastructure. It was a standard practice to work in plan layers. Each layer described a different functional element of a site (such as different land uses, circulation, and open space) at city, district, and neighbourhood scale. Arduous data collection was made on-site and only updated intermittently, with the drawings based on abstractions that were understood primarily by those within the built-environment professions (Moore, 2015, p. 12).

As a pioneering example of hand-drawn social cartography in the nineteenth century, Charles Booth's descriptive map of London poverty (Figure

I), published in 1889, aimed to rebut socialist allegations that 25% of London's population lived in poverty (Booth, 1889). With each street colour-coded to represent the income and social class of its inhabitants, Booth's poverty map enabled analysis of the socio-economic dynamics and spatial structure of areas frequently stigmatised as ghettos (Vaughan, 2007, p. 231).

Despite the long-standing history of the hand-drawn process, Computer-Aided Design (CAD) drafting has been adopted as a replacement for two-dimensional (2D) drawings since the 1980s, and for three-dimensional (3D) isometric drawings over the last two decades (Coates et al., 2010; Deniz, 2018). While drawn representations have changed, the nature of information exchange has remained the same. However, the rise of information technology and the advancement of computer software and hardware have propelled the adoption of Building Information Modelling (BIM). As a collaborative tool, BIM has been largely used to support the intelligent interrogation of design; enhance coordination of documentation; and improve the communication between professionals involved in the construction and operation process (Coates et al., 2010, p. 1037).

## TECHNOLOGY AS AN ENABLER TO CITY PLANNING

Standing at the intersection of our current urban challenges (for instance, waste management, pollution, congestion, crime, and climate change-related cataclysms) the adoption of technologies as enablers to solve such system-level issues has brought the planning of the city into a new dimension that calls for system-based solutions and strategies. This has manifested in combining 3D modelling with dynamic digital technology to create digital twins (DT) for cities (Figure II) (Deren, Wenbo, and Zhenfeng, 2021; World Economic Forum, 2022).

A DT (digital twin) refers to a virtual, dynamic, and 3D replica that represents the systems and processes of the physical entity (physical twin), in which both are interconnected through real-time data exchange (Centre for Digital Built Britain, 2022a; Singh et al., 2021). By integrating with other systems of the cities,

the DT allows for system-based thinking and forms a new concept upon which smart cities and their infrastructure can be built. Assisted with Geographic Information Systems (GIS), activities within cities can be mapped to provide spatial and temporal data to DTs for visualisation, analysis, and prescribing city functions (Moore, 2015, p. 12–13).

It has become evident that the application of DTs for urban governance and planning has acquired a central place in recent years as smart interventions and urban big data have grown rapidly in tandem (Charitonidou, 2022, p. 4). However, the application of urban scale DTs will only redefine most problems in cities as a matter of data collection, data assembly, and data analysis in a data-driven society (Moore, 2015, p. 12). While DT technologies have been critically explored in different disciplines, a 'product-focused', state-driven, 'top-down' approach has often been widely adopted (Stanford Engineering, 2020).

This book sets out to grasp a theoretical understanding of urban scale DTs from socio-technological perspectives that go beyond product-focused and technology-oriented practices, to identify the knowledge gaps in existing DTs. It is hoped that this will lay the foundation for urban scholars and industry professionals to shift from using DTs as siloed, automated policy formulation and implementation tools, to a more comprehensive, connected DT paradigm. Putting the resultant advanced theoretical understanding of DTs into practice, this book illustrates a new DT paradigm that could be deployed in existing and new cities, districts, and neighbourhoods (Figure III).

The new DT paradigm is designed to go beyond the mirroring of the 'physical world' in the digital realm, but one that is able to learn of the practices found within the 'social world' in order for meaningful adaptations to be made to the built environment that can enhance people's lives. Ultimately, the new DT paradigm endeavours to address and deliver social, spatial, environmental, technological, cultural, and economic benefits to transform the natural and built environment into one that is smarter, future-proofed, and more inclusive. Chapter One seeks to establish the broader context

**Figure I** Charles Booth's descriptive map of London poverty (Source: Photo by LSE Library and Charles Booth collection, LSE Library on Unsplash, 2020).

**Figure II** Digital Twin Cities (Source: Photo by tungnguyen0905 via Pixabay, 2021).

with regard to current DT technologies, building a comprehensive overview of DTs across a few selected disciplines. The review is in three parts:

1. DTs across different industries;
2. The different concepts of DTs; and
3. The key stakeholders involved in the co-creation of DT platforms.

This understanding of DTs is followed by the identification of gaps in existing DTs, as well as the challenges they face in a data-driven society. This seeks to provide insights into rethinking the implementation of existing urban scale DTs that are designed for urban governance and smart city development, which is discussed in Chapter Two.

Having established a conceptual understanding of DTs, Chapter Two introduces an analytical framework, which is used to ensure an objective assessment is made for a series of global DT case studies. The analytical framework seeks to create a more detailed and structured comparative analysis of eight urban-scale DT case studies from six regions: namely Europe, North America, the Middle East, Asia, and Oceania. While a product-focused, top-down approach has often been widely adopted by many existing urban-scale DTs, this chapter poses a series of prompts for onward thinking that calls for a new DT paradigm.

Developing a contextually relevant DT framework requires a thorough understanding of a particular nation, city, region, district, or neighbourhood's digitisation process. Chapter Three uses a European case study in the form of Slovakia to highlight the digital transformation process. The chapter covers the process of reviewing the open data portals of the eight Slovakia regions, understanding the types of datasets that have been collected and the data classification approach in each region. A 'six-pillar' framework (Pomeroy, 2020a, p. 2–3) is then introduced to develop a purpose-led DT for Slovakia. The 'six-pillar' framework does not only encapsulate the broad range of datasets available in the on-going digitisation process across the eight regions, but also addresses the knowledge gaps identified in other

existing urban scale DTs that are often lacking in the socio-cultural and economic data aspects.

Understanding the needs of a nation (especially where a DT strategy is required) is key to identifying opportunities and challenges for enabling the digital twin platform at a national level. Chapter Four demonstrates stakeholder engagement via a two-step process, primarily through a series of short lectures and round-table discussions, that provide a platform to facilitate dialogues amongst stakeholders from the 'four spheres of influence' (i.e., state, academia, industry, and civil society) in different domains (Pomeroy, 2020b, p.201–202). The whole process is guided by a purpose-driven approach (Craig and Snook, 2014) that translates sectoral and regional aspirations into a common purpose and purpose-to-impact plan, in ways that are essential to consolidate the appropriate data and enable the national DT.

Enabling a national DT underscores the need for a paradigm shift, guided by a common information management framework in response to the socio-technological changes required. Chapter Five discusses the ultimate goal of this framework, which is to align stakeholders from the 'four spheres of influence' who are wishing to be part of the digital twinning journey. Different levels of change and best practices principles, which seek to achieve the right level of data maturity and ensure data interoperability for the national DT, are also discussed in this chapter.

Chapter Six brings life to the DT by way of scenario-planning narratives and Proof of Concepts (PoCs) identified by Slovakia. An incremental layering of data, pertinent to different stakeholder needs, demonstrates the case of how scenarios involving corporations, state agencies, academia, and civil society groups can not only test the efficacy of the DT but also its user friendliness to multiple stakeholders, their respective desired task(s), and needs. This chapter concludes with a monitoring and evaluation plan, which includes systematic procedures to track the progress and quantify impacts of the national DT implementation in Slovakia; along with concluding thoughts as to the future of global DTs.

**INTRODUCTION**

**1** **CONTEXT**
- DIGITAL TWINS ACROSS DIFFERENT INDUSTRIES
- DEFINITIONS OF DIGITAL TWINS
- KEY STAKEHOLDERS INVOLVED IN THE CO-CREATION OF A DT PLATFORM
- KNOWLEDGE GAPS & CHALLENGES
- KEY CONSIDERATIONS

**2** **CASE STUDIES**
- ANALYTICAL FRAMEWORK
- CASE STUDIES
- SUMMARY OF COMPARATIVE ANALYSIS
- KEY CONSIDERATIONS

**3** **DIGITAL TRANSFORMATION**
- A NEW DIGITAL TWIN PARADIGM
- RESEARCH METHODOLOGY
- DATA CATEGORISATION ACROSS SIX PILLARS
- FOUR SPHERES OF INFLUENCE IN SLOVAKIA

**4** **ENABLING THE DIGITAL TWIN**
- EXECUTIVE SUMMARY
- PART ONE STAKEHOLDER ENGAGEMENT
- OBSERVATIONS & PROMPTS FOR THINKING
- PART TWO STAKEHOLDER ENGAGEMENT
- OBSERVATIONS & PROMPTS FOR THINKING

**5** **A NATIONAL PARADIGM SHIFT**
- EXECUTIVE SUMMARY
- THEORY OF CHANGE
- INFORMATION MANAGEMENT FRAMEWORK

**6** **IMPLEMENTING THE DIGITAL TWIN**
- EXECUTIVE SUMMARY
- PROOF OF CONCEPT (PoCs) & SCENARIO PLANNING
- MONITORING AND EVALUATION PLAN

**CONCLUSION**

**Figure III** Chapter outline: a visual guide to the contents of the book.

# CHAPTER 1.0
## CONTEXT

# DIGITAL TWINS ACROSS DIFFERENT INDUSTRIES

## LATERAL APPLICATIONS & CAPABILITIES OF DIGITAL TWINS

While the terminology of DT has arguably gained popularity in recent years, the technology itself actually has a more enduring history (Qi *et al.*, 2021, p. 4; Singh *et al.*, 2021, p. 2). Singh *et al.* (2022) identify 13 major industrial sectors where DTs have been extensively applied in the midst of the digital transformation. Aerospace and aeronautics, manufacturing, healthcare, and smart city planning have been selected for further discussion in this book, owing to their relevance in operational efficiency, benefits, and ethical considerations that can be drawn into urban governance.

### Aerospace and Aeronautics

Initial DT technology was rooted in the aerospace and aeronautics fields, where the National Aeronautics and Space Administration (NASA) designed and adapted a DT to match actual spacecraft conditions, employing it as a simulator to train astronauts and mission controllers (Allen, 2021). Continuously serving as high-fidelity models, the DT applications have been expanded to assist operation and maintenance: a DT replicates fleet history, produces vast amounts of data that mirrors its flying twin, and forecasts upcoming maintenance requirements based on an aircraft's maintenance history and previous experience (Phanden, Sharma and Dubey, 2021). In essence, the DT applications in the aerospace and aeronautics field primarily include:

1. Optimising spacecraft and aircraft performance and reliability;
2. Modelling and predicting failure scenarios for forensic analysis;
3. Resolving failure scenarios with forecast results or mitigating damage by activating self-healing mechanisms;
4. Making missions safer for the crews; and
5. Increasing mission success probability (Allen, 2021; Glaessgen and Stargel, 2012).

### Manufacturing

The manufacturing industry is known for its well-established DT technology (Singh *et al.*, 2022). Different DT approaches are applied while going through the four stages in the product's lifetime:

1. Creation (concept generation, product design and development, material selection, and raw material procurement);
2. Production (manufacturing, quality testing);
3. Operation (product delivery, sustainment, sales, utilisation, after-sales service); and
4. Recycling or disposal (Grieves and Vickers, 2017; Tao *et al.*, 2018).

At the creation phase, different product iterations and conflicts related to its form are explored and resolved virtually (Grieves and Vickers, 2017). A DT also improves product design by allowing designers to analyse data from past product versions (e.g. customer feedback), and optimise material selection based on cost, environmental impact, and physical properties (Singh *et al.*, 2022). During the manufacturing phase, a DT is applied for resource management, production planning and monitoring, quality testing, and process control (Tao *et al.*, 2018).

At the operation phase, a DT enables manufacturers to optimise logistics for efficient delivery using inventory, order, and geo-location data. It also enables monitoring of product status and user behaviour for better maintenance strategies. At the disposal stage, a novel DT-based system can be used for product remanufacturing with data to improve the next generation of the product (Wang and Wang, 2019; Singh et al., 2022). Through testing, monitoring, and data stored at all stages, a DT ensures a product's feasibility, safety, efficiency, and reliability (Rosen *et al.*, 2015; White *et al.*, 2021), thus leading to economic, environmental, and societal benefits.

## Healthcare

Healthcare is another sector that aptly demonstrates DT applications (Saracco, 2019), from hospital processes to human organs or virtual patients. For instance, the American multi-national conglomerate General Electric is developing DT command centres, using predictive simulations to improve hospital operations, operational strategy, and patient care delivery models, such as medical pathway planning optimisation (Ricci, Croatti, and Montagna, 2021); surgical block schedule optimisation; and design for new and existing facilities (GE Healthcare Partners, 2023).

Another salient application is the DTs individualised approach in medicine, where a DT of the human heart is employed for diagnostic purposes and to tailor cardiological treatment to individual patients in a more targeted way, improving the chances of success (Siemens Healthineer, 2019). Furthermore, DTs are widely applied to predict health issues and test solutions to avoid or mitigate health complications (Bhavnani and Sitapati, 2019). This is made possible given the rise of 'quantified-self' – a cultural phenomenon to self-track and collect lifestyle data with technology, in terms of physical activity, sleep quality, heart rate, diet, weight, productivity, social interaction, and working environment (White, Liang, and Clarke, 2019; White et al., 2021).

Bruynseels, Santoni de Sio, and Van den Hoven (2018) pinpoint the duality of DT in this particular application. On the one hand, it has the potential to deliver significant societal benefits by allowing effective equalising treatments or enhancements. On the other hand, it has the potential to drive inequality if there is unequal access to quantified-self and DTs, given economic pressures or punitive costs.

## Smart City, Urban Planning, & Construction

For smart city design and urban planning, DTs offer great potential when geographic and built contexts represent a city's ecosystem by bringing together different data and information models (Esri, 2021, p. 4). This allows for sensing, analysing, predicting, and making informed decisions corresponding to the different needs of the city and citizens. This is based on geo-locations and the best information available, leading to cities that are potentially more economically, socially, environmentally, and technologically sustainable (Centre for Digital Built Britain, 2022b). A DT of smart cities helps to create interventions that address the health of the natural systems. It takes environmental cost into account in order to inform circular and net zero interventions, and to manage and optimise resource supplies and consumptions (e.g. water, energy, oil, and gas).

From a holistic economic perspective, a DT is applied to evaluate trade-offs between resilience (e.g. disaster management; emergency response plans) (Fan et al., 2021; Ford and Wolf, 2020; Singh et al., 2022), efficiency (improved accessibility; exploration of building designs and construction materials) (National Research Foundation, 2021), and cost (Centre for Digital Built Britain, 2022b). It is estimated that 'every £1 invested in information management could potentially secure up to £6 of labour time savings while boosting government efforts to reach net zero carbon emissions by 2050' (Centre for Digital Built Britain, 2022b, p. 5). A DT can also be used to facilitate democratic processes by providing a common platform for stakeholders' participation and informing better planning and design decisions with a greater collective societal benefit (Centre for Digital Built Britain, 2022b; Fuldauer, 2019).

Melbourne city. 2021 © Photo by Jesse G-C on Unsplash

# KEY TAKEAWAYS

## AEROSPACE & AERONAUTICS

### ADVANTAGES

- Safer missions
- Maximises the mission success
- Cheaper spacecraft
- Lowers operational and maintenance costs

### APPLICATIONS

- Optimising performance and reliability of the spacecraft/aircraft
- Predicting and resolving maintenance issues
- Continuous mirroring of the actual flight to predict future scenarios
- Designing and testing of product
- Simulating and optimising product and production systems

## MANUFACTURING

### ADVANTAGES

- Better-designed products
- Faster and cheaper production
- Increases reliability of equipment and production lines
- Reduces downtime
- Improves decision support
- Lowers maintenance costs
- Reduces wastage

### APPLICATIONS

- Designing and testing of product
- Material selection
- Optimising production planning and control
- Predicting maintenance issues and developing a maintenance strategy
- Real-time monitoring of production and service
- Remote troubleshooting of equipment
- Analysing user behaviour
- Recovering the waste
- Validation tool for Hazard Risk Categories (HRC) safety standards
- Collaboration tool

## HEALTHCARE

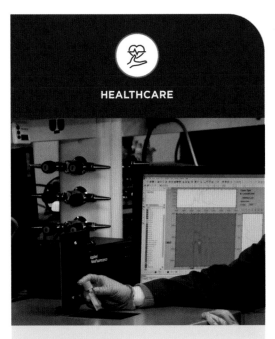

### ADVANTAGES

- Efficient patient care
- Improves success of the treatments
- Shorter waiting times
- Faster patient turnaround
- Better equipment utilisation
- Lowers staffing costs

### APPLICATIONS

- Optimising the care, cost, and performance of hospitals, operations, staff
- Enabling informed and strategic decision making
- Facilitating personalised cure and care
- Detecting and diagnosing disease

## SMART CITY, URBAN PLANNING, & CONSTRUCTION

### ADVANTAGES

- Improves accessibility of specific areas
- Promotes stakeholders' participation in decision making
- Improves city services
- Fosters sustainable development
- Reduces overall design process and associated cost

### APPLICATIONS

- Test-bed for new ideas
- Enabling decision-making process, including resource planning, feasibility of project and sustainability issues
- Real-time monitoring of construction progress, mobility and traffic, environment, and wellness of the city
- Problem-solving against real-life scenarios and planning emergency response for disaster management
- Analysing city's infrastructure and assessing any future risks
- Facilitating comments and suggestions by every stakeholder

# KEY TAKEAWAYS

## AEROSPACE & AERONAUTICS

## MANUFACTURING

Initial 'DT' technology was rooted in the aerospace and aeronautics fields, where the National Aeronautics and Space Administration (NASA) employed it as simulators to train astronauts and mission controllers.

### MAINTENANCE

- Replicating continuous fleet history and producing vast amounts of data corresponding to its flying twin
- Providing insights into what an aircraft has undergone to forecast upcoming maintenance requirements

### HIGH-FIDELITY MODEL

- Optimising spacecraft and aircraft performance and reliability
- Modelling and predicting failure scenarios for forensic analysis
- Resolving failure scenarios with forecasts of results; mitigating damage by activating self-healing mechanism
- Making the missions safer for the crews
- Increasing mission success probability

Different DT approaches are applied in manufacturing while going through the four stages in the product's lifetime.

### CREATION

Exploring product design iterations and resolving form-related conflicts virtually. Gleaning insights from product data record (e.g. customers' preferences and feedback). Optimising material selection based on cost, environmental impact, and physical properties.

### PRODUCTION

Resource management, production planning, and process control.

### OPERATION

Monitoring products status and user behaviour for better maintenance strategies.

### RECYCLING / DISPOSAL

Supporting and improving product re-manufacturing based on product data record.

## HEALTHCARE

DT applications in healthcare range from hospital processes to human organs or virtual patients.

### HOSPITAL PROCESSES

Developing DT command centres, using simulation and prediction to improve hospital operations and patient care: optimising medical pathway planning; maximising surgical block schedule; designing new and existing facilities.

### HUMAN ORGANS

Tailoring cardiological treatment to individual patients in a more targeted way, improving the chances of success.

### VIRTUAL PATIENTS

Predicting health issues and testing solutions to avoid or mitigate health complications, given the rise of quantified-self in terms of physical activity, sleep quality, heart rate, diet, weight, productivity, social interaction, and working environment.

## SMART CITY, URBAN PLANNING, & CONSTRUCTION

By representing a city's ecosystem with different data and information models, a DT allows for sensing, analysing, predicting, and making informed decisions according to citizens' needs based on geo-locations, leading to cities that are more sustainable in many ways.

### ENVIRONMENTAL

Managing and optimising resource supplies and consumptions to inform circular and net-zero interventions.

### ECONOMIC

Evaluating trade-offs between resilience, efficiency, and cost.

### TECHNOLOGICAL

Optimising data access to ensure decisions are made based on the best information available.

### SOCIAL

Facilitating more democratic processes by creating a common user-friendly platform for stakeholders' participation to inform better planning and design decisions.

# DEFINITIONS OF DIGITAL TWINS

## UNDERSTANDING THE (DIFFERENT) CONCEPTS OF DIGITAL TWINS

Whilst the nomenclature of DTs has changed over time, the basic concept of DTs has remained unchanged and invariably consists of three crucial parts: physical entity, virtual space, and the connections tying them through information flow (Deng, Zhang and Shen, 2021, p. 126; Grieves and Vickers, 2017, p. 93). Despite their similarities in these three parts, the nuances in the concepts of DTs are found across different disciplines owing to their objectives and implementation, coupled with the ongoing expansion of DT concepts in each discipline.

### Manufacturing

The DT concept was put forth by Professor Michael Grieves, and was interchangeably referred to as a 'conceptual ideal' or the 'mirrored spaces model' in his course on Product Life Cycle Management (PLM) at the University of Michigan in 2003 (Grieves and Vickers, 2017, p. 93). He subsequently referred to it as the information mirroring model in his seminal PLM book (Grieves, 2006). The term DT was only created by his co-author, John Vickers, as its concept was extensively expanded by Professor Grieves in 2011 (Grieves, 2011).

The term DT has since been used until today. As the physical product is tied to its virtual representation throughout the four stages of the product's life cycle, Grieves and Vickers (2017, p. 94) define the DT as 'a set of virtual information constructs that fully describes a potential or actual physical manufactured product from the micro atomic level to the macro geometrical level. At its optimum, any information that could be obtained from inspecting a physical manufactured product can be obtained from its DT'. To this end, the foundation of the DT concept has been laid with three fundamental components: a 'virtual model', a 'physical entity', and a description of the connections between the two.

### Aerospace & Aeronautics

As research on various aspects of DTs continues to advance, they are anticipated to perform as a digital platform that provides processed information and valuable insights rather than a description that simply describes the connections between the physical entity and virtual model. This leads to the importance of having an ultra-high fidelity DT model in the aeronautics and aerospace field to ensure mission success and safety, considering space launch itself is an expensive and challenging mission.

As the DT serves as a 'living model' or a virtual flying vehicle, it is expected to experience every event that its flying twin experiences, supported by continuous statistical and physical testing in every aspect of a mission (Allen, 2021; Glaessgen and Stargel, 2012). Given the mathematical and physical emphasis in this field, Glaessgen and Stargel (2012, p. 7) refer to the DT as 'an integrated multi-physics, multi-scale, probabilistic simulation of an as-built vehicle or system that uses the best available physical models, sensor updates, fleet history, to mirror the life of its corresponding flying twin'.

### Healthcare

Considering its diverse applications, the concepts of DT can be considerably varied within the healthcare sector. From the hospital processes perspective, a DT is conceptualised as a digitised hospital to provide a safe testing environment for optimising system performance, enabling objectivity in decision-making for operational strategy, capacities allocation, staffing, and care delivery models (GE Healthcare Partners, 2023). When applied to medical practices, a DT provides a 'conceptual framework for analysing data-driven healthcare practices and the conceptual and ethical implications for therapy, preventative care, and human enhancement' (Bruynseels, Santoni de Sio, and Van den Hoven, 2018, p. 1).

A DT is also defined as an advanced technology that constructs 'in silico representations of an individual that dynamically reflect molecular status, physiological status and lifestyle over time' (Bruynseels, Santoni de Sio, and Van den Hoven, 2018, p. 1).

## Smart City, Urban Planning & Construction

For smart citiy design, urban planning, and construction, the definitions of urban scale DTs available in literature reviews reveal that the DT is a virtual, dynamic, three-dimensional (3D) representation of the real world, including physical objects, processes and systems between social, economic, and digital infrastructure, as well as the natural environment (Centre for Digital Built Britain, 2022a, p. 3–4; Esri, 2021, p. 4; Mott Macdonald, 2023, p. 1).

It is also known as a 'collaborative data platform for virtual experimentation and test-bedding' (National Research Foundation, 2021), using 'technology and at the same time establishing bidirectional links with the physical world' (Stanford Engineering, 2020). By going through the information value chain, DTs can be far more efficient decision-making systems that lead to better outcomes for people, nature, and society (Centre for Digital Built Britain, 2022a). Figure 1.2 illustrates the information value chain as defined respectively by government-led initiative, industry, and research community. The Centre for Digital Built Britain (2022a, p. 7) also refers to a connected DT as a 'system of systems' approach to understand inherent complexities of the elements within the physical world. This approach allows for system-based thinking while addressing systemic vulnerabilities in cities.

**Figure 1.1** Bird's eye view of a city (Source: Photo by yeyalpha on Pixabay, 2020).

# KEY TAKEAWAYS

## AEROSPACE & AERONAUTICS

Initially born at NASA in the 1960s as a 'living model' of the Apollo mission, a DT was referred to as a 'simulator or high fidelity model to explore solutions and predict results' for its flying twin. It was developed to evaluate Apollo 13's oxygen tank explosion and the damages brought about to the main engine. By allowing a continuous ingestion of data, it modelled the episodes leading up to the incident for forensic analysis and identification of next steps (Allen, 2021).

Given the mathematical and physical emphasis in the aerospace and aeronautics field, and the realisation of the important role of an analytical model for information processing, a DT is defined as 'an integrated multi-physics, multi-scale, probabilistic simulation of an as-built vehicle or system that uses the best available physical models, sensor updates, fleet history, etc., to mirror the life of its corresponding flying twin' (Glaessgen and Stargel, 2012, p. 7).

## MANUFACTURING

The concept of a DT was interchangeably referred to as a 'conceptual ideal' or the 'mirrored spaces model' in the context of Product Life Cycle Management (PLM) in 2003; and subsequently as an 'information mirroring model' in 2006 (Grieves and Vickers, 2017; Grieves, 2006).

The term DT was officially introduced by John Vickers while its concept was extensively expanded by Professor Grieves in 2011 (Grieves, 2011).

The physical product is tied to its virtual representation throughout the four stages of the product's lifecycle – creation, production, operation, recycling / disposal. Hence, a DT is referred to as 'a set of virtual information constructs that fully describes a potential or actual physical manufactured product from the micro atomic level to the macro geometrical level. At its optimum, any information that could be obtained from inspecting a physical manufactured product can be obtained from its DT' (Grieves and Vickers, 2017, p. 94).

## HEALTHCARE

The concepts of DT can be considerably varied within the healthcare sector.

### HOSPITAL PROCESSES:
A DT is the digitisation of a hospital, serving 'as a safe environment to test changes in system performance', allowing decisions and actions to be made for operational strategy, capacities, staffing, and care-delivery models (GE Healthcare Partners, 2023).

### MEDICAL PRACTICES:
A DT provides a 'conceptual framework for analysing data-driven healthcare practices and the conceptual and ethical implications for therapy, preventative care and human enhancement' (Bruynseels, Santoni de Sio, and Van den Hoven, 2018, p. 1).

### VIRTUAL PATIENTS:
A DT constructs 'in silico representations of an individual that dynamically reflect molecular status, physiological status and lifestyle over time' (Bruynseels, Santoni de Sio, and Van den Hoven, 2018, p. 1).

## SMART CITY, URBAN PLANNING, & CONSTRUCTION

A DT is generally defined as a virtual, dynamic, three-dimensional representation of the real world – including physical objects and systems between social, economic, and digital infrastructure, as well as the natural environment (Centre for Digital Built Britain, 2022a; Esri, 2021; Mott Macdonald, 2023).

It is also known as a 'collaborative data platform for virtual experimentation and test-bedding', using 'technology and at the same time establishing bidirectional links with the physical world' (National Research Foundation, 2021; Stanford Engineering, 2020).

By going through the information value chain (Figure 1.2), a DT can be seen as a far more efficient decision-making system, using a 'system of systems' approach to understand inherent complexities of the elements within cities. This allows for system-based thinking while addressing systemic vulnerabilities in cities (Centre for Digital Built Britain, 2022a, p. 7).

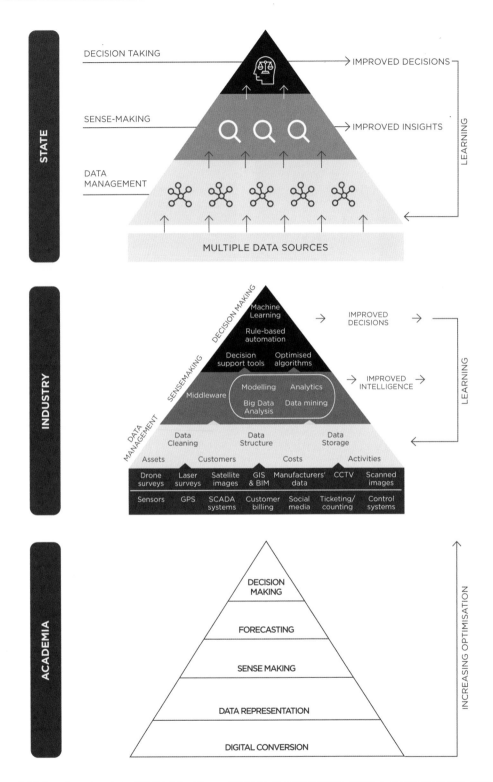

**Figure 1.2** Information value chain of Digital Twins (Source: Centre for Digital Built Britain, 2022a, p. 5; Mott Macdonald, 2023, p. 3; Pomeroy Academy, 2022)

# DEFINITIONS

| | | |
|---|---|---|
| **SMART CITY & URBAN PLANNING** | **CENTRE FOR DIGITAL BUILT BRITAIN (2022A)** | 'A digital twin is a digital representation of a physical asset, process or system. It is distinguished from any other digital model by its dynamic connection to the physical twin. A digital twin unlocks value by supporting improved decision making'. |
| | **MOTT MACDONALD (2023)** | 'Digital twins are realistic digital representations of physical things. They unlock value by enabling improved insights that support better decisions, leading to better outcomes in the physical world. What distinguishes a digital twin from any other digital model is its connection to the physical twin. Based on data from the physical asset or system, a digital twin unlocks value by supporting improved decision making, which creates the opportunity for positive feedback into the physical twin'. |
| | **ESRI (2021)** | 'Digital twins are virtual representations of the real world including physical objects, processes, relationships, and behaviours. A digital twin in a geographic context represents real-world assets or natural systems along with information models, data, reports, analyses, and behaviours in spatial context to the natural and built world. Digital twins may be used to represent the current, past, or even future state of assets. Digital twins mirror what exists in the real world today, but also can forecast what may exist in the future'. |
| | **NATIONAL RESEARCH FOUNDATION (2021)** | '"Virtual Singapore" is a dynamic three-dimensional (3D) city model and collaborative data platform, including the 3D maps of Singapore...It will enable users from different sectors to develop sophisticated tools and applications for test-bedding concepts and services, planning and decision-making, and research on technologies to solve emerging and complex challenges for Singapore'. |
| | **CHARITONIDOU (2022)** | '"Digital twin" is a term used to refer to the digital representation enabling comprehensive data exchange and can contain models, simulations and algorithms describing their counterpart and its features and behaviour in the real world'. |
| **CONSTRUCTION** | **STANFORD ENGINEERING (2020)** | 'A digital twin is a virtual representation of the world which enables us to use technology and at the same time establishes bidirectional links with the physical world'. |

**Table 1.1** Definition of DT in the field of smart city design, urban planning, and construction.

# KEY STAKEHOLDERS INVOLVED IN THE CO-CREATION OF A DIGITAL TWIN PLATFORM

An understanding of DT applications and concepts reveals the multi-scale, multi-functional, and interdependent complexities of the models that require strong integration and collaborations between government, academia, and industry (Centre for Digital Built Britain, 2022c). In the aerospace and aeronautics industry, the building of high-fidelity DTs involves inputs from aerospace systems researchers, engineers, and designers, as well as aerospace manufacturing contractors and maintainers in the whole gamut of modelling, visualisation, and infrastructure of DT models (Li *et al.*, 2021). Twinning in the manufacturing industry integrates different views of stakeholders, such as product manager, systems engineer, developer, and data scientist throughout the entire product life cycle (Rasor *et al.*, 2021, p. 229). In the healthcare sector, key stakeholders like clinicians, IT professionals, and data scientists are essential throughout the DT development process: co-evaluating model feasibility, clinical impacts, and data availability, as well as data governance concerns that arise (Lu, C. *et al.* 2020).

For smart cities across all stages of development, the multi-stakeholders collaboration model includes governments, Information and Communication Technology (ICT) service providers, transportation industries, utility suppliers, building developers, and city operators; and finally citizens at the post-project evaluation stage (Esri, 2021, p. 5; World Economic Forum, 2022, p. 25–26).

The existing DT process can, therefore, be evaluated as a co-creation process of a strategic partnership model that primarily involves:

1.  State and local government to regulate the twinning process and smart city development;
2.  Academia to research and develop state-of-the-art technologies and digital innovations; and
3.  Industry to champion and/or co-fund 'proof of concepts' while providing services to the cities (Pomeroy, 2020b, p. 201–202) (Figure 1.3).

This strategic partnership represents a series of expert inputs and discourses that span across organisational and sectoral boundaries, and eventually enact them in practice in the digital equivalents (Jasanoff, 2004; Solman *et al.*, 2022, p. 273). In other words, the twinning decisions collectively hold consequences for what objects and systems are included and excluded in the DT. This involves various experts and their expertise; and stakeholders' and their stakes (Henderson, 1991; Latour, 2004; Solman *et al.*, 2022). This in turn creates a greater collective societal benefit in the physical twin (Centre for Digital Built Britain, 2022b; Fuldauer, 2019).

Examining factors that contribute to successful stakeholder collaborations is crucial when considering the multitude of stakeholder involved in co-creating DTs. According to the Centre for Digital Built Britain (2022c, pp. 1–6), a successful strategic partnership is premised on the following:

1.  Right culture of strong leadership and collaboration across government, academia, and industry to deliver a DT for public good;
2.  Right values and ethics to deliver genuine public benefit in perpetuity;
3.  Right delivery vehicle to find alignments and foster stakeholder collaborations through a top-down and bottom-up approach; and
4.  Right resources developed in the open with community feedback to ensure they are useful and adoptable.

In summary, effective collaboration and integration among government, academia, and industry are essential in co-creating DTs, as they bring unique perspectives and expertise to the whole process. This leads to a more holistic approach that considers the system's entire life-cycle while developing sustainable, effective, and tailored solutions that ultimately benefits all stakeholders involved.

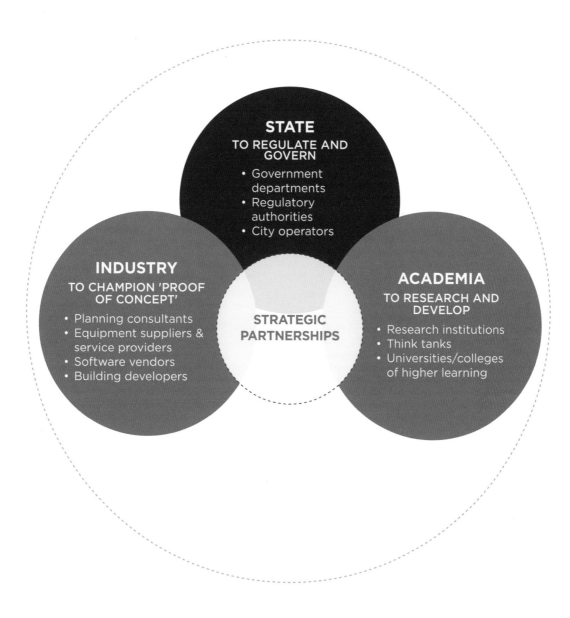

**STATE**
**TO REGULATE AND**
**GOVERN**
- Government
  departments
- Regulatory
  authorities
- City operators

**INDUSTRY**
**TO CHAMPION 'PROOF**
**OF CONCEPT'**
- Planning consultants
- Equipment suppliers &
  service providers
- Software vendors
- Building developers

**STRATEGIC**
**PARTNERSHIPS**

**ACADEMIA**
**TO RESEARCH AND**
**DEVELOP**
- Research institutions
- Think tanks
- Universities/colleges
  of higher learning

**Figure 1.3** Strategic partnership model of existing digital twins for urban governance (Source: adapted from Pomeroy, 2020b, p. 202).

# KNOWLEDGE GAPS & CHALLENGES IN EXISTING DIGITAL TWINS & A DATA-DRIVEN CITY

Stanford Engineering (2020) has identified two significant problems that are yet to be explicitly addressed by many implemented DTs:

1. There is a need for a sustained 'top-down' and bottom-up leadership to discuss and prioritise opportunities in order to realise DT benefits
2. The existing DTs have widely adopted a 'product-focused approach'

These two points are further unpacked in the following sections.

## SUSTAINED TOP-DOWN AND BOTTOM-UP LEADERSHIP

The Centre for Digital Built Britain (2022c, p. 2) stresses the significance for adopting a 'middle-out approach' that brings together state-led, top-down and community-led, bottom-up approaches in enabling an ecosystem of connected DTs. While the former seeks to ensure strong governance to achieve comprehensive master plans, the latter allows industry practitioners and academia from relevant fields to identify knowledge gaps and potentially find 'proof-of concepts' in solving real-life issues that are pertinent to cities.

The author (2020b, p. 201–202) goes further to highlight an additional 'sphere of influence' – civil society, alongside state, academia, and industry – that can form better strategic partnerships and reflect the needs of citizens (Figure 1.4). This places a greater emphasis on perceiving civil society as an equally important stakeholder. Their equitable contributions offer additional socio-cultural insights into the eventual product (in this case, the DT), which are currently missing in most existing DTs. Such a strategic partnership with a 'middle-out' approach seeks to ensure a level of sustainability essential for long-term city development and urban governance (Centre for Digital Built Britain, 2022c; Stanford Engineering, 2020; Wataya and Shaw, 2019).

The inherent benefits of a middle-out approach that engages 'four spheres of influence' may seem apparent to certain scholars. However, the intangible knowledge and values that could be brought particularly by community-led, bottom-up approaches are challenged by pressures to tangibly demonstrate its potential of creating spill-over positive outcomes (Wataya and Shaw, 2019, p. 107). Despite existing efforts in enhancing citizens' participation in the decision-making processes of urban planning strategies, questions are raised regarding what extent the application of a DT can contribute to achieving such an objective. This may be due to two reasons:

3. The creation of urban scale DTs is based on a limited set of variables and processes
4. The ways in which they abstract sets of variables and processes neglect the social-cultural aspects of urban contexts (Charitonidou, 2022, p. 12)

The effectiveness of DT applications for efficient and sustainable urban solutions can only be achieved if the essential roles and contributions of each sphere of influence – state, academia, industry, and civil society – are acknowledged as equally important throughout the DT development process. Despite the challenges in acknowledging civil society as an equally significant stakeholder, additional effort is required to devise different measurement methods to quantify their contributions. When this is mapped with contextual information (e.g. tracking civil society's input aggregated at the local level), it enables a more effective DT for urban governance and management, as well as identification of community capital and community mobilisation. Furthermore, more action is needed to operationalise the additional socio-cultural perspectives that can contribute to a DT model and thus shape a more sustainable built environment that ultimately benefits everyone.

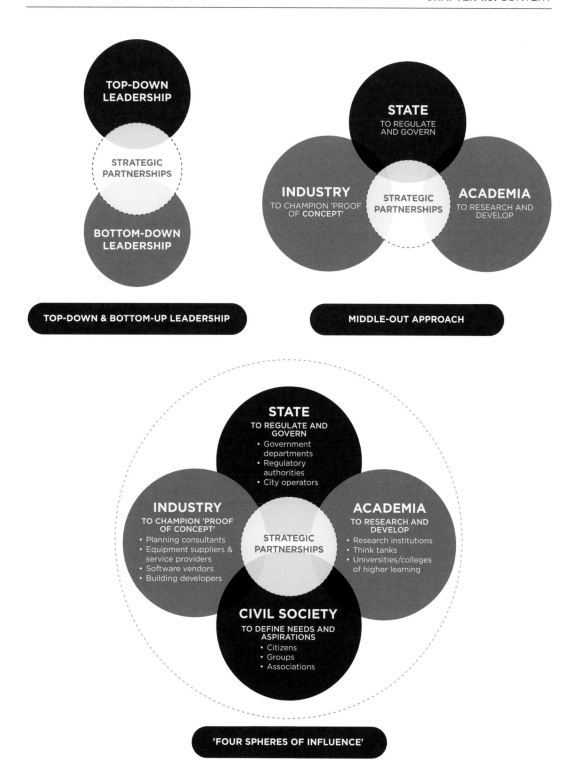

**Figure 1.4** (Top left) A sustained top-down and bottom-up leadership; (top right) state-led, top-down and community-led, middle-out approach; (bottom) the 'four spheres of influence'.

## PRODUCT-FOCUSED APPROACH

The growing availability of big data, coupled with emerging knowledge in urban data science and analytics, has inevitably encouraged cities to undergo unprecedented transformative changes. This has involved the rise of urban scale DTs as a means for urban governance and management. Charitonidou (2022, p. 4–5) highlights the potential of urban-scale DTs that mainly come from their capacity to collect and analyse massive quantums of urban data to monitor activities and simulate different scenarios for any interventions introduced to the city: leading to more efficient and sustainable design solutions.

Smart cities, which rely on large amounts of urban data, are celebrated for their ability to tackle complex urban issues. However, there are concerns about the way in which (urban) big data is collected, analysed, and translated to make informed decisions. As remarked by Loukissas (2019, p. 16), 'aspiring to the ideology of big data means seeking to collect everything on a subject, downplaying the importance of data's origins, and assuming that data alone can entirely supplant other ways of knowing'. Therefore, it is worth noting that all data is local and attached to the built environment and social-cultural context that creates them.

Charitonidou (2022, p. 5) continues to highlight that the trends of building a data-driven city has led to smart approaches that are 'largely ignorant of people and what relates to them'. This results in the product-focused approach found in many urban scale DTs. Regarding the entities that relate to people, Batty (2018, p. 819) highlights that 'one of the quests in city modelling is to merge social and economic processes with the built environment and to link functional and physical processes to socio-economic representations'. Likewise, Wataya and Shaw (2019, p. 107) highlight the necessity to not only look at improving the efficiency of tangible (hard) infrastructure and basic services, but also to adopt a people-centric approach to deliver the less visible or intangible (soft) benefits that ensure the welfare and well-being of the people (Figure 1.5).

To move away from a product-focused approach and adopt a more people-centric approach, the afore-mentioned highlights the necessity to further unpack the entangled relationships between people, what relates to them, and the context in which they live in to create the massive quanta of urban data.

Human interactions play a vital role in defining the 'social world' in which people engage – they allow like-minded individuals to create groups and communities bound by ethics, social contracts, laws, and the codes of civil society. These social interactions, which also reflect our traditions and cultural practices, then have the ability to shape places, buildings, and infrastructure which form the 'physical world' (Figure 1.6). In this digitally-enabled age, digital technologies have since been adopted to model the physical world and create what we can refer to as the 'digital world'. This results in the emergence of the DT, serving as a predictive tool to enhance performance of the built and natural environments, but is often devoid of connection to our social-cultural practices. As remarked by Charitonidou (2022, p. 5), the data-driven approach in urban governance, and the informed decision-making process of using a DT, often neglects the importance of the soft assets – 'social interactions, social norms, culture, history, democracy, politics, human rights, ethics and essential non-material qualities, laws and regulations' – that are essential in supporting city functions.

In today's digital age, the potential for DT technology, as manifested in the digital world to enhance the performance of the physical world, is immense. For the digital world to be a useful and accurate representative model of the physical world, it would seem essential for the DT to learn of the practices, as well as the soft assets, found within the social world. Ultimately, the success of the digital world, enabled by urban big data on DT models in improving the physical world, highly relies on their ability to learn from, and meaningfully adapt to, the practices and behaviours of the people who inhabit it.

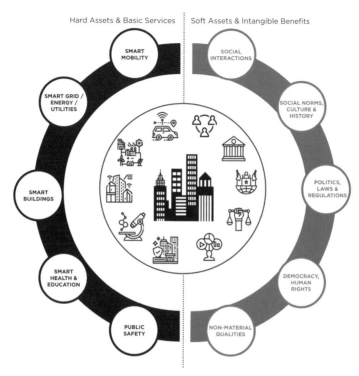

**Figure 1.5** Hard and soft assets that support city functions.

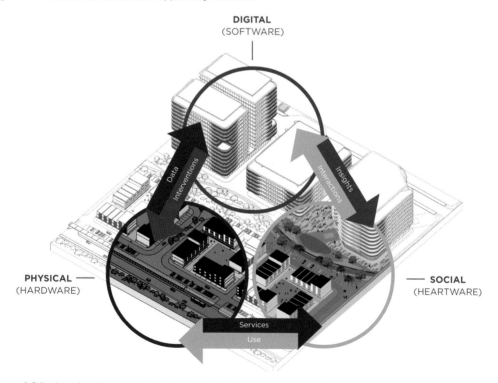

**Figure 1.6** Socio-cultural practices are needed to effectively integrate social, digital, and physical spheres.

## REDEFINING SUSTAINABILITY THROUGH SIX PILLARS

Whilst the definition of sustainability and sustainable development can find its roots in many texts that range from Carl von Carlowitz's forest management tome *Silvicultura* (1713) to Rachel Carson's impassioned plea against the use of pesticides in *A Silent Spring* (1962), the academic Andrew Basiago suggests its emergence in the text *A Blueprint for Survival* (1972), a decade later (Basiago, 1995). The date of publication coincided with the United Nations Conference on the Human Environment, held in Stockholm, following which the UN established the United Nations Environment Programme (UNEP) as the world's principal international environmental organization (United Nations, 1972). At the time, scientific data also emerged that demonstrated chlorofluorocarbons (CFCs) were depleting the ozone layer, which later led to the ban of CFCs with the Montreal Protocol in 1987 (United Nations, n.d.).

The debilitating effects of pesticides on the environment, CFCs on the ozone layer, the nuclear contamination of Chernobyl, and the subsequent scientific evidence that the continued emission of greenhouse gases exacerbate global warming, and cause long-lasting changes in all components of the climate system (Intergovernmental Panel on Climate Change, n.d.), are just a few examples of the environmental cataclysms that shaped various summits, conferences, and subsequent discourse on sustainability.

However, the catalyst for change may have taken place in 1992 with the United Nations Framework Convention on Climate Change, in Rio de Janeiro. The Earth Summit became the largest ever gathering of Heads of State, with an agreement signed by 154 states. Since then, governments have collectively signed accords in combating climate change. In 2015 the Paris Agreement was adopted for climate protection after 2020, which set a target for limiting warming to 1.5–2 degrees above pre-industrial levels by monitoring the emissions produced by various industries (Pomeroy, 2016).

Such protocols and global commitments over time have reaffirmed the need for a combined response to the global environmental problem. They have in turn become enshrined in environmental laws and policies and continued the discourse around the definition of sustainability and sustainable development: a term first coined in 1987. The World Commission on Environment and Development sought to address concerns regarding the accelerating deterioration of the human environment and natural resources as well as the consequences of that deterioration for economic and social development (Brundtland, 1987), and published its findings in *Our Common Future*. It is from this report that sustainable development was first defined as 'meet[ing] the needs of the present without compromising the ability of future generations to meet their own needs' (Brundtland, 1987, p. 41). It is also where we start to understand the 'environment' as the place 'where we all live; and "development"...[being] what we all do in attempting to improve our lot within that abode' (Brundtland, 1987, p. 7).

The notion of 'environment' and 'development' being inseparable, and their outcomes being predicated upon socio-economic actions across local and global, rural and industrial, developing and developed nations, has yielded a variety of other definitions. These have mostly expanded on the presence of social, economic, and environmental pillars: either weighted towards environmental preservation or a greater socio-economic agenda. The results often highlight the multi-faceted and sometimes conflicting nature of the term sustainability and its multiple interpretations held by different groups, sectors, disciplines, and governments (Johnston *et al.*, 2007).

According to Purvis, Mao, and Robinson, 2019 (p. 681), there has been 'no single point of origin of this three-pillar conception, but rather a gradual emergence from various critiques in the early academic literature of the economic status quo from both social and ecological perspectives on the one hand, and the quest to reconcile economic growth as a solution to social and ecological problems on the part of the United Nations on the other'.

Despite the multiple interpretations of what constitutes sustainability it has been commonly argued that a balance between the needs of man and nature, through the careful trade-off between social, economic, and environmental parameters of equal weighting, is required if a development is to be truly sustainable (Mawhinney, 2002). This in itself has yielded a plethora of sustainability rating tools that seek to deliver more sustainable developments through the consideration of a balance of indicators across social, economic, and environmental pillars.

This has inevitably led to complexities in defining the term in the wake of further principles or pillars. Consequentially, some scholars have argued that we are no closer to a singular definition of sustainability and that the irreversible rates of human-induced biodiversity loss, increase in per-capita resource consumption, and global climate change should resist the call to define the term and instead consider resilience thinking (Benson and Craig, 2014). Others have argued that there is a need to go back to the original tenets of the Brundtland report: 'where sustainability is concerned with the well-being of future generations and in particular with irreplaceable natural resources—as opposed to the gratification of present needs which we call well-being' (Kuhlman and Farrington, 2010, p. 3436).

There is also the view that additional pillars are necessary for a more nuanced definition of sustainability that addresses contemporary issues of the early twenty-first century. Loach, Rowley, and Griffiths (2017) highlight the cultural role museums and libraries play in preserving a communities' heritage and argue for more explicit coverage of cultural sustainability for their survival. The academic Hillier (2009, p. 1) posited a spatial sustainability of cities as they are often regarded as a 'system of systems': a 'foreground network of linked centres at all scales set into a background network of mainly residential space, is already a reflection of the relations between environmental, economic and socio-cultural forces, that is between the three domains of sustainability.'

Probably more contentious is the consideration given to a technological sustainability, especially as technology may be perceived as a tool to achieving social, economic, environmental, spatial, or cultural objectives. Yet it has formed part of the critical debate of weak and strong sustainability: whereby 'weak sustainability postulates the full substitutability of natural capital, whereas the strong conception demonstrates that this substitutability should be seriously limited due to the existence of critical elements that natural capital provides for human existence and well-being' (Pelenc, Ballet, and Dedeurwaerdere, 2015, p. 1). A weak sustainability may propagate technological innovations that may seek to reduce waste and pollution and yet come at the expense of further environmental degradation.

If previous environmental cataclysms were the catalyst for transformative change in both legislation and sustainable systems thinking, it would seem logical to assume that the present era's cataclysms will similarly shape sustainability discourse, rating tools and policy. With an estimated three quarters of the world's population living in inner city centres by 2050 and a continued trend toward urban migration, there will be an inextricable spatial strain on our urban spatial infrastructure. The need to transmigrate as a result of climate change, territorial conflict, socio-political unrest, or economic circumstance will also lead to more heterogeneous environments and necessitate greater cultural understanding and acceptance. In the wake of the COVID-19 pandemic and the Industrial Revolution 4.0, we have witnessed an unprecedented embrace of technology to enhance the way we can live, work, play, and learn.

In *Cities of Opportunities*, the author (2020a, p. 2–3) argues that in a trans-migratory, post-pandemic, digitised age, the need to look both critically and holistically at the concept of sustainable development necessitates looking beyond social, economic, and environmental factors to also consider space, culture, and technology as equally important pillars. These 'six pillars' (Figure 1.7), similarly encapsulate both hard and soft infrastructure assets; and are inextricably linked to the design and implementation of more smart and sustainable cities in the future. They can form the basis upon which more holistic sustainable DTs can potentially be made.

The concept of social sustainability covers a diverse range of societal issues that broadly calls for greater equality amongst mankind. This lends itself to fostering greater liveability prospects for all, regardless of gender, race, age, sexual orientation, and better health and well-being, community engagement, and increasing social capital. The legislative mechanisms of ensuring social support, human rights, labour rights, social responsibility, and social justice similarly depend upon the relationship between people and the environment in which they occupy; and in these terms, social sustainability encompasses all human activities and should be read in conjunction with spatial sustainability.

Beyond the notion of a city's spatial network being a reflection of the relationship between social, economic, and environmental forces, space is a commodity in need of preservation, yet continues to be re-distributed, privatised, and depleted as a consequence of urbanisation and population increase. It can be problematic to have a discourse about society and the way people interact without also discussing the space in which they occupy – be that virtually or physically. Spatial sustainability as a counterpoint to social sustainability would seem inseparable in our discourse if there is continued physical migration to urban centres and / or the greater use of virtual space for mankind's social interaction.

The concept of an environmental sustainability considers the needs of the planet as an equally important dimension to the needs of its people. Healthy ecosystems provide vital goods and services to humans and other organisms and this necessitates the reduction of the negative impact of humans on our ecosystem. There is the need to preserve and manage our environment for present and future generations largely based on environmental science and conservation biology. There is also the need for a cultural step change in the way mankind consumes via conventional linear practices, necessitating new 'circular' ways of thinking that treats waste as a systems 'flaw'.

Society's continued and increasing use of technology depends not just on the inherent characteristics of a particular technology but also on the way it is perceived, used, or its ability to transform the context. An appropriate technological sustainability that acknowledges the existence of an energy-efficient, environmentally-sound, people-centred approach can permit more community-focused activity to work in symbiosis with citywide technological interventions. In addressing the weak and strong sustainability debate, a technological sustainability should ensure that environmental technologies, when used sparingly, can seek to reduce waste and pollution from our man-made systems whilst optimising our approach to preserving nature's ecological systems.

Cultural identity is increasingly challenged by globalisation. Whilst technology has helped bring people together and promoted the cross-fertilisation of cultures, innovations, and ideas, it has also arguably contributed to a transcendence of modernisation and commercialisation that need not relate to people, place, or culture. Spaces, which may have once been imprinted by cultural practices and time-tested rituals, are also being compromised through the process of urbanisation, which potentially undermines the cultural identity of a place. If globalisation means globalising modernity, and modernity represents the harbinger of identity, the cultural sustainability discourse may be strengthened in its ability to form a localised counterpoint to globalisation.

The concept of economic sustainability refers to the economic well-being and quality of life of a nation, region, local community, or an individual, which is improved according to targeted goals and objectives that do not compromise the needs of the people or the planet. This translates to greater fiscal conscientiousness and a more acute understanding of societal value as opposed to societal cost. It can therefore be seen that an economic sustainability can correlate to the health and well-being of a nation or a business, and necessitates a fiscal prudence to remain in power, or in business. It has become increasingly important to ensure that economic development through public demand and government mandate does not compromise environmental conservation.

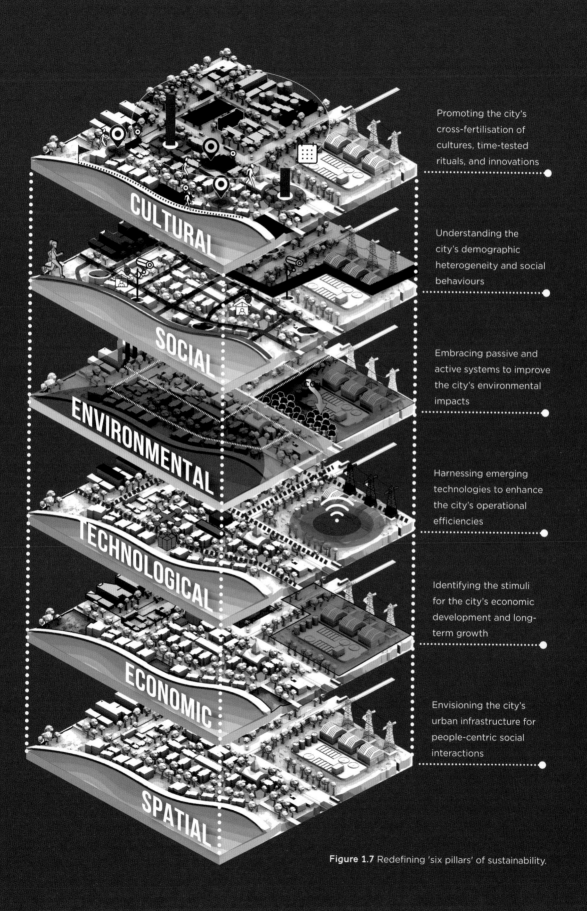

CULTURAL

Promoting the city's cross-fertilisation of cultures, time-tested rituals, and innovations

SOCIAL

Understanding the city's demographic heterogeneity and social behaviours

ENVIRONMENTAL

Embracing passive and active systems to improve the city's environmental impacts

TECHNOLOGICAL

Harnessing emerging technologies to enhance the city's operational efficiencies

ECONOMIC

Identifying the stimuli for the city's economic development and long-term growth

SPATIAL

Envisioning the city's urban infrastructure for people-centric social interactions

**Figure 1.7** Redefining 'six pillars' of sustainability.

# KEY CONSIDERATIONS

This chapter has sought to provide an overview of DTs – from their different applications, to how the usage of DTs can lead to varying concepts and definitions of DT technology across different industries. Recognising its origin and benefits in the aerospace and aeronautics field, DT technology has been adopted to revolutionise other industries in the midst of digital transformation in the past few decades, and it is envisaged to continue to flourish in the coming years (Singh *et al.*, 2021).

The review in this chapter has demonstrated the value brought forth by DTs in different industries – ensuring safer missions and maximising mission success; safeguarding products' feasibility, safety, efficiency, and reliability; improving hospital processes and patient-care efficiency; predicting health issues and testing individualised medical treatments; and, last but not least, creating cities that are potentially more economically, socially, environmentally, and technologically sustainable.

Nonetheless, in consideration of urban governance and planning perspectives, the product-focused and piecemeal solutions offered by potentially siloed decision-making tools have yet to solve the problems involved in the tangible and intangible complexities of cities. It is, therefore, critical to contemplate the lessons that can be drawn from DTs in different disciplines, identifying their commonalities and knowledge gaps in order to rethink the implementation of urban scale DTs, which will be discussed in Chapter Two.

Within this scope, this chapter reaffirmed that the product-focused approach in many existing DTs (digital world) is 'ignorant of people and what relates to them' (Charitonidou, 2022, p. 5), particularly the socio-cultural practices that shape the social world and take place in the physical world of cities. Additionally, this chapter substantiated the advocacy of a quadripartite relationship between civil society, state, industry, and academia in the co-creation of DTs (Pomeroy, 2020b, p. 201–202), which appears to be critically important in ensuring inclusive and sustainable urban governance and planning processes.

The review in this chapter also reasserted the importance of collating, filtering, and categorising both tangible hard infrastructure and intangible soft assets, potentially across 'social, economic, environmental, spatial, cultural, and technological pillars' on DT platforms for a more holistic and integrated mapping approach, when adopting smart urban governance and planning (Charitonidou, 2022; Pomeroy, 2020a; Wataya and Shaw, 2019). The above-mentioned justifies the need to shift from a 'product-focused' to a 'people-centric', 'middle-out' approach to measure both tangible and intangible assets when developing a DT for smart city urban governance and development (Centre for Digital Built Britain, 2022c, p. 2; Stanford Engineering, 2020).

In this regard, it is anticipated that the DT can be more than just a spatial-digital representation of the physical world. The DT can imbue a greater richness of data that can capture economic, technological, environmental, social, and cultural idiosyncrasies to enable a greater understanding of both people and place for a broader range of stakeholders to reap its benefits. In order to consider such potential, we will review a series of DT case studies for various cities in the next chapter, which will enable us to test this hypothesis using the 'six-pillar' framework and with due consideration given to the stakeholders engaged in the DTs creation and onward participation.

# CHAPTER 2.0
## CASE STUDIES

Toronto Financial District, 2017 © Photo by Davi Rezende on Unsplash

# ANALYTICAL FRAMEWORK & CASE STUDY COMPARISON OF URBAN SCALE DIGITAL TWINS

To break from the prevailing DT applications that have widely adopted a 'product-focused', top-down approach, it was necessary to consider whether this phenomenon was similarly found in urban-scale DTs. This necessitated a review of urban scale DTs in which the evaluation criteria consisted of two components for consideration:

1. The presence of strategic partnerships between the 'four spheres of influence' within the DT; and
2. The presence and cross comparison of both hard infrastructure and soft infrastructure assets within the DT.

In the evaluation of the first component, an analytical framework (Figure 2.1) was developed by adapting the information value chain pyramid (Figure 1.2) (Centre for Digital Built Britain, 2022a; Mott Macdonald, 2023) and the strategic partnership model of the 'four spheres of influence' (Figure 1.4).

To evaluate the second component, the different data layers gleaned from the eight identified case studies were categorised into the 'six-pillars' (Figure 1.7) (Pomeroy, 2020a, p. 2–3). These are intrinsically linked parameters that similarly represent the complexities of urban systems and whose sub-criteria may or may not be represented in the DT models considered in the study.

In response to the knowledge gaps and challenges identified in Chapter One, this comparative analysis provided a more detailed and structured understanding of the extent of civil society, state, academic, and corporate involvement and influence in the planning and implementation process, as well as the comparative data gaps in the systems represented by the urban scale DTs. It also sought to verify the urban scale DT as a 'purpose-led technology' instead of a 'technology-led change' (Centre for Digital Built Britain, 2022a).

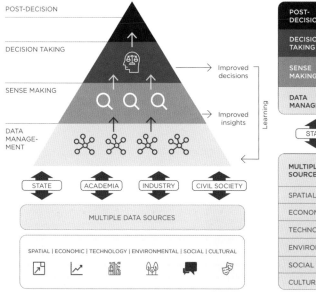

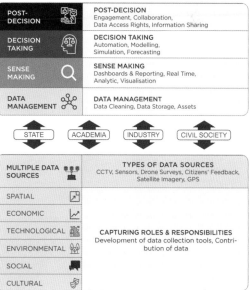

**Figure 2.1** Analytical framework to facilitate comparative analysis of case studies.

## GLOBAL CASE STUDIES

After evaluating the collective practices of existing urban scale DTs, case studies were selected from Asia, Europe, North America, Oceania, and the Middle East (Figure 2.2), and analysed using the analytical framework.

**DIGITAL TWIN SMART CITY**
DUBLIN, IRELAND

A digital twin to transform city planning and community engagement

**DIGITAL 3D MODEL OF BOSTON**
MASSACHUSETTS, USA

A 3D model of the city for analysing shadows and evaluating the impact of new zoning and development

**GREENTWINS**
TALLINN, ESTONIA

A digital twin to connect built environment, green infrastructure, and people

**TASMU PLATFORM**
Qatar

A smart platform to drive sustainable digital economic diversification while improving the quality of life and enhancing the delivery of public services

**Figure 2.2** Case studies of urban scale digital twins by region.

## DIGITAL TWIN CITY
### XIONG'AN NEW AREA, CHINA

A digital twin city with deep learning capabilities for synchronised planning and construction of the city

## PLATEAU
### JAPAN

3D city models for activity monitoring, disaster management, and smart planning

## VIRTUAL SINGAPORE
### SINGAPORE

A dynamic 3D city model and collaborative data platform for virtual experimentation, virtual test-bedding, planning and decision-making, and research and development

## DIGITAL TWIN OF DARWIN
### NORTHERN TERRITORY, AUSTRALIA

A digital twin of Darwin to monitor city operations and investigate the impacts of changes in urban planning

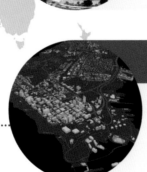

# CASE STUDY 1
## VIRTUAL SINGAPORE, SINGAPORE

**Figure 2.3 (Left)**
Representational image of Virtual Singapore (Source: Google Earth, 2016).

**Figure 2.4 (Overleaf)**
Jurong East Station, Singapore (Source: Photo by Shawnanggg on Unsplash, 2020).

## CASE OVERVIEW

'Virtual Singapore' (VSg) is a collaboration between the National Research Foundation (NRF), Prime Minister's Office, Singapore, the Singapore Land Authority (SLA), the Government Technology Agency of Singapore (GovTech), and the French company Dassault Systèmes, with the intention to enhance the following:

1. Virtual experimentation to test new ideas;
2. Virtual test-bedding to validate services provision;
3. Analytical tool for planning and decision-making; and
4. Research and development avenues for new technologies and capabilities (National Research Foundation, 2021).

## SCENARIOS

VSg adopts a multi-source, multi-modal data collection approach, including data from government agencies, 3D models, information from the Internet, and real-time dynamic data from Internet of Things (IoT) devices. By collecting multi-source, multi-model city data, e.g. demographics, movement, climate, VSg renders a number of potential uses in tackling liveability issues in Singapore, manifested in three main use cases on the platform:

1. Spatial and urban planning through semantic 3D modelling, visualisation, and simulation of the effects of new interventions;
2. Enhancing green energy efforts through advanced analysis to identify suitable locations for solar panel installations; and
3. Examining routes to improve accessibility.

### Semantic 3D Modelling and Visualisation for Planning & Building Design

Special attention has been paid to the semantic 3D modelling and visualisation in VSg (Figure 2.5), which enables the simulation of the effects of new interventions. It provides insights into how ambient temperature and sunlight vary throughout the day in response to a particular intervention. Additionally, a semi-automated planning process is made possible with an in-built filtering feature, allowing planners to efficiently filter buildings of interest according to specific parameters. For instance, when exploring residential blocks suitable for solar panel installation, VSg allows planners to quickly specify desired criteria, such as height of building, amount of sunlight received, roof type, orientation, and number of storeys, to name a few.

### Analysis on Potential for Solar Energy Production

To enhance efforts in green energy and achieve more efficient energy consumption, VSg allows the identification of suitable buildings for solar panel installation by recognising buildings that have higher potential for solar energy production. The platform also supports further analysis to simulate cost and energy savings, as well as the amount of energy produced on typical, cloudy, or rainy days (Figure 2.6) (National Research Foundation, 2021). Potential simulation platforms, such as tree modelling with biological, spatial, and semantic representations (Gobeawan *et al.*, 2018), and urban canopy modelling (UCM) for assessment of micro-climate condition (Ignatius *et al.*, 2019), have also been proposed by government-led initiatives and the research community, which have yet to be integrated into VSg.

### Improved Accessibility

The representation of the physical landscape and terrain attributes (e.g. water bodies, vegetation) on VSg allows for a more detailed analysis and visualisation that shows curbs, stairs, and steepness of a slope while assessing accessibility. Coupled with pedestrian movement data, VSg allows planners to perform socio-spatial analysis by identifying the most accessible and convenient routes while planning for inter- and intra-neighbourhood connectivity (National Research Foundation, 2021). For instance, by specifying two point locations (points A and B), the platform can perform estimation of travel distance and time for both pedestrians and wheelchair users. This enables planners to assess and improve equity in accessibility.

## CASE SUMMARY

VSg allows the government to explore impacts of interventions as well as to develop evidence-based solutions according to the needs of the city. There is the intention to show citizens future physical upgrades to their estates and a forthcoming plan where they can voice their feedback to the relevant agencies at the post-decision stage. However, the platform has yet to be made publicly available, and citizens appear not to be fully represented on the platform. This implies a government-driven DT that limits the participation of the other spheres of influence, particularly at the planning phase. The assessments of the effects of new interventions mainly focuses on the variation of temperature and sunlight, yet there is the potential to consider the adverse effects on human thermal comfort levels in the future.

As Singapore is envisioned as a 'City in Nature' (National Park Board, 2022), the urgency to integrate tree modelling and urban greenery as an equally important planning and design parameter (Gobeawan *et al.*, 2018) into VSg becomes increasingly apparent. Known as a global business hub, it would also seem essential to expedite the upcoming plan to enable the development of a global industry network on VSg, allowing for real-time geo-positioning of assets and processes of global operating business (Dassault Systèmes, 2015). While it seems efficient in establishing urban planning solutions, it would seem important for VSg to represent the interactions between the hard infrastructure and soft assets, such as social interactions and cultural practices.

**Figure 2.5** Screenshot shows the semantic 3D modelling and visualisation in VSg (Source: National Research Foundation, 2016 [2:27]).

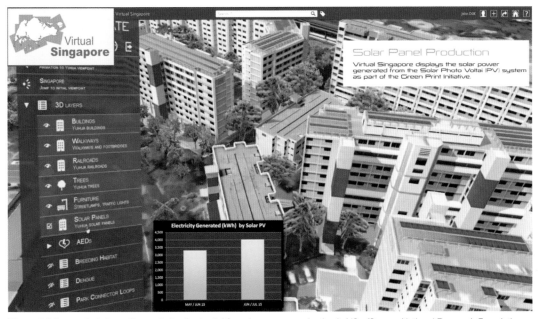

**Figure 2.6** Screenshot shows the analysis of potential for solar energy production in VSg (Source: National Research Foundation, 2016 [3:59]).

# CASE STUDY 1
## VIRTUAL SINGAPORE, SINGAPORE

| | STATE | ACADEMIA |
|---|---|---|
| **POST-DECISION** Engagement, Collaboration, Data Access Rights, Information Sharing | N.A. | N.A. |
| **DECISION TAKING** Automation, Modelling, Simulation, Forecasting | • Visualising effects of proposed new buildings or installations, creating more comfortable and cool living environments for citizens<br>• Identifying residential buildings with higher potential for solar energy production and solar panels installation<br>• Identifying the most accessible and convenient routes | • Tree modelling (UPCOMING)<br>• Urban canopy modelling (UPCOMING) |
| **SENSE MAKING** Dashboards & Reporting, Real Time, Analytic, Visualisation | • Overlaying heat and noise maps<br>• Understanding variation in ambient temperature, sunlight, rooftops surface, and heights of buildings<br>• Visualising terrain attributes and accurate representation of physical landscape | • Creating new innovations (UPCOMING)<br>• Developing sophisticated tools for multi-party collaboration, complex analysis, and test-bedding (UPCOMING) |
| **DATA MANAGEMENT** Data Cleaning, Data Storage, Assets | • Championing the development of VSg<br>• Operating and owning VSg<br>• Providing expertise and management of ICT | N.A. |

 STATE  ACADEMIA

| | STATE | ACADEMIA |
|---|---|---|
| **MULTIPLE DATA SOURCES** | • Aerial photography; airborne LiDAR; vehicle-mounted laser scans; geo-spatial and non-geospatial platforms; BIM; CIM; ICT<br>• Mobile LiDAR scanning (MLS) data; satellite imagery; airborne imagery (UPCOMING) | • Airborne LiDAR scanning (ALS); mobile LiDAR scanning (MLS) data; satellite imagery; airborne imagery; IFC-BIM<br>• Urban canopy model (UCM) (UPCOMING) |
| SPATIAL | • 3D topographical mapping data; 2D data and information; BIM; CIM<br>• Tree data (UPCOMING) | • Tree data (UPCOMING) |
| ECONOMIC | N.A. | N.A. |
| TECHNOLOGICAL | • ICT | N.A. |
| ENVIRONMENTAL | • Climate data | • Urban Heat Island (UHI) data; urban micro-climatic data (UPCOMING) |
| SOCIAL | N.A. | N.A. |
| CULTURAL | N.A. | N.A. |

**Table 2.1** Analytical Framework of Case Study 1, Virtual Singapore, Singapore.

N.A.

- Visualising upgrades to housing estates (UPCOMING)
- Providing timely feedback to the relevant agencies (UPCOMING)

- Planning and managing resources (UPCOMING)
- Specialising services & new business models (UPCOMING)

N.A.

- Performing business analytic (UPCOMING)

N.A.

- Developing VSg

N.A.

INDUSTRY

CIVIL SOCIETY

- Aerial photography; airborne LiDAR; vehicle-mounted laser scans

- Citizen data (demographic, movement)
- Citizen data (feedback) (UPCOMING)

| | |
|---|---|
| • 3D topographical mapping data | N.A. |
| • Global industry networks (UPCOMING) | N.A. |
| • IoT | N.A. |
| N.A. | N.A. |
| N.A. | • Demographic data; movement data<br>• Feedback (UPCOMING) |
| N.A. | N.A. |

# CASE STUDY 2
## DIGITAL TWIN OF THE DOCKLANDS AREA IN DUBLIN, IRELAND

**Figure 2.7 (Left)**
Digital Twin Smart City of the Docklands
area, Dublin, Ireland (Source: White *et al.*,
2021. p. 103069).

**Figure 2.8 (Overleaf)**
The Docklands area, Dublin, Ireland
(Source: Google Maps, 2022).

## CASE OVERVIEW

Dublin's Docklands 'DT smart city' is part of the 'Smart Dublin' project, aiming to transform city planning and community engagement using 3D modelling and digital representation of six layers of information in the city (Figure 2.9):

1. Terrain;
2. Buildings;
3. Infrastructure;
4. Mobility;
5. Digital layer / smart city; and
6. Virtual layer / DT

The data layers enable four types of DT simulations. (Smart Dublin, 2020; White *et al.*, 2021).

## SCENARIOS

### Skyline Simulation

The skyline simulation allows the addition and removal of newly proposed buildings to be made conveniently on the DT using BIM files, which is made available online for public access. This enables users (including citizens and public officials), to run simulations and evaluate the impacts of proposed interventions in the city, as well as on the city skyline. Besides, the interplay between the BIM files and sunlight information on the DT enables the simulation of sunlight access in nearby parks or public spaces. With its citizen-centric approach, citizens are also allowed to vote, approve, or disapprove the proposed interventions displayed on the DT, accompanied by a text box where citizens are allowed to share their feedback or explanation on the decisions made.

### Green Space Simulation

Considering the importance of green space for promoting health and well-being, the Green Space simulation is developed to enable the identification of suitable locations for green space development. Facilitated with the simulation, planners can make informed decisions for green space development in the city by cross-analysing environmental data (e.g. air pollution, noise pollution, amount of direct sunlight) and pedestrian traffic flow data. Citizens are also given a platform to vote for facilities selection (e.g. benches, vegetation diversity) or to propose new suggestions. To evaluate the success of the developed green space or allocated facilities, sensors are installed to track pedestrian traffic in the designated green space, which will then help planners to make the necessary improvements.

### User-tagging & Flooding Simulation

The User-tagging Simulation allows citizens to tag objects and reflect real-life problems of the city, while incorporating the exact geo-location(s) as they walk around the Building Information Model (BIM). In disaster mitigation scenarios, the user-tagging feature also allows citizens to share their geo-location as they seek municipal assistance. The platform allows the interactions between citizens and the relevant authorities, industries, and research community on the online DT. The data generated over time will then inform more detailed flooding simulations on the DT with regard to citizens' different needs: based on their geo-locations and supported with actual water-level and rainfall data. The simulation results can be used to develop long-term flood prevention mechanisms by cross-analysing urban mobility and identifying flood-prone areas in the city.

### Crowd Simulation

Crowd Simulations are also enabled in the DT by adopting an agent-based model, allowing for more realistic reactions across different social demographics to any introduced stimuli. The simulation results can then be used to derive insights into connectivity and traffic flows of the city.

## CASE SUMMARY

The DT of the Docklands area deserves merit for its people-centric approach, as well as its effort in leveraging citizens to collect crowd-sourced data, which is then used to complement other simulations on the DT. Despite its merit in delivering optimal people-centred services, White *et al.* (2021) highlight that their flooding simulation solely focuses on urban mobility and identifying flood-prone areas within the city. Serving as the country's economic hub and known as a flood-prone city, this underscores the need for the DT to incorporate models with a capacity to forecast flood-induced economic cost (Pyatkova *et al.*, 2019). Moreover, with existing software products, it is possible to extend flood simulation beyond forecasting economic cost to create flood-hazard mapping for different areas, including cultural heritage sites in the city. In light of increased occurrence of heat waves, simulations of heatwave-fuelled forest fires will also be key to establish early warning systems of high-temperature records, as well as to inform advanced fire management and municipal preparedness and mitigation plans (Gutierrez *et al.*, 2021; Lau and Nath, 2014).

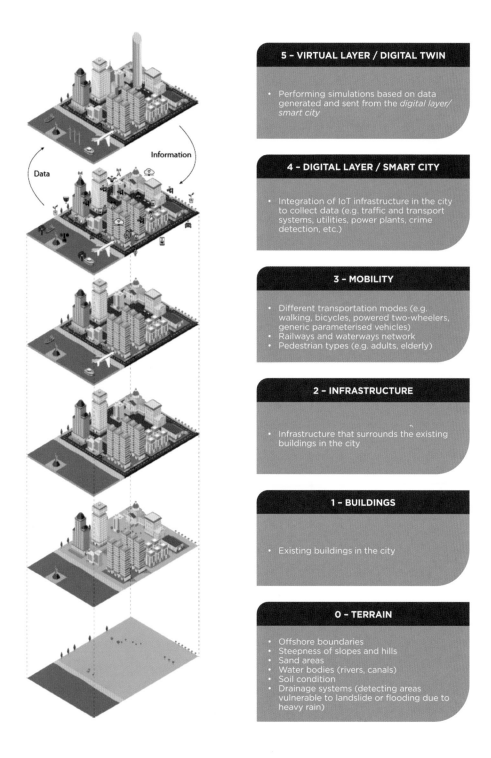

**5 – VIRTUAL LAYER / DIGITAL TWIN**

- Performing simulations based on data generated and sent from the *digital layer/ smart city*

**4 – DIGITAL LAYER / SMART CITY**

- Integration of IoT infrastructure in the city to collect data (e.g. traffic and transport systems, utilities, power plants, crime detection, etc.)

**3 – MOBILITY**

- Different transportation modes (e.g. walking, bicycles, powered two-wheelers, generic parameterised vehicles)
- Railways and waterways network
- Pedestrian types (e.g. adults, elderly)

**2 – INFRASTRUCTURE**

- Infrastructure that surrounds the existing buildings in the city

**1 – BUILDINGS**

- Existing buildings in the city

**0 – TERRAIN**

- Offshore boundaries
- Steepness of slopes and hills
- Sand areas
- Water bodies (rivers, canals)
- Soil condition
- Drainage systems (detecting areas vulnerable to landslide or flooding due to heavy rain)

**Figure 2.9** Layers required to develop a digital twin smart city for the Docklands area in Dublin, Ireland (Source: building on White *et al.*, 2021, p. 103066).

# CASE STUDY 2
## DIGITAL TWIN OF THE DOCKLANDS AREA IN DUBLIN, IRELAND

| | STATE | ACADEMIA |
|---|---|---|
| **POST-DECISION** Engagement, Collaboration, Data Access Rights, Info Sharing | N.A. | N.A. |
| **DECISION TAKING** Automation, Modelling, Simulation, Forecasting | • Urban planning and policy-making based on citizens' feedback<br>• Flood planning, flood prevention mechanisms<br>• Removing / adding of newly proposed buildings to evaluate its effect on the skyline<br>• Developing green spaces in suitable areas based on pollution levels (air, noise), traffic flow, and amount of direct sunlight | • Simulating urban mobility by different transportation modes (walking, bicycles, powered two-wheelers, and generic parametrized vehicles) and pedestrian types (adult, elderly)<br>• Modelling urban mobility based on citizens' feedback<br>• Identifying vulnerable citizens based on geo-locations, predicting water level based on rainfall |
| **SENSE MAKING** Dashboards & Reporting, Real Time, Analytic, Visualisation | • Optimising traffic flow based on real-time traffic data<br>• Improving urban IoT data based on citizens' feedback | N.A. |
| **DATA MANAGEMENT** Data Cleaning, Data Storage, Assets | • Championing the development of DT | • Developing urban mobility model |

| | ⬍ STATE | ⬍ ACADEMIA |
|---|---|---|
| **MULTIPLE DATA SOURCES** | • Aerial photography; airborne LiDAR; (moisture) sensors; CCTV cameras; anemometry; sensors (wind, seismic, people counting) | • Soil survey |
| SPATIAL | • Terrain | • Terrain |
| ECONOMIC | N.A. | N.A. |
| TECHNOLOGICAL | • Public surveillance and crime-related data | N.A. |
| ENVIRONMENTAL | • Vegetation moisture level; wind data; seismic data; water level / rainfall data | N.A. |
| SOCIAL | • Visitors' count to (new) green spaces | N.A. |
| CULTURAL | N.A. | N.A. |

**Table 2.2** Analytical Framework of Case Study 2, Digital Twin of the Docklands area in Dublin, Ireland.

N.A.

- Providing feedback on new urban policy and planning decisions
- Accessing to skyline simulation to visualise the effect of a new building would have on the skyline and sunlight access of its surroundings
- Accessing to green space simulation to choose or propose new suggestions
- Providing feedback or voting on newly proposed buildings or green spaces or propose new ideas
- Accessing to disaster alerts

- Modelling 3D buildings based on citizens' feedback

N.A.

N.A.

- Visualising areas and roads affected by flooding
- Reporting current location and seeking assistance in disaster scenarios

- Developing of 3D building models

N.A.

| INDUSTRY | CIVIL SOCIETY |
|---|---|
| • BIM; stereoscopic aerial photography; 5G cell tower | • Ground surveys; GPS unit; digital camera; citizen data; cellular; central monitoring system |
| • BIM | • Infrastructure data |
| N.A. | N.A. |
| • City-wide internet access | • Real-time traffic data |
| N.A. | N.A. |
| N.A. | • Mobility; feedback; smoke detection |
| N.A. | N.A. |

# CASE STUDY 3

## DIGITAL TWIN CITY OF XIONG'AN NEW AREA, CHINA

**Figure 2.10 (Left)**
Representational image of Digital Twin city of the Xiong'an new area, China (Source: Pomeroy Academy, 2023).

**Figure 2.11 (Overleaf)**
West facade of Xiong'an Railway Station, Xiong'an New Area, North China's Hebei province (Source: Photo by N509FZ on Wikimedia Commons, 2020).

## CASE OVERVIEW

Xiong'an New Area (XNA), in North China's Hebei Province, is the first in China to become a national-level 'new area' and is now a DT city with deep learning capabilities (World Economic Forum, 2022; Xinhua News Agency, 2018). The XNA has been established with the aim to build a new metropolis that is green, smart, cultural, and creative from the ground up. As a collaborative effort, the project involves the government of Hebei Province, its major universities, scientific design / research institutions, and engineering / construction companies in sectors such as information, construction, transportation, and finance (Chen, Lai, and Zhang, 2021).

## SCENARIOS

The DT city is intended to fuse the physical and digital cities through synchronised planning and construction (Zou *et al.*, 2021), using the DT for digital supervision of urban planning, construction, management, maintenance, and repair while building the city. The DT city is designed to proceed on the basis of four city information platforms (Figure 2.12):

1.  Construction of Traditional Urban Infrastructure: integrating city infrastructure, transportation systems, energy data, and computerisation processes to monitor public and infrastructure safety, ecological environment conservation, disaster prevention, and emergency response;

2.  Construction of Infrastructure for a New Style of Intelligent (DT) City: setting up city-wide intelligent sensing systems (the Internet of Things [IoT]) and

next-generation telecommunication networks (5G) to support XNA's computing capacity and an intelligent hub;

3.  Digital City, Double Infrastructure Integration Platform: leveraging the power of AI and DT through an information management centre for big data resources management systems and enhancing trust and security; and

4.  Innovation Platform: integrating both scientific research centres and open innovation centres to test scientific innovations and allow for business incubations.

Facilitated by the four information platforms, the planning of the XNA, as a leading-edge future city, is done deliberately to reflect the metropolis as an:

1. Innovation City;
2. Intelligent City;
3. Green City; and
4. Liveable City (Chen, Lai, and Zhang, 2021).

### Innovation City

The XNA's Innovation City fosters synergy amongst academia and industry experts in healthcare, finance, and technology. Leveraging the city's DTs platforms, it aims to become an innovation hub to enable start-ups' establishment, as well as to attract and train talent.

### Intelligent City

The XNA synchronises planning and construction of both physical and digital cities. This is made possible by appropriating traditional urban infrastructure, ensuring its compatibility with an Intelligent City that thrives on urban cloud, big data platforms, 5G networks, and IoT.

### Green City

While using DT to guide the planning and management of the XNA, the platform is deliberately set to adhere to the principles of green ecological development. This results in the establishment of the XNA that seamlessly interweaves both the blue (wetlands) and green (forests, farmland, and grass).

### Liveable City

Considering the concepts of liveability and walkability, the DT is used in the planning of community and public services on three different levels – community, district, and neighbourhood. The DT is optimised to design six 15-minute living zones: each consisting of residential areas, as well as community and public services (e.g. transportation services, educational institutions, healthcare centres) that are within a 1-km radius.

## CASE SUMMARY

The DT city of XNA is perceived as a utopian urban living environment that epitomises the Chinese system's efficiency, digital capabilities, and foresightedness in the field of urban planning. Building on the four city information platforms, the DT serves as an enabler for synchronised planning and construction, as well as for real-time monitoring, early warning, and condition assessments of the city (World Economic Forum, 2022). The collaborative effort in incubating different business start-ups to establish an economic landscape in the city is also commendable. However, there is a lack of evidence regarding the use of the economic data to monitor and manage the city's economy. While the urban planning in XNA has been set out with principles to establish itself as an innovative, intelligent, green, and liveable city (Chen, Lai, and Zhang, 2021), more information is needed to understand the multi-dimensional data collected in order to achieve the principles through the DT.

Noting the XNA's aspirations to be a green, smart, cultural, and creative metropolis that reflects trends in future cities of China, it may prove challenging to reconcile the aspiration of reflecting traditional cultural heritage with a modern smart city identity from its inception. It is also observed that citizen participation, as well as the collection of citizen data, appears to be absent throughout the master plan of the XNA's DT smart city. This may not be surprising since the planning of the XNA has been committed as a 'top-down design' and that 'Beijing's administrative orders and state-owned enterprises have taken the lead in building up the New Area' at its initial stage (China Briefing, 2019).

**GREEN, EFFICIENT ENERGY**

Public facilities, community, buildings, homes

**SMART, PUBLIC SECURITY**

Medical health and monitoring, disaster prevention and response

**SOCIAL CONNECTIVITY**

Social PF, care for the elderly, activity analysis and unattended retail

**FUTURE MOBILITY**

Sharing and diversity, fully automated, real-time management

**FUTURE CITY SCENARIOS**

---

Scientific research centres of national importance, OI centres; international level technology innovation PF, and science & technology education; infrastructure and PF

**INNOVATION PF**

Next-generation information and telecommunication technology industries, modern life science, biotechnology, new materials, eco-agriculture, advanced service businesses

---

City brain (AI); intelligent city information management centre

**DIGITAL CITY, DOUBLE INFRASTRUCTURE INTEGRATION PF**

Trust and security; big data resource management system

---

Next-generation telecommunication network (5G); all-encompassing intelligent sensing PF (IoT)

**CONSTRUCTION OF INFRASTRUCTURE FOR NEW STYLE OF INTELLIGENT CITY**

Computing capacity (cloud, big data); intelligent hub (X-hub)

---

City infrastructure, transportation, hydro, energy, cyclic regeneration, and computerisation processes

**CONSTRUCTION OF TRADITIONAL URBAN INFRASTRUCTURE**

Ecological environment conservation, under-grounding, disaster prevention, emergency response, public safety, and infrastructure safety processes

---

PF: platform     OI: open innovation     AI: artificial intelligence     5G: 5th generation

**Figure 2.12** Overview of work on Xiong'an New Area Digital Twin city (Source: after Chen, Lai, and Zhang, 2021).

# CASE STUDY 3

## DIGITAL TWIN CITY OF XIONG'AN NEW AREA, CHINA

| | STATE | ACADEMIA |
|---|---|---|
| **POST-DECISION** Engagement, Collaboration, Data Access Rights, Info Sharing | N.A. | N.A. |
| **DECISION TAKING** Automation, Modelling, Simulation, Forecasting | • Synchronising planning, design, and construction<br>• Examining social connectivity<br>• Optimising clean energy supply system with photovoltaic power generation<br>• Providing demand-responsive customised public transport systems and smart-driving vehicles<br>• Developing enhanced response to public emergencies<br>• Assessing future city scenario planning | N.A. |
| **SENSE MAKING** Dashboards & Reporting, Real Time, Analytic, Visualisation | • Real-time transit information systems<br>• Intelligent social security prevention and control system<br>• Real-time environmental monitoring | • Innovation & complex analysis<br>• Test bedding |
| **DATA MANAGEMENT** Data Cleaning, Data Storage, Assets | • Championing the development of DT<br>• Building the Financial Service Innovation Centre and the blockchain infrastructure platform<br>• Developing intelligent industries and services | • Developing and operating CIM |
| | **STATE** | **ACADEMIA** |
| **MULTIPLE DATA SOURCES** | • Object-linked sensing; mobile interconnection; AI and BIM Management Platform | • CIM |
| **SPATIAL** | • BIM Management Platform; air-soil heat exchange data | • CIM Platform |
| **ECONOMIC** | N.A. | N.A. |
| **TECHNOLOGICAL** | N.A. | N.A. |
| **ENVIRONMENTAL** | N.A. | N.A. |
| **SOCIAL** | N.A. | N.A. |
| **CULTURAL** | N.A. | N.A. |

**Table 2.3** Analytical Framework of Case Study 3, Digital Twin city of Xiong'an New Area, China.

*Limited information is available on the data layers required.*

N.A.                                                          N.A.


N.A.                                                          N.A.


- Monitoring utilities infrastructure
- Monitoring and supervising construction of project site (people,
  machines, materials, methods, and the environment)           N.A.
- Supervising traffic and vehicles


- Constructing a full-time, global and multi-dimensional data
  fusion urban safety monitoring system
- Building the Financial Service Innovation Centre and the
  blockchain infrastructure platform                           N.A.
- Developing intelligent industries and services

INDUSTRY                                              CIVIL SOCIETY

- Sensors; drone surveys; cloud computing; AI;
  telecommunication network infrastructure; video monitoring;    N.A.
  access control intercom and anti-theft alarm; 5G network;
  Internet of Things (IoT)

| | |
|---|---|
| - Utilities data; site info | N.A. |
| N.A. | N.A. |
| - Traffic & vehicle data, information technology infrastructure; big data and telecommunications data | N.A. |
| N.A. | N.A. |
| - Social security prevention data | N.A. |
| N.A. | N.A. |

# CASE STUDY 4
## THE PLATEAU PROJECT, JAPAN

**Figure 2.13 (Left)**
3D city model of PLATEAU, Japan (Source: Ministry of Land, Infrastructure, Transport and Tourism website, 2023).

**Figure 2.14 (Overleaf)**
Aerial view of the Shiba-koen district of Minato, Tokyo, Japan (Source: Google Earth, 2022).

## CASE OVERVIEW

Japan's Ministry of Land, Infrastructure, Transport, and Tourism (MLIT) is leading the PLATEAU project to create 3D city models in 50 cities for developing sustainable and human-centric urban policy. The project employs 3D city models to visualise city data and develop towns with citizen participation. Collaboration between government, research institutions, industries, and citizens allows knowledge sharing through downloadable open data (Obi and Iwasaki, 2021). Use cases (Figure 2.15) on the PLATEAU are broadly grouped into disciplines such as:

1. Activity Monitoring;
2. Disaster Management; and
3. Smart Planning (MLIT website, 2023).

# SCENARIOS

### Activity Monitoring

In view of the high population in Japan, the 'Activity Monitoring' adopts a multi-pronged approach, using data collected from cameras and sensors to understand the complexities of a city's mobility. This ranges from outdoor roadside situations; indoor, underground and overground people flow; movement and retention of people in between point of interests; urban activities and human flow at shopping streets and markets; congestion status in public spaces; and social distancing measurement. The data collected enables simulations of social mobility, in the public and private domain as well as major stations of high-speed railways. This subsequently provides insights into improving pedestrian safety and design, as well as identifying efficient placement of outdoor facilities around the city.

### Disaster Management

Considering the emergence of COVID-19 and Japan's vulnerability to natural disasters, the PLATEAU is developed to bridge top-down and bottom-up efforts in disaster management. From top-down perspectives, the platform allows planners to run simulations of disaster impacts and predict waste generation, in which the results can be used to inform disaster preparedness, restoration, and reconstruction. The platform also allows the visualisation of indoor-outdoor evacuation plans, enabling authorities to develop protocols and facilitate evacuation training for citizens in cyberspace. From a bottom-up perspective, the PLATEAU provides citizens with a platform to receive disaster prevention information by raising disaster awareness and promoting disaster prevention plans led by citizens.

## Smart Planning

PLATEAU's smart planning is a unique interface where both top-down and bottom-up efforts meet. For top-down planning, smart planning is used for:

1. Streamlining administrative affairs as well as development permission procedures;
2. Identifying suitable site for developments based on pre-set city planning regulations, disaster risks, natural ventilations, Urban Heat Island, and photovoltaic power generation;
3. Visualising changes in pedestrian flow in response to new developments;
4. Developing and simulating sensor installation master plan for city management;
5. Understanding pedestrian flow (moving route, staying time);
6. Visualising effects of planning measures on urban structures; and
7. Prescribing land and building uses based on shifting urban and population structures.

From bottom-up perspectives, PLATEAU allows all individuals to create use cases and contribute to the government's database; participate in community development using simulation games to interact with the design layouts and communicate with agencies; receive regional information regarding events and disaster evacuation plans; and, lastly, identify walking routes and exercise intensity based on individual health data (MLIT website, 2023).

# CASE SUMMARY

The PLATEAU positions itself as a collaborative, digital platform for building resilient cities across Japan (Obi and Iwasaki, 2021). This is evident in the platform's holistic use cases generated with a middle-out approach. Not only does it allow municipal authorities to run simulations and develop city management plans, but it also provides a wide range of applications for scholars, industry professionals, and citizens in all industries. The efforts in promoting community participation by gamifying community development have also contributed to more inclusive planning processes. Additionally, elaborated and tangible methods are meticulously employed to investigate pedestrian behaviours of the cities.

Despite its quantitative methods in creating extensive use cases and measuring pedestrian behaviours, the official website of the PLATEAU does not appear to show the integration of economic development and its unique Japanese cultural impact onto the platform (MLIT website, 2023). Given Japan's influence on the global economy though cultural and technological goods and services (Abe and Fitzgerald, 1995; Japan Economic Foundation, 2009), it would seem essential to demonstrate the coexistence of these two layers and their social, spatial, environmental, and technological impact on Japan's national development.

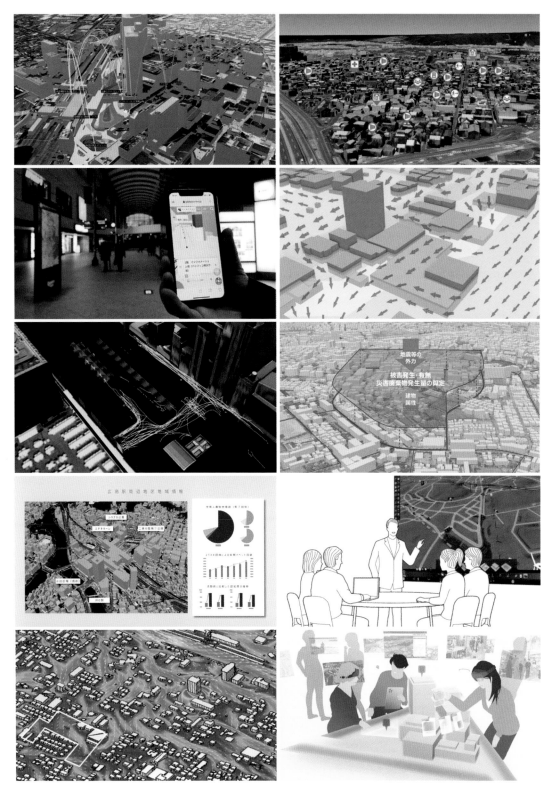

**Figure 2.15** Use cases for activity monitoring, disaster management, and smart planning (Source: Ministry of Land, Infrastructure, Transport and Tourism website, 2023).

# CASE STUDY 4
## THE PLATEAU PROJECT, JAPAN

| | | |
|---|---|---|
| **POST-DECISION** Engagement, Collaboration, Data Access Rights, Info Sharing | • Sharing of regional information platform | • Sharing congestion information for crowd avoidance |
| **DECISION TAKING** Automation, Modelling, Simulation, Forecasting | • Urban roads safety & connectivity measures<br>• People-centric town development measures; development permissions<br>• Disaster countermeasures & waste disposal plan<br>• Security strategies; crime prevention measures<br>• Regional de-carbonisation policies | • Simulating people flow & measures<br>• Simulating efficiency of security equipment & evacuation routes<br>• Simulating environmental factors for development site<br>• Forecasting urban planning impacts |
| **SENSE MAKING** Dashboards & Reporting, Real Time, Analytic, Visualisation | • Visualising vehicle traffic volume and speed<br>• Visualising effects of (implemented) urban development plans<br>• Visualising emergency- / disaster-induced building damage<br>• Visualising efficiency of security strategies and infrastructure | • Identifying trouble spots & risks on roads<br>• Grasping real-time people flow / congestion status<br>• Measuring people count and retention time at public events & point of interests (PoIs)<br>• Understanding change in people flow before & after development / intervention; verifying the impact of large-scale development |
| **DATA MANAGEMENT** Data Cleaning, Data Storage, Assets | • Championing the development of PLATEAU<br>• Collaborating in the development of roadside sensing system; people flow analysis; snow damage countermeasures; security equipment installation plan support tool; disaster waste generation simulation | • Developing roadside sensing system<br>• Developing people flow and congestion monitoring system<br>• Developing security equipment installation plan support tool |

| | STATE | ACADEMIA |
|---|---|---|
| **MULTIPLE DATA SOURCES** | • Information models; vehicle-mounted sensors, camera images, WiFi, Census; 3D city information model | • Sensors (vehicle-mounted, people flow sensors, people-counting; WiFi packet); radio waves; AI; IoT; ICT; Census; 3D WebGIS; BIM |
| SPATIAL | • Road-related data; use cases; city planning information & regulations; landscape & environmental regulations | • Road-related data; 3D building data; city planning information & regulations; topographical data; land-use status |
| ECONOMIC | N.A. | N.A. |
| TECHNOLOGICAL | N.A. | • Telecommunications; AI; IoT; ICT; pedestrian & bicycle traffic |
| ENVIRONMENTAL | N.A. | • Hazard maps; wind data; thermal data |
| SOCIAL | • District disaster prevention plans; pedestrian & bicycle traffic | • People flow & congestion; retention time at PoIs; population density; occupancy & dereliction; evacuation facilities capacity |
| CULTURAL | N.A. | N.A. |

**Table 2.4** Analytical Framework of Case Study 4, the PLATEAU Project, Japan.

- Sharing congestion information for crowd avoidance
- Sharing issues of the city and building consensus among various actors
- Sharing of hazard maps & risk assessment
- Performing disaster prevention drills with residents

- Accessing congestion situation
- Receiving updates on improvement work status
- Obtaining disaster prevention information, evacuation training tool
- Accessing upcoming development and regional activities

- Building consensus for people-centric planning
- Planning public health & safety measures
- Modelling disaster risks and waste, evacuation behaviours & plans
- Simulating efficiency of security equipment
- Modelling photovoltaic power generation

- Defining voluntary disaster prevention activities of self-help and mutual assistance amongst residents

- Identifying trouble spots & risks on roads
- Measuring effects of urban development plans
- Monitoring movement patterns, social distancing status & facilities usage; identifying traffic obstacles
- Visualising disaster risks and risk reduction improvement work; identifying potential obstacles to evacuation routes

- Visualising congestion status to avoid crowd
- Visualising disaster risks, identifying appropriate evacuation routes

- Developing roadside sensing system
- Establishing people-monitoring techniques combining multiple technologies
- Developing 3D hazard maps & evacuation routes models; visualising improvement work effects
- Developing security strategies support tool

- Developing district disaster prevention plan

| Sensors (vehicle-mounted, people-counting); CCTV cameras; WiFi; laser sensor (3D LiDAR); Census; BIM; AI; 3D WebGIS | Citizen data (community development plan, disaster prevention plans, health data, use cases, mobility); 3D WebGIS |
| --- | --- |
| • Road-related data; 3D building data; topographical data; land use status | • Use cases |
| N.A. | N.A. |
| • Telecommunications; pedestrian & bicycle traffic | N.A. |
| • Historical disaster data; wind data; snow data; seismic data; disaster waste storage capacity | N.A. |
| • People flow & congestion; retention time at PoIs; social distancing measures; population density; occupancy & dereliction; evacuation behaviours, action plan, & facilities capacity | • Mobility; demographics; health data; community development plan; disaster prevention plan |
| N.A. | N.A. |

# CASE STUDY 5
## DIGITAL TWIN OF DARWIN, NORTHERN TERRITORY, AUSTRALIA

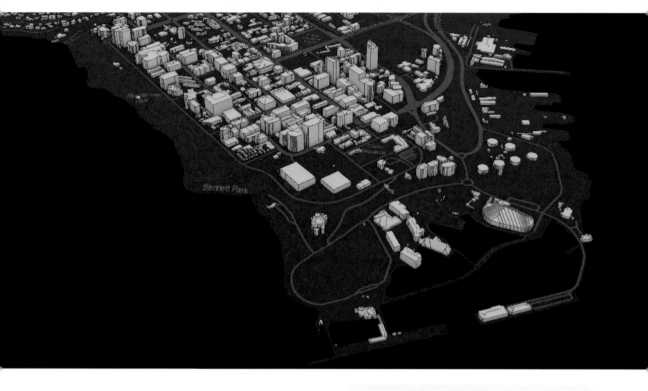

**Figure 2.16 (Left)**
Screenshot shows the 3D Darwin's Digital Twin platform (Source: CSIRO, Darwin Living Lab, Australia, 2023).

**Figure 2.17 (Overleaf)**
Basemap of 3D Darwin (Source: CSIRO, Darwin Living Lab, Australia, 2023).

## CASE OVERVIEW

Darwin's DT is a collaboration between the Commonwealth Scientific and Industrial Research Organisation (CSIRO), Australian and Territory Governments, and the City of Darwin. The DT integrates various forms of information, serving as a tool to monitor city operations and inspect the impacts of changes in urban planning. Built on a spatial data layer, the platform has five types of datasets (Figure 2.18):

1.  Buildings;
2.  Private and public open space;
3.  Road and road verges;
4.  LiDAR data; and
5.  Aerial photography (Williams, Meharg, and Muster, 2020).

## SCENARIOS

The DT of Darwin stands out as a platform for enviro-economic analysis, which involves the evaluation of economic value and return on investments of cooling and greening initiatives. This is done by quantifying a selected set of social, environmental, spatial, and economic information, followed by monitoring changes in key indicators such as Canopy Cover, Land Surface Temperature (LST), and Air-Quality.

### Canopy Cover Monitoring

Urban Monitor is designed to establish monitoring baselines for land cover information according to a detailed time-series. By comparing surface covers (e.g. irrigated and non-irrigated roofs, lawns) change over time using spatio-temporal statistics, analysis can be made to understand the impact of their variations on the ecosystem services (CSIRO, 2021a). The monitoring outcomes can be used to:

1.  Support state and local government authorities to develop urban forest strategies (e.g. defining areas that need replanting programmes);
2.  Plan, enhance, and support tree-canopy design objectives and climate-change policies; and
3.  Identify local areas of potential bushfire risks.

### Temperature Monitoring

The Temperature Monitoring allows the modelling and visualisation of heat distribution patterns against several built and natural urban features. Combining the heat distribution maps together with population and housing data, it enables the identification of heat-health vulnerable neighbourhoods, contributing to building evidence-based guides for climate adaptation plans in Darwin. Understanding features such as surface temperatures can assist planners in selecting materials or land cover types that can reduce urban heat. For large-scale planning, the temperature monitoring helps to determine varying contributions of different urban features (e.g. dwelling density, distance from the coast, etc.) to LST in residential neighbourhoods (Meyers *et al.*, 2020).

### Air-Quality Monitoring

The Air-Quality Monitoring mobile application – a public-access version of the DT – has been developed for all citizens to track environmental hazards, such as high temperatures, poor air quality, and pollen (where available) (Figure 2.19). The application aims to increase awareness (particularly amongst outdoor workers) of environmental hazards, reducing health impacts and ultimately improving workplace health outcomes. The application directly links environmental conditions to an individual's health and symptoms, building up a picture of an individual's symptoms attributed to environmental factors. With live tracking of temperature and air quality, the application sends notifications to individuals when the triggers of symptoms are elevated. The application disseminates real-time data regarding air quality, enabling people to make informed decisions about working during heat events and severe air pollution (CSIRO, 2021b).

## CASE SUMMARY

Darwin's tropical climate, and distinct wet and dry seasons, explains the DTs with a strong focus on environmental factors, particularly concerning the well-being of its citizens. By integrating a wealth of information from social, spatial, economic, and environmental data layers, the DT has taken a well-rounded approach to tackling local environmental challenges, which has led to effective and informed decisions to improve the liveability of the city. The people-centric approach of Darwin's DT is exemplified by its focus on understanding the stocks and flows of ecosystem services, using the international System of Environmental and Economic Accounting (SEEA) framework to quantifiably measure the direct and indirect benefits that urban vegetation generates for human well-being, and to develop urban forest strategies accordingly. Another people-centric facet of the DT is illustrated by the publicly available air-quality monitoring mobile app, which is mainly for improving citizens' well-being. As extreme environmental conditions (i.e. temperature and relative humidity) would significantly affect the state of cultural heritage artefacts (Lombardo *et al.*, 2019), it would seem essential for Darwin's DT to expand its scope and investigate how to better conserve the cultural elements of the city despite its extreme climate and weather.

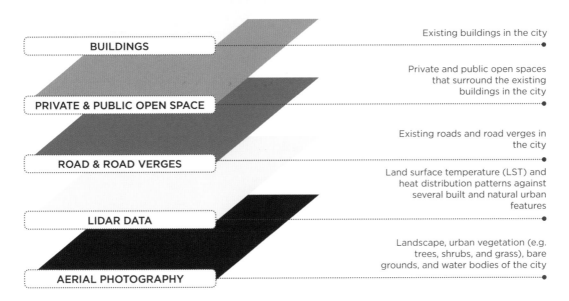

**Figure 2.18** Schematic of spatial layers of different types of datasets, the foundation of Digital Twin for Darwin (Williams, Meharg, and Muster, 2020, p. 121772).

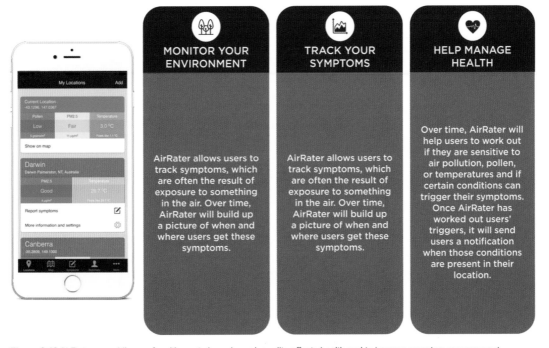

**Figure 2.19** AirRater, a mobile app for citizens to learn how air quality affects health and to improve symptom management (Source: AirRater, 2023).

# CASE STUDY 5
## DIGITAL TWIN OF DARWIN, NORTHERN TERRITORY, AUSTRALIA

| | | |
|---|---|---|
| **POST-DECISION** Engagement, Collaboration, Data Access Rights, Info Sharing | N.A. | • Distributing up-to-date information about air quality (smoke, pollen, temperature, humidity) |
| **DECISION TAKING** Automation, Modelling, Simulation, Forecasting | • Supporting state and local government authorities to develop urban forest strategies (i.e. areas that need replanting programme; policies and strategies to protect urban canopy)<br>• Planning, enhancing, and supporting tree canopy design objectives, water-sensitive cities' program, and climate-change policies<br>• Defining local areas subject to bushfire risks<br>• Providing evidence-based guide for climate adaptation plan | • Supporting people to reduce health impacts of environmental conditions, e.g. extreme heat and poor air quality<br>• Helping people better manage symptoms related to heat and poor air quality, and improve quality of life |
| **SENSE MAKING** Dashboards & Reporting, Real Time, Analytic, Visualisation | • Performing urban green space and heat island assessment<br>• Estimating direct and indirect ground water recharge<br>• Off-site monitoring of land cover / elevation change from oil and gas operations<br>• Identifying land surface temperature 'hot spots' and 'cool spots'<br>• Visualising heat-distribution patterns against built and natural urban features<br>• Identifying heat-health-vulnerable neighbourhoods | N.A. |
| **DATA MANAGEMENT** Data Cleaning, Data Storage, Assets | • Championing the development of DT<br>• Developing canopy-cover-monitoring model<br>• Mapping of land-surface temperatures and heat-health vulnerability | • Developing an air-quality monitoring free mobile app |

| | STATE | ACADEMIA |
|---|---|---|
| **MULTIPLE DATA SOURCES** | • Aerial photography; aerial and space-borne sensors; LiDAR scan; temperature / humidity data logger; pollen dispersal model | • Temperature / humidity data logger; pollen-dispersal model |
| SPATIAL | • Terrain; roads & road verges; private & public open space; buildings; land surfaces (roofs, irrigated & non-irrigated roofs, bushes, trees, lawns) | N.A. |
| ECONOMIC | • Stocks and flows of ecosystem services provided by urban vegetation | N.A. |
| TECHNOLOGICAL | • IoT-enabled sensors | N.A. |
| ENVIRONMENTAL | • Urban vegetation; seasonal land-surface temperature; heat-distribution patterns; air quality; air temperature; humidity level; pollen; tree inventory | • Air quality; air temperature; humidity level; pollen |
| SOCIAL | N.A. | N.A. |
| CULTURAL | N.A. | N.A. |

**Table 2.5** Analytical Framework of Case Study 5, Digital Twin of Darwin, Northern Territory, Australia.

- Identifying and testing new ideas and approaches for innovation in urban heat mitigation

- Having an increased awareness of extreme heat and poor air quality, leading to a reduction in health impacts and ultimately to better health outcomes

- Making informed decisions about working during heat events and severe air pollution

N.A.

- Tracking environmental hazards such as temperature, air quality, and pollen (where available)

N.A.

- Developing DT of Darwin

N.A.

INDUSTRY

CIVIL SOCIETY

N.A.

- GPS; citizen data (health and fitness, contact information); census (socio-economic data)

| | |
|---|---|
| N.A. | N.A. |
| N.A. | N.A. |
| N.A. | N.A. |
| N.A. | N.A. |
| N.A. | - Location; health & fitness; contact information; socio-economic data |
| N.A. | N.A. |

# CASE STUDY 6
## DIGITAL 3D MODEL OF BOSTON, MASSACHUSETTS, USA

**Figure 2.20 (Left)**
Screenshot shows the digital 3D Model of Boston, Massachusetts, USA (Source: Boston Planning & Development Agency GIS Lab, 2023).

**Figure 2.21 (Overleaf)**
Downtown Boston, Massachusetts, USA (Source: Google Earth, 2022).

## CASE OVERVIEW

An active real-estate market prompted the Boston Planning & Development Agency (BPDA) to create a DT for understanding the impact of interventions and expediting the design review processes with an agile, 3D digital model of the city. In collaboration with Esri, the DT has been made publicly available and it provides information on buildings, transportation, urban vegetation, daylight and shade, and points of interest within the city. The BPDA currently uses the DT for three main use cases:

1.  Shadow Analysis;
2.  Project Evaluation; and
3.  Flood Modelling (Esri, 2018).

# SCENARIOS

### Shadow Analysis

Comprising both quantitative and qualitative analysis work flows, the Shadow Analysis of the DT is a great tool for BPDA and developers to negotiate proposed projects: ensuring that the projects are compliant with the Boston Common Shadow Law to limit the amount of time any new building could cast shadows on the surroundings. While the quantitative assessment provides in-depth measurements (e.g. extent and duration) of shadows through the seasons, the qualitative evaluation allows BPDA to perform quick simulations and visual analytics to visualise shadows cast by any new building(s). This subsequently allows BPDA to share their views with relevant stakeholders and offer concrete advice on minimising the impacts of the proposed building(s) on the city (Figure 2.22).

### Project Evaluation

The Project Evaluation feature of the DT of Boston allows BPDA to make sure the proposed projects adhere to Boston's Zoning Code (e.g. height, density, and usage requirements) and to visualise their effects on their surrounding neighbourhoods (in terms of housing, zoning, and parking) before they take effect in the real-world. For instance, BPDA can virtually overlay Urban Heat Island (UHI) data to visualise temperatures corresponding to the proposed projects, impervious surfaces, and tree canopies; and subsequently guide planning decisions. The Project Evaluation interface also serves as a platform to coordinate the project review process and facilitate dialogues between BPDA planning and urban design personnels, relevant officials, city authorities, and even the community.

### Flood Modelling

As climate change continues to accelerate in recent years, Boston as a coastal city is highly vulnerable to the impacts of rising sea level. To this end, the Flood Modelling of Boston's DT is articulated to reveal flood-prone areas in Boston, as well as areas that would be critically impacted by a 100-year flood of 40 inches or more (Figure 2.23) (Marani, 2018). The simulation results provide a clear visualisation of the flood impacts across the city, which can then guide the local government to develop flood-management and evacuation plans.

Boston has been witnessing one of its greatest growth periods, seeing a lot of development in the city in the last few years. Moving forward, BPDA anticipates using the planning and shadow tools to visualise and facilitate a wide variety of decision-making tasks, including integrating developers' project submissions into the platform, as well as line-of-sight evaluation. Furthermore, BPDA is in the process of exploring how the DT can provide real-time data of city services, given the emerging demand for ride-sharing and self-driving vehicles (Esri, 2018).

## CASE SUMMARY

Boston's dense concentration of skyscrapers justifies its DTs emphasis on shadow analysis. Made publicly available, it allows citizens to visualise buildings' impacts on citywide light exposure through the seasons. As it enables citizens to access the buildings, and landscape of the city, special attention has been paid to juxtapose different types of building (existing, under construction, approved, and under reviewed) using a colour scheme sequenced to reflect the building's development status.

Despite having a user-friendly interface, the DT seems to have omitted the participation of other spheres of influence, specifically academia and civil society. Despite the wealth of information in the DT, citizens appear to be perceived as passive users, with their roles limited to only information search. It would seem essential to integrate citizens' social trends into the DT so that planners and citizens will have a more holistic view of how Boston's urban landscape and design responds to not only the spatial cues of new and existing development, but also the social cues of how the city is being inhabited.

**Figure 2.22** Visualising shadow casting of Downtown Boston around 4pm in fall (Source: Boston Planning & Development Agency GIS Lab, 2023).

**Figure 2.23** Flood modelling showing the entire city of Boston and areas prone to flooding (Source: Boston Planning & Development Agency GIS Lab, 2023).

# CASE STUDY 6
## DIGITAL 3D MODEL OF BOSTON, MASSACHUSETTS, USA

| | STATE | ACADEMIA |
|---|---|---|
| **POST-DECISION** Engagement, Collaboration, Data Access Rights, Info Sharing | • Sharing of buildings status of the city (existing, under construction, approved, and under reviewed) | N.A. |
| **DECISION TAKING** Automation, Modelling, Simulation, Forecasting | • Simulating shadow castings of proposed projects<br>• Automated checking of proposed projects adhere to zoning codes<br>• Flood modelling<br>• Planning and development (UPCOMING)<br>• Line-of-sight evaluation (UPCOMING) | N.A. |
| **SENSE MAKING** Dashboards & Reporting, Real Time, Analytic, Visualisation | • Performing visual analytic of shadow cast by proposed projects | N.A. |
| **DATA MANAGEMENT** Data Cleaning, Data Storage, Assets | • Championing the development of Boston's DT | N.A. |

| | STATE | ACADEMIA |
|---|---|---|
| **MULTIPLE DATA SOURCES** | • GIS | N.A. |
| SPATIAL | • Road-related data; use cases; city planning information & regulations; landscape & environmental regulations | N.A. |
| ECONOMIC | • Parcel ownership | N.A. |
| TECHNOLOGICAL | N.A. | N.A. |
| ENVIRONMENTAL | • Shadow data; UHI | N.A. |
| SOCIAL | N.A. | N.A. |
| CULTURAL | N.A. | N.A. |

Table 2.6 Analytical Framework of Case Study 6, Digital 3D Model of Boston, Massachusetts, USA.

*Limited information is available on the data layers required.*

N.A.

- Accessing the DT to visualise current landscape of buildings (existing, under construction, approved, and under reviewed), trees, daylight and shadows, points of interest

N.A.

N.A.

N.A.

- Visualising daylight and shadows at specific date and time

- Co-developing Boston's DT

N.A.

INDUSTRY

CIVIL SOCIETY

- GIS, BIM; aerial photography

N.A.

| | |
|---|---|
| • 3D buildings data; topography | N.A. |
| N.A. | N.A. |
| N.A. | N.A. |
| N.A. | N.A. |
| N.A. | N.A. |
| N.A. | N.A. |

# CASE STUDY 7
## GREENTWINS, TALLINN, ESTONIA

**Figure 2.24 (Left)**
Screenshot shows the digital 3D web application / digital twin of Tallinn, Estonia (Source: Estonian Land Board, 2023).

**Figure 2.25 (Overleaf)**
Downtown Tallinn, Estonia
(Source: Photo by Jaanus Jagomäg on Unsplash, 2019).

## CASE OVERVIEW

Estonia's status as a digital nation has enabled the development of the Estonian National DT, as well as the GreenTwins pilot project – an urban digital twin of Tallinn. The GreenTwins project is a public – private collaboration involving the FinEst Centre (based at TalTech), Aalto University, Forum Virium Helsinki, and the Estonian government. With a great focus on integrating a dynamic layer of green infrastructure into its urban digital twin, the GreenTwins project aims to develop sustainable solutions to address issues of urban vegetation and urban ecosystems while contributing to the development of participatory urban planning (Dembski, 2021; Kern, Dembski, and Wössner, 2021).

# SCENARIOS

### CityHUB

The CityHUB, located in the downtown of Tallinn, is a built structure that aims to connect different stakeholders, including citizens, urban planners, city administrators, industry professionals, and researchers as key decision-makers. The venue and its systems encourages inclusivity across the 'four spheres of influence'. The CityHUB facilitates the participatory process by using VR, providing visualisations and simulations of proposed developments in a more realistic and accurate manner. This helps to ensure the proposed developments are interpretable by all stakeholders in order to encourage more citizen participation. It also promotes democratic decision-making in urban planning (FinEst Centre, n.d.; Petrone, 2021).

### 3D Digital Plant Library

The GreenTwin's inventory of plant species and their characteristics, as a dynamic layer on the DT platform, advances the interplay between built and natural environments throughout the planning processes (Figure 2.26). Such accurate modelling allows urban planners to:

1. Predict UHI corresponding to the built environment and green space expansion;
2. Forecast climate change and seasonal impacts within the natural environment;
3. Monitor changes of urban greenery over time and their impacts on the city's ecosystems and humans' well-being; and
4. Track urban-street-side vegetation and visibility of traffic signs (Dembski, 2021; FinEst Centre, n.d.; Petrone, 2021).

## Co-planning App

The Co-planning app is developed in consideration of GreenTwins' focus on open-access, open-source, and open-science approaches. Accompanied by visualisation tools in virtual and augmented reality, the Co-planning app serves as a platform to reach diverse communities (especially those that have so far been little considered), providing additional information and opportunity for citizen participation to encourage more democratic and sustainable planning processes (Figure 2.27a).

## Urban Tempo App

Serving as a platform to enable simulations and visualisations, the Urban Tempo app empowers different public and private stakeholders, planners, and citizens to experience the interplay between the urban and natural environments (Figure 2.27b). The Urban Tempo app provides its users with realistic visualisations and immersive experiences throughout the planning process, allowing stakeholders to gain a greater understanding of the impacts of proposed interventions on the environment and subsequently lead to better and more informed decisions.

## Virtual Green Planner

The Virtual Green Planner is developed as an interactive tool that enables different stakeholders, including citizens, to co-create different planning scenarios digitally. To facilitate better communication and idea exchange, the platform offers an interface where stakeholders and citizens are able to virtually overlay different data and sketches of design ideas on the platform. This will eventually serve as a basis for planners and decision-makers while developing democratic and sustainable urban planning solutions (Petrone, 2021).

# CASE SUMMARY

The Estonian digital capabilities are clearly evident in the GreenTwins project that recognises the pressing need to develop and integrate the natural environment into urban digital twins. The GreenTwins platform's focus on the interplay between the built and natural environment will become increasingly relevant in the face of climate change and global challenges: as it opens up more dynamic, in-depth analysis on the impacts of the built environment on urban vegetation and vice versa. The platform's significant emphasis on making urban planning processes more inclusive is also commendable, as it encourages citizen participation and provides citizens with user-friendly tools to share their design ideas with planners and decision-makers.

Despite the DTs contribution to the development of participatory urban planning, further efforts in civic engagement could include other socio-cultural scenarios for greater civic participation. Furthermore, as more than half of the Estonian GDP is created in Tallinn, the need for integrating economic data layers into the platform has become apparent. By interplaying socio-economic and green infrastructure data, it allows planners and decision-makers to assess the equity of accessibility to urban green space. Scholars have also extensively studied the importance of urban green space for cultural ecosystem services (Dushkova et al., 2021). This underscores the need to expand the GreenTwins' scopes to include cultural data layers into the platform for a more comprehensive analysis of its urban ecosystems.

**Figure 2.26** A dynamic layer of green infrastructure that enables analysis of the interplay between the built and natural environment in GreenTwins (Source: Pomeroy Academy, 2023).

**Figure 2.27a** (left) Vision of the CityHUB for participatory processes using VR (Source: Fabian Dembski / High-Performance Computing Center Stuttgart, 2021); **Figure 2.27b** (right) The Urban Tempo App for the simulation and visualisation of seasonal and temporal change showing the effect of the environment to the urban atmosphere (Source: Lauri Lemmenlehti, 2021).

# CASE STUDY 7

## GREENTWINS, TALLINN, ESTONIA

| | | |
|---|---|---|
| **POST-DECISION** Engagement, Collaboration, Data Access Rights, Info Sharing | • Engaging stakeholders and promoting democratic decision-making in planning processes via CityHUB | • Engaging stakeholders and promoting democratic decision-making in planning processes via CityHUB |
| **DECISION TAKING** Automation, Modelling, Simulation, Forecasting | • Co-creating planning scenarios | • Projecting growth trajectories of digital plants, species interaction, plants mortality, soil humidity, and changes in access to sunlight<br>• Predicting urban heat islands corresponding to the built environment and green space expansion<br>• Forecasting climate change and seasonal impacts on urban greenery<br>• Co-creating different planning scenarios |
| **SENSE MAKING** Dashboards & Reporting, Real Time, Analytic, Visualisation | • Visualising proposed developments more realistically and accurately | • Monitoring changes of urban greenery overtime<br>• Visualising impacts of urban vegetation on the cityscape, urban space and microclimate, and human well-being<br>• Monitoring of urban-streetside vegetation and visibility of traffic signs<br>• Visualising proposed developments more realistically and accurately |
| **DATA MANAGEMENT** Data Cleaning, Data Storage, Assets | • Co-developing GreenTwins<br>• Creating 3D map of Estonia (Land Board) | • Championing the developmemt of GreenTwins<br>• Developing a Co-planning app<br>• Developing Urban Tempo app<br>• Building a 3D Digital Plant Library<br>• Developing Virtual Green Planner |

 STATE                  ACADEMIA

| MULTIPLE DATA SOURCES | • Archived database; LiDAR scan; expert knowledge | • Remote sensing; drone flight data; expert knowledge |
|---|---|---|
| SPATIAL | • 3D data (buildings); ground elevation model; electric land cables and overhead lines; heating and cooling pipes; sewer and water drainage pipes; water pipes; road network; transportation infrastructure; planning scenarios | • Planning scenarios |
| ECONOMIC | N.A. | N.A. |
| TECHNOLOGICAL | • 5G access points | N.A. |
| ENVIRONMENTAL | • Urban vegetation | • Inventory of plant species and characteristics (3D digital plant library) |
| SOCIAL | N.A. | N.A. |
| CULTURAL | N.A. | N.A. |

**Table 2.7** Analytical Framework of Case Study 7, GreenTwins, Tallinn, Estonia.

- Having access to information and opportunity for participatory planning processes

- Co-creating planning scenarios

- Visualising proposed developments more realistically and accurately

- Co-developing GreenTwins

- Having access to information and opportunity for participatory planning processes

- Co-creating planning scenarios

- Visualising proposed developments more realistically and accurately

N.A.

INDUSTRY

CIVIL SOCIETY

- BIM; expert knowledge

- Citizen data

| BIM models; planning scenarios | Planning scenarios |
|---|---|
| N.A. | N.A. |
| N.A. | N.A. |
| N.A. | N.A. |
| N.A. | N.A. |
| N.A. | N.A. |

# CASE STUDY 8
## TASMU PLATFORM, QATAR

**Figure 2.28 (Left)**
Representational image of Qatar's new initiative TASMU platform to enhance the digital economy (Source: GCC Business News, 2021).

**Figure 2.29 (Overleaf)**
The Pearl-Qatar, Doha, Qatar (Source: Photo by Visit Qatar on Unsplash, 2022).

## CASE OVERVIEW

The Qatari government's commitment to making Qatar a world-class smart nation has culminated in the development of the TASMU platform, which is part of the larger 'TASMU Smart Qatar' project. The platform is led by the Minister of Communications and Information Technology (MCIT), previously the Ministry of Transport and Communications (MOTC). As a digital response to achieving the Qatar National Vision 2030, the platform harnesses state-of-the-art smart technologies to drive sustainable digital economic diversification, improve quality of life, and enhance the delivery of public services across five strategic sectors: transportation, logistics, environment, healthcare, and sports (Figure 2.30) (Joseph, 2021; Villegas-Mateos, 2023).

## SCENARIOS

The TASMU platform is highly regarded as the enabler of the Smart Qatar vision, as it enables cross-sectoral collaborations to deliver use cases while leveraging a growing data ecosystem via dynamic data sharing. The platforms' use cases (Figure 2.31) are broadly categorised into the five strategic sectors as follows (Ministry of Communications and Information Technology, 2023; TASMU Digital Valley, 2022).

### Transportation
The TASMU platform supports Qatar's transportation sector in facilitating mobility to create a safe, reliable, and environmentally friendly transport network. Its Real-time Crowd Analytics generates insights for transportation systems, metro stations, and airport terminals. The platform analyses crowd density, passenger numbers, and vehicle locations to offer demand-based recommendations for transportation services. These updated transportation services are disseminated to commuters through a mobile application as a digital travel guide, thereby enabling them to make informed travel decisions.

### Environment
The TASMU platform promotes sustainable consumption and safeguards water and food security. A Digital Farmer Community, hosted on the platform, offers local agriculture information and crop-specific advice to farmers, improving their chances of success and ensuring food security. Additionally, the platform's sensors monitor household electricity and water consumption, enabling residents to conserve natural resources. The platform promotes sustainability for Qatar by empowering citizens and informing farmers.

### Healthcare

The healthcare sector aims to enhance accessibility to affordable and high-quality healthcare services while mitigating the risk of chronic diseases. To achieve this goal, the TASMU platform offers virtual consultation services, allowing doctors to check on patients in case of medical emergencies regardless of location. This telemedicine technology provides nationwide and personalised access to clinics, making it convenient for patients to receive the medical care they need.

### Logistics

The TASMU platform supports Qatar's logistics sector by promoting international trade and business development. It incorporates a National Supply and Demand Dashboard that monitors national supply and demand information, enhancing awareness of product availability. The platform also facilitates National Food Security Analytics by balancing food imports against local supply. Additionally, it provides intelligent rating algorithms for customs authorities to perform selective screening of inbound shipments. These features support the growth of Qatar's logistics industry, ensure food security, and facilitate efficient customs clearance.

### Sports

The sports sector is envisioned to establish a world-class destination for sports enthusiasts, athlete training, and sports innovation in Qatar. To support this goal, the TASMU platform incorporates crowd-management solutions that provide unique visibility to prevent overcrowding and bottlenecks, particularly in preparation for upcoming mega-events or tournaments.

## CASE SUMMARY

The use cases from the five strategic sectors, enabled by the TASMU platform, showcase Qatar's commitment to becoming a world-class smart nation. Not only does it allow its citizens to reap the benefits of a digital country in the palms of their hands, the platform is also anticipated to be the cornerstone of Qatar's digital transformation and Smart Qatar Vision.

As Qatar faces the challenges of a harsh climate and limited food resources, the government's adoption of the TASMU platform to ensure food security is commendable. However, construction in Qatar is challenged by an arid climate, sandstorms, and harsh terrain. While MOTC has pledged to enhance cooperation with the Lean Construction Institute Qatar (LCI-Qatar) (Joseph, 2021), it would seem essential for these agencies to explore ways to include topographical and environmental studies in the platform, allowing the assessment of building performance in consideration of local environmental factors.

Qatar also boasts rich islamic influences, which have shaped Qatari citizens' social norms and cultural practices that they take pride in (Al-Ammari and Romanowski, 2016; Elshenawy, 2017). Striking a balance between culture and innovation would seem essential and necessitates the incorporation of socio-cultural data / indicators into the platform to enhance the quality of life in a way that is meaningful for Qatari citizens. Embracing both traditional and modern influences with TASMU can provide the digital solutions that align with its citizens' cultural identity.

**ENVIRONMENT**
Drive sustainable consumption of natural resources, and ensure water and food security

**LOGISTICS**
Grow a competitive logistics sector that promotes international trade and drives business development

**HEALTHCARE**
Increase population access to high-quality and affordable healthcare and reduce the risk of chronic diseases

**SPORTS**
Establish a world-class destination for sports fan experience, athlete training, and sports innovation

**TRANSPORT**
Facilitate people mobility through a safe and environmentally friendly transport network

ENVIRONMENT
LOGISTICS
HEALTHCARE
SPORTS
TRANSPORT

Vertical Farming
City Pollution Tracker
Drone Delivery
Smart Building
Smart Health Booth
Dynamic Route Management
Mobile Clinic
Technology Enhanced Athletic Training
Smart Vehicle Monitoring
Smart Parking
National Sports e-Hub
Digital Travel Guide

TASMU PLATFORM AT THE HEART OF THE PROGRAM

**Figure 2.30** A diagram showing the five strategic sectors to be enhanced by the TASMU platform.

TRANSPORT

LOGISTICS

ENVIRONMENT

HEALTHCARE

SPORTS

**Figure 2.31** Cross-sectoral use cases categorised into the five strategic sectors (Source: Photo on Unsplash by Ross Sneddon 2022; Frank McKenna, 2017; Katrien Van Crombrugghe, 2021; National Cancer Institute, 2019; Thomas Serer on Unsplash, 2017).

# CASE STUDY 8
## TASMU PLATFORM, QATAR

| | | STATE | ACADEMIA |
|---|---|---|---|
| **POST-DECISION** Engagement, Collaboration, Data Access Rights, Info Sharing | | • Providing commuters access to a digital travel guide that is delivered through a mobile application<br>• Providing localised agriculture information and crop-specific advice for farmers | N.A. |
| **DECISION TAKING** Automation, Modelling, Simulation, Forecasting | | • Enhancing awareness of product availability and make informed-decisions for food imports<br>• Enabling analytics-driven insights for transportation systems, metro stations and airport terminals<br>• Allowing dynamic route management for transportation services | N.A. |
| **SENSE MAKING** Dashboards & Reporting, Real Time, Analytic, Visualisation | | • Monitoring national-level outlook on the demand and supply of food<br>• Monitoring real-time crowd data<br>• Visualising infrastructure setup in order to plan operation procedures and enhance efficiency of fault identification and rectification | N.A. |
| **DATA MANAGEMENT** Data Cleaning, Data Storage, Assets | | • Championing the development of TASMU platform | N.A. |

 STATE    ACADEMIA

| | STATE | ACADEMIA |
|---|---|---|
| **MULTIPLE DATA SOURCES** | • SQL; sensors; geospatial services APIs; 3D city models | N.A. |
| SPATIAL | • Locations; map-related capabilities; buildings; roads; point of interest; planned urban projects | N.A. |
| ECONOMIC | • Food source; food imports; international trade and business development | N.A. |
| TECHNOLOGICAL | N.A. | N.A. |
| ENVIRONMENTAL | N.A. | N.A. |
| SOCIAL | N.A. | N.A. |
| CULTURAL | N.A. | N.A. |

**Table 2.8** Analytical Framework of Case Study 8, TASMU Platform, Qatar.

- Allowing the Smart Water Network to provide real-time water usage information and targeted maintenance interventions
- Enabling Drone Delivery to share delivery status with its customers
- Allowing Smart Parking to share the parking location's details with customers
- Allowing Flexible Delivery to provide recipients with flexible delivery services by accommodating needs and schedules and providing information about deliveries
- Providing doctor consultation through telemedicine

- Having access to information regarding real-time transportation services; localised farming and agriculture guide; telemedicine; delivery services; real-time water consumption and maintenance schedules; parking facilities

N.A.

N.A.

N.A.

N.A.

- Allowing Smart Parking to establish connections with devices/sensors at various parking locations to highlight parking utilisation
- Enabling Smart Building to transfer data to optimise heating, cooling, lighting, air quality, and water usage through sensor monitoring technologies
- Allowing Precision Agriculture to establish a connection with devices/sensors to provide an overview of the field operations to crop yield farmers to manage their agricultural input resources effectively

N.A.

INDUSTRY

CIVIL SOCIETY

| • Internet of Things (IoT); sensor | • GPS, Citizen data (health) |
|---|---|
| N.A. | N.A. |
| N.A. | N.A. |
| • Networked devices data; sensor data | N.A. |
| • Utilities data; crop yield | N.A. |
| N.A. | • Location; health |
| N.A. | N.A. |

# SUMMARY OF COMPARATIVE ANALYSIS

| CASE STUDIES | SG | DUB IRL | XNA CHN | JPN | DAR AUS | BOS USA | TLL EST | QAT | SG | DUB IRL | XNA CHN | JPN | DAR AUS | BOS USA | TLL EST | QAT |
|---|---|---|---|---|---|---|---|---|---|---|---|---|---|---|---|---|
| **POST-DECISION** Engagement, Collaboration, Data Access Rights, Info Sharing | | | | ✓ | | ✓ | ✓ | ✓ | | | | ✓ | ✓ | | ✓ | |
| **DECISION TAKING** Automation, Modelling, Simulation, Forecasting | ✓ | ✓ | ✓ | ✓ | ✓ | ✓✓ | ✓ | ✓ | ✓ | ✓ | | ✓ | ✓ | | ✓ | |
| **SENSE MAKING** Dashboards & Reporting, Real Time, Analytic, Visualisation | ✓ | ✓ | ✓ | ✓ | ✓ | ✓ | ✓ | ✓ | ✓ | | ✓ | ✓ | | | ✓ | |
| **DATA MANAGEMENT** Data Cleaning, Data Storage, Assets | ✓ | ✓ | ✓ | ✓ | ✓ | ✓ | ✓ | ✓ | | ✓ | ✓ | ✓ | ✓ | | ✓ | |

STATE ⬍                      ACADEMIA ⬍

| | SG | DUB IRL | XNA CHN | JPN | DAR AUS | BOS USA | TLL EST | QAT | SG | DUB IRL | XNA CHN | JPN | DAR AUS | BOS USA | TLL EST | QAT |
|---|---|---|---|---|---|---|---|---|---|---|---|---|---|---|---|---|
| **MULTIPLE DATA SOURCES** | ✓✓ | ✓ | ✓ | ✓ | ✓ | ✓ | ✓ | ✓ | ✓✓ | ✓ | ✓ | ✓ | ✓ | | ✓ | |
| SPATIAL | ✓✓ | ✓ | ✓ | ✓ | ✓ | ✓ | ✓ | ✓ | ✓ | ✓ | ✓ | ✓ | | | ✓ | |
| ECONOMIC | | | | | ✓ | ✓ | | ✓ | | | | | | | | |
| TECHNO-LOGICAL | ✓ | ✓ | | | ✓ | | ✓ | | | | | | ✓ | | | |
| ENVIRON-MENTAL | ✓ | ✓ | | | ✓ | ✓ | ✓ | | ✓ | | | ✓ | ✓ | | ✓ | |
| SOCIAL | | ✓ | | ✓ | | | | | | | | ✓ | | | | |
| CULTURAL | | | | | | | | | | | | | | | | |

**Table 2.9** Summary of comparative analysis or urban scale DT case studies.

✓   *Current Features*
✓   *Upcoming Features*

**INDUSTRY**

| SG | DUB IRL | XNA CHN | JPN | DAR AUS | BOS USA | TLL EST | QAT |
|----|---------|---------|-----|---------|---------|---------|-----|
|    |         |         | ✓   | ✓       |         | ✓       | ✓   |
| ✓  | ✓       |         | ✓   |         | ✓       |         |     |
| ✓  |         | ✓       | ✓   |         | ✓       |         |     |
| ✓  | ✓       | ✓       | ✓   | ✓       | ✓       | ✓       | ✓   |

**CIVIL SOCIETY**

| SG | DUB IRL | XNA CHN | JPN | DAR AUS | BOS USA | TLL EST | QAT |
|----|---------|---------|-----|---------|---------|---------|-----|
| ✓  | ✓       |         | ✓   | ✓       | ✓       | ✓       | ✓   |
|    |         |         | ✓   | ✓       |         | ✓       |     |
|    |         |         | ✓   | ✓       | ✓       | ✓       |     |
|    |         |         | ✓   |         |         |         |     |

**INDUSTRY**

| SG | DUB IRL | XNA CHN | JPN | DAR AUS | BOS USA | TLL EST | QAT |
|----|---------|---------|-----|---------|---------|---------|-----|
| ✓✓ | ✓       | ✓       | ✓   |         | ✓       | ✓       | ✓   |
| ✓  | ✓       | ✓       | ✓   |         | ✓       | ✓       |     |
| ✓  |         |         |     |         |         |         |     |
| ✓  | ✓       | ✓       | ✓   |         |         | ✓       |     |
|    |         |         | ✓   |         |         | ✓       |     |
|    |         | ✓       | ✓   |         |         |         |     |

**CIVIL SOCIETY**

| SG | DUB IRL | XNA CHN | JPN | DAR AUS | BOS USA | TLL EST | QAT |
|----|---------|---------|-----|---------|---------|---------|-----|
| ✓✓ | ✓       |         | ✓   | ✓       |         | ✓       | ✓   |
|    | ✓       |         | ✓   |         |         | ✓       |     |
|    |         |         |     |         |         |         |     |
| ✓  |         |         |     |         |         |         |     |
|    |         |         |     |         |         |         |     |
| ✓✓ |         | ✓       | ✓   | ✓       |         |         | ✓   |

*Limited information is available on the data layers required for DT, XNA, CHN and DT, BOS, USA.*

**VIRTUAL SINGAPORE, SINGAPORE**

**DIGITAL TWIN SMART CITY OF THE DOCKLANDS AREA, DUBLIN, IRELAND**

**DIGITAL TWIN CITY OF THE XIONG'AN NEW AREA, CHINA**

**PLATEAU, JAPAN**

**DIGITAL TWIN DARWIN, NORTHEN TERRITORY, AUSTRALIA**

**DIGITAL 3D MODEL OF BOSTON, MASSACHUSETTS, USA**

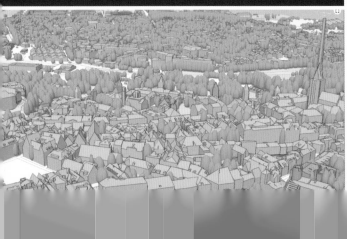

# KEY CONSIDERATIONS

The analytical framework developed in this chapter sought to provide a more detailed and structured comparative analysis of urban scale DTs. The framework identified strategic partnerships and considered both hard and soft assets that are vitally important in not only planning a (physical) city, but also its (digital) counterpart.

Taking stock of the eight case studies selected, the summary of the comparative analysis (Table 2.9) reveals that the utilisation of civil society for citizen data collection and co-creation is still an uncommon practice in many DTs (except for the cases in Ireland and Japan). Despite the effort of some DTs to understand and improve social mobility, there is a lack of tangible methods for measuring social trends and socio-cultural practices, such as collective behaviours, social interactions, and social norms, which are also essential to inform cities' functions and design.

What can be further observed from these case studies is how municipalities are increasingly adopting DTs as a tool to sense, analyse, predict, and make informed decisions regarding a city's infrastructure in the interests of improving the operability of the city for which it serves. They tend to be tools of the state, with the active participation of ICT industry partners and occasionally academic institutions who act as enablers of proof-of-concepts for commercial and academic interests respectively.

It was also observed that the complexity of the DT models can be seen to vary across the case studies, though the commonality lies in their ability to be a predominantly spatial model, with greater regard to solving municipal 'hardware' issues. The DT has often been used as a means to test new innovations or urban scenarios before becoming the physical reality within the city, and, to a lesser extent, capturing social-economic and cultural behavioural patterns of its citizens.

Therefore, a future research agenda could advocate the quadripartite relationship in urban scale DTs, with greater emphasis to perceive and empower civil society as an equally important stakeholder, as well as recognising their equitable contributions to smart city governance and planning. There is also a pressing need to develop tangible methods in order to quantifiably measure social trends by leveraging on predictive, algorithmic-based pedestrian modelling software (e.g. Depth Map), Global Positioning System (GPS) tracking devices, and social media analytics, to name a few, to further examine people-environment relationships and enhance the decision-making process using DTs.

Additionally, while cities are seen to be highly influential in cultural development and powerhouses of economic growth, it is evident that the majority of DTs have yet to fully integrate cultural and economic elements and consider their spill-over impacts on the spatial, environmental, social, and technological systems of the cities.

Lastly, more effort is required to explore and understand methods to operationalise, quantify, integrate, and represent the layers that are still absent (especially cultural and economic data layers / sets) in the majority of existing urban scale DTs, as well as to create scenarios that can accurately represent the interactions between the tangible and intangible elements: just as they are in the physical world. Only by unleashing the true potential of a more inclusive, all-encompassing DT will smarter cities emerge that are fit for a dynamic population, resilient in times of crisis, and adaptable to climate change.

# CHAPTER 3.0
## DIGITAL TRANSFORMATION

BRATISLAVA

PREŠOV

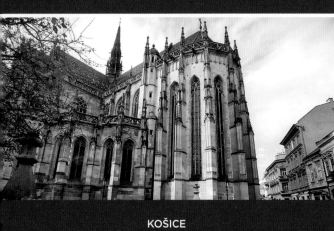

KOŠICE

TRENCÍN

BANSKÁ BYSTRICA

NITRA

TRNAVA

ŽILINA

# A NEW DIGITAL TWIN PARADIGM

In 2023, Slovakia celebrated its 30th anniversary of independence. Despite its relative youthfulness as a nation, its central geographical location in Europe made it an important historical transit hub for centuries. The country is today perceived as one of the major manufacturing hubs in the world. In a 2020 International Organization of Motor Vehicle Manufacturers report, Slovakia was still the world's leading car manufacturing nation by vehicle produced per 1000 people. The country manufactured a total of 1.1 million cars in 2019, representing 43% of its total industrial output (International Organization of Motor Vehicle Manufacturers, 2023).

Yet despite what would seem to be post-Soviet prosperity through a combination of a market economy and a comprehensive social security system, which provides citizens with universal health care, free education, and one of the longest paid parental leaves in the OECD, the Republic ranked 23rd out of 27 European countries in the EU Digital Economy and Society Index (DESI) in 2022 (European Commission, 2022). The index is an indicator of digital performance and integration across EU countries and highlighted the opportunities for the Republic's transformation from analogue to digital systems.

Statutory planning and building application processes, as a case in point, were mired in analogue-driven bureaucracy, which led to protracted approval times that stagnated the built-environment industry. In light of this, the Slovak government established new laws on spatial planning and construction that replaced the 1976 Construction Act in Slovakia. A new Authority for Spatial Planning and Construction of the Slovak Republic, established to administer the new laws, also reflected Slovakia's 2030 digital transformation process and electronicisation (Lexante Law Firm & Advisory, 2022). This formed the act's foundation.

Part of the transformation process would be a new DT paradigm for Slovakia: forged by a quadripartite relationship between civil society, state, academia, and industry, and with greater emphasis on empowering civil society as an equally important stakeholder. This would recognise their equitable contributions to smart city governance and planning, and similarly yield tangible benefits for the Slovak people. Whilst existing open data platforms are available across the eight regions of Slovakia (Figure 3.1), the data available lacks a streamlined framework for efficient interoperability. This is a significant barrier to the implementation of a working DT, where complexity or even inability of data integration is brought about by incompatible data types and structures.

With the implementation of the new 'Spatial Planning and Construction Law', the following agenda was set in action to digitally transform Slovakia:

1.  Interoperability of processes and actions;
2.  Availability of high-quality, real-time data, that is reflected in the DT;
3.  Electronic services to ensure execution of end-to-end processes of spatial planning and building permit; and
4.  Information technology service management of the spatial planning and construction information system 'myUrbium' (Authority for Spatial Planning and Construction of the Slovak Republic, 2022).

**Figure 3.1** Eight Regions in Slovakia.

# RESEARCH METHODOLOGY

## A MULTI-LAYERED APPROACH

To adopt a more people-centric approach, a DT could aspire to go beyond the spatial, technological, and environmental considerations often found in the majority of DTs today, by encapsulating the author's broader 'six pillars' of sustainability (Pomeroy, 2020a). This was verified and expanded on through a five-step process-driven approach (Figure 3.2):

1. Analysis of case studies from literature review;
2. Analysis of existing open data available in Slovakia;
3. Data extraction and filtering;
4. Data categorisation; and
5. Stakeholder validation.

This multi-layered process has been adopted to ensure the establishment of a broad-based, sustainable, and contextual framework that is unimpeded by spatial and temporal dimensions. It further balances quantitative and qualitative data findings to offer a strategy (and eventually a Proof of Concept [PoC], tested through scenario planning) for an effective and efficient DT in Slovakia.

### Step 1: Analysis of Case Studies from Literature Review

A study of existing urban scale DTs in different regions of the world (Asia, Europe, North America, Oceania, and the Middle East) was undertaken to assess the required baseline data layers and indicators. This informed the initial repository of potential data layers for the DT, which were aggregated and mapped to one of the six corresponding pillars.

### Step 2: Analysis of Existing Open Data Available in Slovakia

Beyond the literature review, a contextual investigation of available data in Slovakia was imperative to assess areas of readiness for data integration into the DT. Through desktop research of open-data platforms in the eight regions of Slovakia, the types of datasets and classification approaches were investigated and populated in the data layer repository, and similarly aggregated and categorised into one of the six corresponding pillars.

### Step 3: Data Extraction & Filtering

With Steps 1 and 2 providing a two-layered approach for amassing a data layer repository for the digital twin, Step 3 sought to extract critical data relevant to the DT and its uses through a filtering process: screening those that are relevant in the urban context. The curation and selection process provided greater clarity to the DT, and will become richer with more data over time.

### Step 4: Data Categorisation

Having established a repository of data layers from both the literature review of existing DTs and existing open data in Slovakia, it was observed that the data classification approach varies across different DTs and the eight regions. This necessitated a common framework to unify existing data critical for interoperability and collaboration across all regions and the four stakeholder spheres. The author's 'six-pillar' framework was used as a common data classification structure to potentially streamline and standardise the digitisation process across Slovakia, promoting a sustainable smart nation through its digital transformation.

### Step 5: Stakeholder Validation

The intuitiveness of the data layer categorisation was further validated by engaging the four stakeholder spheres. Through qualitative 'card sorting', employed to understand how people organise and categorise information and their choices (Brent et al., 2021), a broad range of feedback was gathered from the four stakeholder groups. This sought to refine the DT data layer and indicator categorisation within the 'six-pillars', culminating in a more inclusive and user-centric DT strategy for Slovakia.

# RESEARCH METHODOLOGY

## 1 DATA LAYERS: CASE STUDIES

- DUBLIN DOCKLANDS, IRELAND
- XIONG'AN, CHINA
- BOSTON, USA
- PLATEAU, JAPAN
- DARWIN, AUSTRALIA
- SINGAPORE
- TALLINN, ESTONIA
- QATAR

## 3 DATA EXTRACTION & FILTERING

| DATA LAYERS | SPATIAL | 1 | 2 | ECONOMIC | 1 | 2 | TECHNOLOGICAL | 1 | 2 |
|---|---|---|---|---|---|---|---|---|---|
| | BUILDINGS | ■ | ■ | SUBSIDIES & INCENTIVES | | ■ | FUTURE PROOF INFRASTRUCTURE | | |
| | OPEN SPACE NETWORK | ■ | | REGIONAL INCOME & EXPENDITURE | ■ | ■ | GREEN ENERGY | | ■ |
| | MOBILITY INFRASTRUCTURE | ■ | ■ | EMPLOYMENT & BUSINESS ECOSYSTEM | | ■ | RESOURCE OPTIMISATION | ■ | ■ |
| | UTILITIES | ■ | ■ | PUBLIC PROCUREMENT | | ■ | IT INFRASTRUCTURE | ■ | ■ |
| | URBAN PLANNING | ■ | ■ | PROPERTY INFORMATION | | ■ | MONITORING, OPERATIONS, & MAINTENANCE | ■ | ■ |
| | TOPOGRAPHY | ■ | ■ | LAND USE | ■ | ■ | SMART PUBLIC INFRASTRUCTURE | ■ | ■ |

**OBSERVATIONS**

Spatial data layers are present and consistent in both steps 1 & 2. The proposed spatial data layers are critical to facilitate the categorisation of existing spatial datasets, from the macro to the micro scale.

While Step 1 has shown that economic data layers are limited in many DTs, Step 2 has shown extensive data is available relating to this pillar in the eight regions of Slovakia. These are extracted, filtered, and categorised to encapsulate economic datasets of both tangible & intangible assets.

Combining results from steps 1 & 2, a repository of technological data layers is built up. What is critical is the need to support this pillar with further future-proofing strategies in the era of automation and robotisation, especially considering the digital transformation strategy of Slovakia 2030.

## 5 STAKEHOLDER VALIDATION

- STATE
- ACADEMIA
- INDUSTRY
- CIVIL SOCIETY

**Figure 3.2** A five-step process-driven approach to establish a broad-based, sustainable, and contextual DT framework for Slovakia.

# 2 DATA LAYERS: SLOVAKIA'S 8 REGIONS

- BRATISLAVA
- PREŠOV
- KOŠICE
- TRENČÍN
- BANSKÁ BYSTRICA
- NITRA
- TRNAVA
- ŽILINA

- EXTRACTION OF CRITICAL DATA FROM STEPS 1 & 2
- FILTERING OF DATA RELEVANT TO THE BUILT ENVIRONMENT

# DATA CATEGORISATION 4

| | ENVIRONMENTAL | 1 | 2 | SOCIAL | 1 | 2 | CULTURAL | 1 | 2 |
|---|---|---|---|---|---|---|---|---|---|
| **DATA LAYERS** | CLIMATE RESILIENCE | | ■ | COMMUNITY ENGAGEMENT | | | CULTURE OF INNOVATION | | ■ |
| | ENVIRONMENTAL HAZARD MONITORING | ■ | | SOCIAL INFRASTRUCTURE & USAGE | | ■ | TOURISM | | |
| | POLLUTION | | ■ | SAFETY & SECURITY | | ■ | PUBLIC SERVICES / SOCIAL MEDIA | | ■ |
| | WASTE MANAGEMENT | | ■ | HEALTHCARE | | | CALENDAR OF CULTURAL EVENTS | | |
| | ENVIRONMENTAL BASELINE STUDIES | ■ | | EDUCATION | | ■ | CIVIC AMENITIES & FACILITIES | | |
| | BIODIVERSITY | | ■ | DEMOGRAPHY | ■ | | LANDMARKS OF NATIONAL IMPORTANCE | | |

**OBSERVATIONS**

The results from Step 1 and Step 2 build up the repository of environmental data layers. The data layers range from understanding natural features to addressing environmental impact and pollution, as well as forecasting unfavourable weather conditions and environmental catastrophes.

The social data layers are derived through Steps 1 & 2. The proposed data layers above start from understanding the population and demographic data, to ensuring welfare & well-being of the population in different aspects of their social life.

It is observed that the DTs studied in Step 1 are lacking in cultural-related data. The extensive results found in Step 2 are processed and summarised into the cultural data layers above, adding a new dimension to the new DT paradigm for Slovakia.

# PILLAR 1: SPATIAL

A geo-spatial visualisation tool for citizens; a planning, development, and construction tool for statutory submissions, academic research, and corporations.

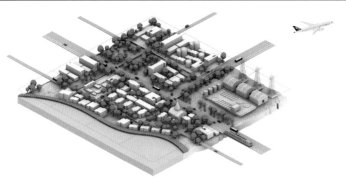

**Figure 3.3** Spatial elements are represented in this pillar to highlight the existing physical environment.

# PILLAR 2: ECONOMIC

A quantity-surveying tool to gauge development and operational costs; a predictive tool to forecast gross development and real estate value for strategic investment.

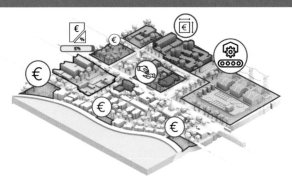

**Figure 3.4** Economic data relating to land use, property, and spending employment data is visualised in this pillar.

# PILLAR 3: TECHNOLOGICAL

A sensing tool to monitor consumption patterns; optimise and manage maintenance and operations of city infrastructure without any technical downtime.

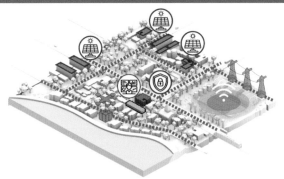

**Figure 3.5** Information Technology and energy infrastructure are highlighted in this pillar to facilitate city operations.

## PILLAR 4: ENVIRONMENTAL

An early warning system and risk management tool to future proof the city through collaboration with state agencies, organisations, academia, and citizens.

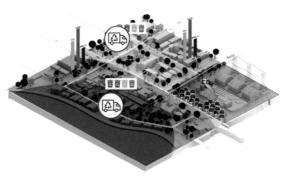

**Figure 3.6** Dynamic environmental data is simulated and visualised to forecast and implement preventive measures.

## PILLAR 5: SOCIAL

A visualisation of socio-demographic shifts and changing social patterns to cultivate citizen participation and identify social gaps and bias to enhance quality of life.

**Figure 3.7** Social data is collected, visualised, and simulated to integrate citizen behaviour into future planning.

## PILLAR 6: CULTURAL

A platform to cultivate community appreciation of cultural heritage through the retracing of historical sites and mining of local stories from crowd-sourced data.

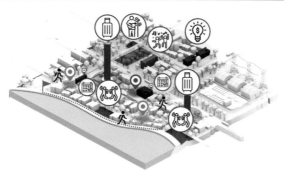

**Figure 3.8** Key heritage sites and cultural events are visualised to cultivate citizen appreciation of arts and culture.

# SPATIAL
## DATA LAYERS | CATEGORISATION OF DATA LAYERS

Spatial elements are represented in this pillar to highlight the existing physical environment, from topography, planning boundaries, utilities, mobility and green infrastructure, to buildings. This will allow the user to get a full picture of the baseline conditions to plan for future developments, identify routes, and ultimately get a sense of the 'static' physical and tangible elements that are represented in the virtual world.

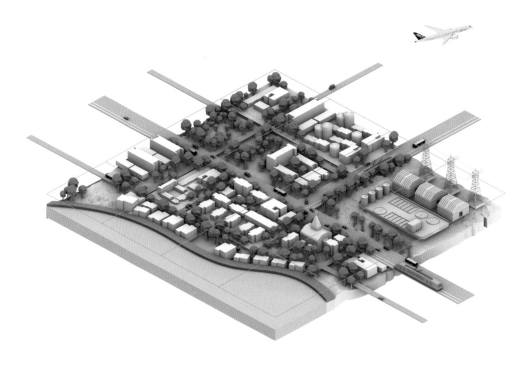

**Figure 3.9** Spatial elements are represented in this pillar to highlight the existing physical environment.

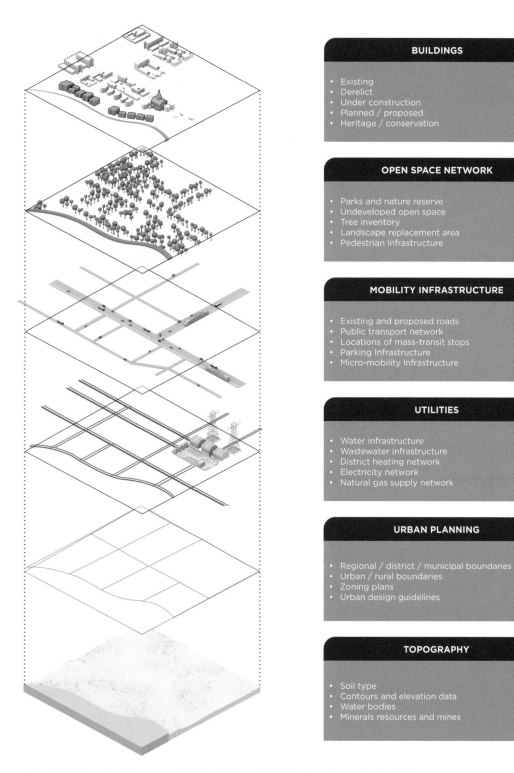

**BUILDINGS**

- Existing
- Derelict
- Under construction
- Planned / proposed
- Heritage / conservation

**OPEN SPACE NETWORK**

- Parks and nature reserve
- Undeveloped open space
- Tree inventory
- Landscape replacement area
- Pedestrian Infrastructure

**MOBILITY INFRASTRUCTURE**

- Existing and proposed roads
- Public transport network
- Locations of mass-transit stops
- Parking Infrastructure
- Micro-mobility Infrastructure

**UTILITIES**

- Water infrastructure
- Wastewater infrastructure
- District heating network
- Electricity network
- Natural gas supply network

**URBAN PLANNING**

- Regional / district / municipal boundaries
- Urban / rural boundaries
- Zoning plans
- Urban design guidelines

**TOPOGRAPHY**

- Soil type
- Contours and elevation data
- Water bodies
- Minerals resources and mines

**Figure 3.10** An exploded axonometric view of the spatial data pillar, showcasing its data layers.

# ECONOMIC

## DATA LAYERS | CATEGORISATION OF DATA LAYERS

It is observed in Chapter One that the economic pillar is seen to be minimally substantiated in other DTs as compared to the other pillars. The DT will be enriched with economic data relating to land use, property, spending patterns, and employment data, to allow users to make informed decisions for strategic investment. Socio-economic information can also be gleaned from the data layers in this pillar, enabling inclusive city planning.

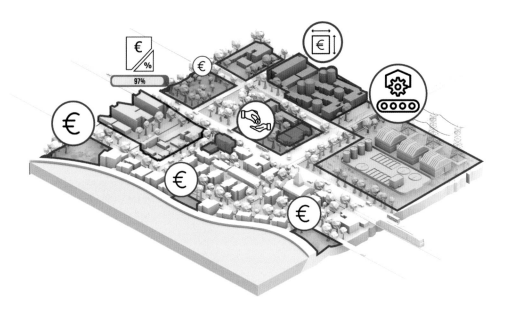

**Figure 3.11** Economic data relating to land use, property, spending employment data is visualised in this pillar.

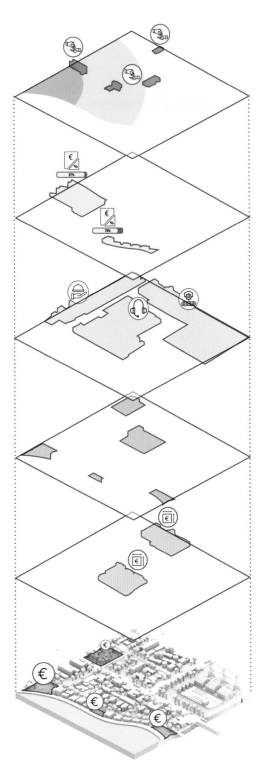

## SUBSIDIES & INCENTIVES

- Subsidies for individuals
- Subsidies for business
- Grant schemes for promoting intangible cultural heritage and cultural awareness activities
- Incentives for digital transformation
- Incentives for sustainable development

## REGIONAL INCOME & EXPENDITURE

- GDP nominal and public – private partnership (PPP)
- Revenue generated per sector
- Property tax collections and status
- Direct / Indirect tax collections
- Spending pattern per sector

## EMPLOYMENT & BUSINESS ECOSYSTEM

- Employment data
- Centralised available jobs repository
- Registered businesses and associated data
- Revenue generated per sector
- Gig business and employment monitoring

## PUBLIC PROCUREMENT

- Construction service tenders
- Goods and services tenders
- Government registered suppliers
- Public-sector panel of consultants

## PROPERTY INFORMATION

- Commercial property for rent / sale
- Residential property for rent / sale
- Industrial property for rent / sale
- Transaction values over a period of five years
- Property taxes & stamp duty
- Gross development value

## LAND USE

- Permitted uses
- Land ownership record
- Land for sale public & private
- Development permit status and conditions

**Figure 3.12** An exploded axonometric view of the economic data pillar, showcasing its data layers.

# TECHNOLOGICAL

## DATA LAYERS | CATEGORISATION OF DATA LAYERS

The technological pillar is critical in the facilitation of city-wide operations, maintenance, and optimisation. This involves the mapping of public infrastructure, including real-time data such as public transport and telecommunications information. This is further enhanced by monitoring facilities such as a Central Command Centre, as well as resource optimisation technologies to future-proof the city and roll out resilient infrastructure.

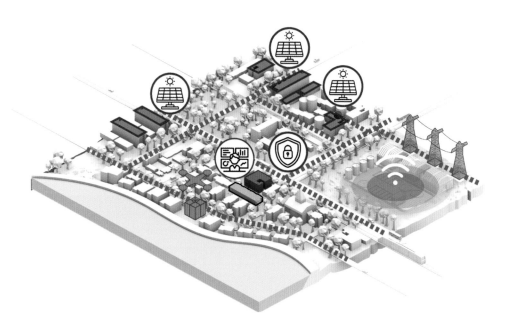

**Figure 3.13** Information Technology and energy infrastructure are highlighted in this pillar to facilitate city operations.

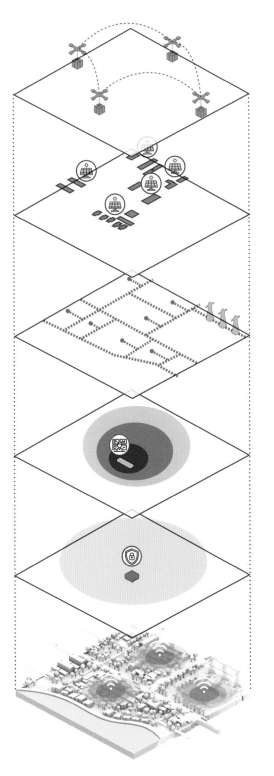

## FUTURE PROOF INFRASTRUCTURE

- Autonomous-vehicle-ready infrastructure
- Air Mobility & delivery
- Water Mobility
- Blockchain technology deployment

## GREEN TECHNOLOGY

- Existing / proposed alternate energy sources infrastructure
- Energy split, pricing, and utilisation
- Off-grid energy production
- National battery storage network

## RESOURCE OPTIMISATION

- Household / industrial water consumption
- Household / industrial electricity consumption
- Irrigation water use for agriculture
- Mining and quarrying extraction / exploration

## IT INFRASTRUCTURE

- Data / cloud storage network and capacity
- Central command centre
- Internet distribution network and usage

## MONITORING, OPERATIONS, & MAINTENANCE

- Gas / water leakage detection and control
- Water quality monitoring
- Public infrastructure maintenance schedules
- Solid waste management
- Cybersecurity monitoring

## SMART PUBLIC INFRASTRUCTURE

- Sensor network
- WiFi hotspots
- Live Traffic Information
- Live Public Transport Information
- CCTV Surveillance network

**Figure 3.14** An exploded axonometric view of the technological data pillar, showcasing its data layers.

# ENVIRONMENTAL

## DATA LAYERS | CATEGORISATION OF DATA LAYERS

Dynamic environmental information is simulated and visualised on the DT to allow for climate-responsive planning interventions. This will support environmental hazard monitoring and serve as an early warning system for citizens in vulnerable regions. Through monitoring of environmental conditions, pollution levels, and waste, risk management measures can be strategically implemented to transform the city into one that is more resilient, healthier, and safer for its inhabitants.

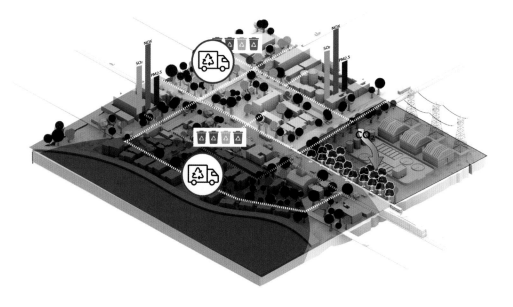

**Figure 3.15** Dynamic environmental data is simulated and visualised to forecast and implement preventive measures.

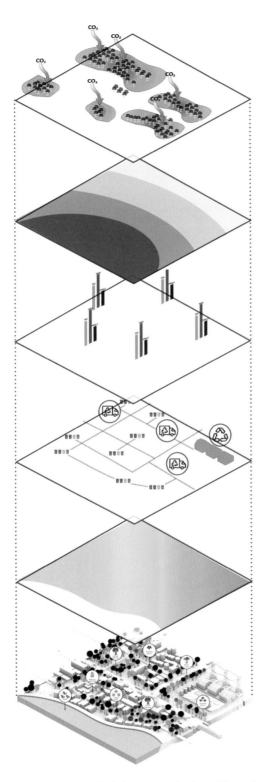

## CLIMATE RESILIENCE

- Carbon credits tracking
- Circular economy monitoring
- Biodiversity index
- Decarbonisation tracking

## ENVIRONMENTAL HAZARD MONITORING

- Landslides
- Forest Fires
- Earthquake Monitoring
- Flood Monitoring
- Radiation and Biohazard

## POLLUTION

- Air pollution
- Water pollution
- Noise pollution
- Soil contamination

## WASTE MANAGEMENT

- Collection data
- Segregation data
- Transportation optimisation
- Processing and recycling
- Dumping / landfill data

## ENVIRONMENTAL BASELINE STUDIES

- Meteorological
- Sunpath and shadow data
- Ambient air quality
- Noise data
- Water quality
- Land environment
- Ambient temperature

## BIODIVERSITY

- Plant data
- Animal data
- Ecosystem data
- Genetic data

**Figure 3.16** An exploded axonometric view of the environmental data pillar, showcasing its data layers.

# SOCIAL

## DATA LAYERS | CATEGORISATION OF DATA LAYERS

The social pillar collects and visualises demographic data, education, healthcare, social infrastructure, and utilisation patterns by citizens. Gauging public acceptance and frequency of use of services and infrastructure will enhance efficiency and advocate a citizen-centric approach to planning of a safer, more sustainable, equitable nation. Social gaps and bias can also be identified to allow for targeted aid to enhance standard of living and quality of life of citizens.

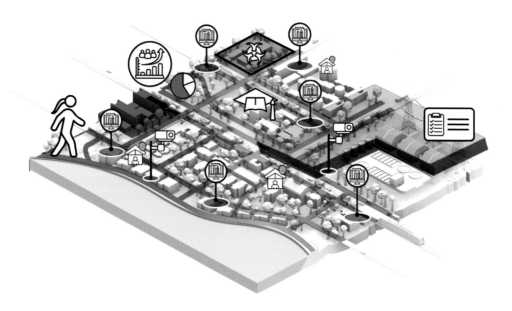

**Figure 3.17** Social data is collected, visualised, and simulated to integrate citizen behaviour into future planning.

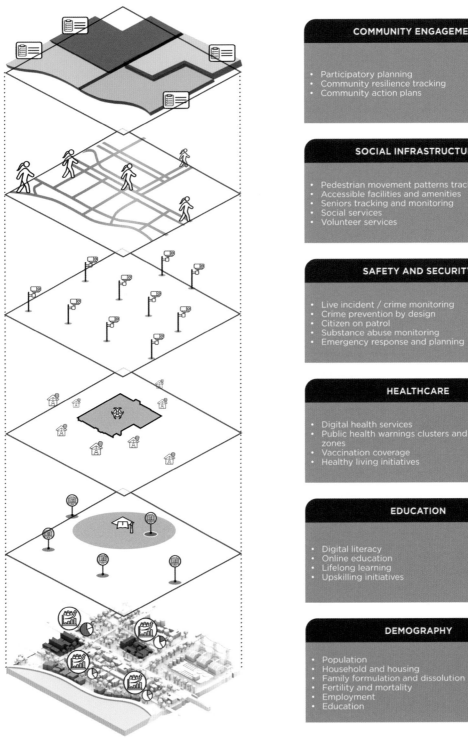

**COMMUNITY ENGAGEMENT**

- Participatory planning
- Community resilience tracking
- Community action plans

**SOCIAL INFRASTRUCTURE**

- Pedestrian movement patterns tracking
- Accessible facilities and amenities
- Seniors tracking and monitoring
- Social services
- Volunteer services

**SAFETY AND SECURITY**

- Live incident / crime monitoring
- Crime prevention by design
- Citizen on patrol
- Substance abuse monitoring
- Emergency response and planning

**HEALTHCARE**

- Digital health services
- Public health warnings clusters and quarantine zones
- Vaccination coverage
- Healthy living initiatives

**EDUCATION**

- Digital literacy
- Online education
- Lifelong learning
- Upskilling initiatives

**DEMOGRAPHY**

- Population
- Household and housing
- Family formulation and dissolution
- Fertility and mortality
- Employment
- Education

**Figure 3.18** An exploded axonometric view of the social data pillar, showcasing its data layers.

# CULTURAL

## DATA LAYERS | CATEGORISATION OF DATA LAYERS

Cultural nodes and points of interest such as heritage monuments and historical sites are highlighted in this pillar, alongside time-based practices such as pop-up events or exhibitions. Local events, festivals and stories are also populated in the DT, cultivating citizen appreciation and engagement with arts and heritage, through crowd-sourced data. The DT also seeks to spur a culture of innovation through the mapping of creative spaces (such as fablabs) and events (such as hackathons).

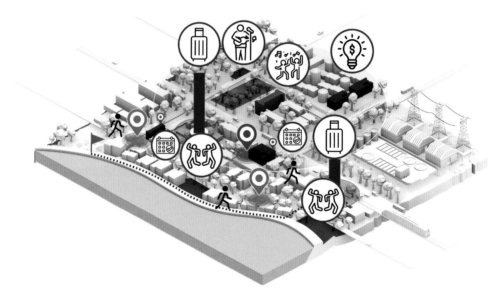

**Figure 3.19** Key heritage sites and cultural events are visualised to cultivate citizen appreciation of arts and culture.

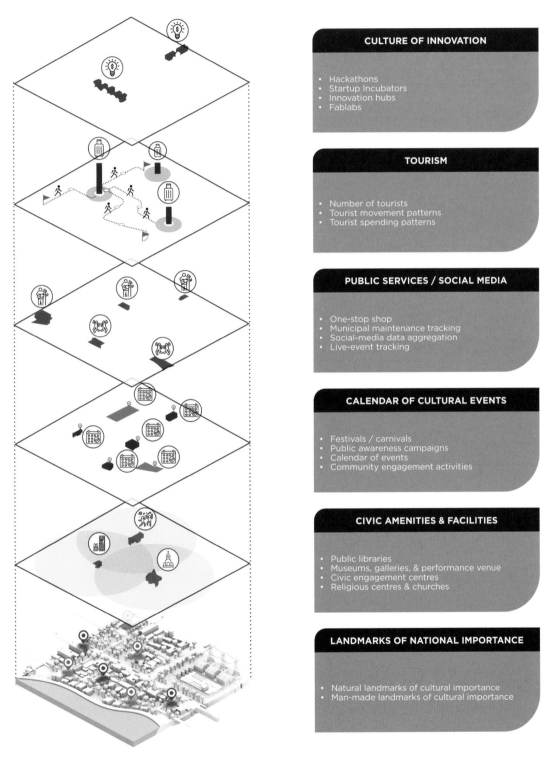

**CULTURE OF INNOVATION**

- Hackathons
- Startup Incubators
- Innovation hubs
- Fablabs

**TOURISM**

- Number of tourists
- Tourist movement patterns
- Tourist spending patterns

**PUBLIC SERVICES / SOCIAL MEDIA**

- One-stop shop
- Municipal maintenance tracking
- Social-media data aggregation
- Live-event tracking

**CALENDAR OF CULTURAL EVENTS**

- Festivals / carnivals
- Public awareness campaigns
- Calendar of events
- Community engagement activities

**CIVIC AMENITIES & FACILITIES**

- Public libraries
- Museums, galleries, & performance venue
- Civic engagement centres
- Religious centres & churches

**LANDMARKS OF NATIONAL IMPORTANCE**

- Natural landmarks of cultural importance
- Man-made landmarks of cultural importance

**Figure 3.20** An exploded axonometric view of the cultural data pillar, showcasing its data layers.

# FOUR SPHERES OF INFLUENCE IN SLOVAKIA

## DATA LAYERS | A PURPOSE-LED DIGITAL TWIN WITH FOUR SPHERES OF INFLUENCE

As discussed in Chapter One, strategic partnerships are critical to creating a successful and sustainable product: in this case, the DT for Slovakia. Through the comparative analysis of urban-scale DT case studies elaborated in Chapter Two, the author's 'four spheres of influence' (Pomeroy, 2020b) have revealed their respective roles and contributions that are equally important in the co-creation of DTs for effective urban governance and development in the long-run. It reflects a paradigm shift from top-down, siloed, one-directional decision-making approaches to a more integrative, middle-out approach that engages the four spheres.

The above-mentioned underscores the necessity to examine the involvement of active and relevant stakeholders across the eight regions in Slovakia. The author's framework of 'four spheres of influence' (depicted in Figure 3.21) was employed as a tool to pinpoint key potential stakeholders from each of the four spheres. In order to ensure a well-rounded group of stakeholders with varied areas of expertise, each stakeholder that was identified was categorised to one of the six corresponding pillars. These stakeholders can then form strategic partnerships for the development of the DT in Slovakia.

The analysis of open data in the eight Slovak regions not only led to the establishment of a repository of data layers for the development of the DT, but also identified a roster of data owners who are accountable for a broad range of data assets throughout the country. It became apparent that the central bodies of state administration, such as the Statistical Office of the Slovak Republic, were the key contributors of consistent data at the national level. These central bodies are assisted by other stakeholders such as government agencies (state) at different levels, corporate stakeholders (industry), universities and research labs (academia), as well as citizens (civil society).

It became clear that having a collaborative framework has enabled Slovakia to yield positive outcomes in creating, maintaining, and protecting the data assets throughout the country, as it is in the midst of digital transformation. Such a collaborative framework can be transposed to the development of the DT to ensure it is attuned to the needs of citizens; feature up-to-date technologies that begin in the realm of academia and industry; and is regulated and protected by state bodies to mitigate risks, such as cybersecurity threats and data protection vulnerabilities. Such partnerships will also allow for more sustained systemic change, where citizens are able to provide feedback and input through the DT that can be screened and conveyed to relevant policy-makers. The DT provides an open channel of communication that is typically closed and limited by bureaucratic red tape.

To progress, the process involves strategic plans to gather an ensemble of stakeholders, and embark on a collaborative journey that will break down the norms of a top-down, product-focused approach that is commonly seen in the majority of urban scale DTs. This is an unprecedented and unparalleled opportunity to reshape the way a smart nation can be represented and governed in this digitally-enabled age, and open new paths for an integrated, people-centric DT strategy for Slovakia: one that advocates the quadripartite relationship between the four spheres of influence, and extends beyond typical spatial, technological, and environmental considerations of existing DTs, incorporating social, cultural, and economic data in the development of a comprehensive and balanced DT.

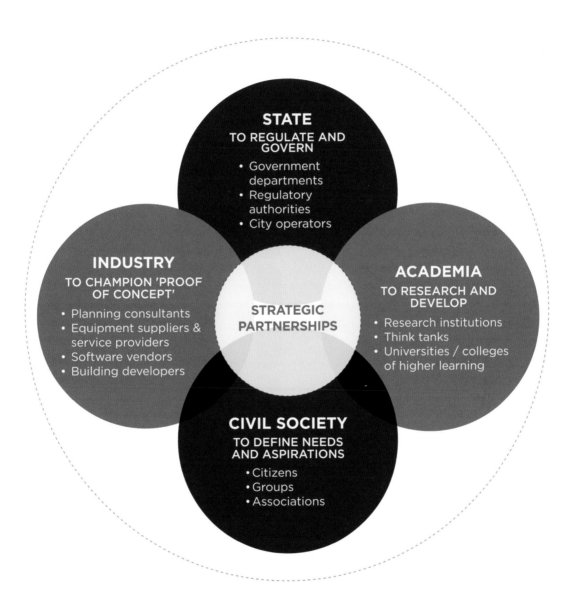

**Figure 3.21** The quadripartite relationship between civil society, state, academia, and industry in Slovakia.

# FOUR SPHERES POTENTIAL STAKEHOLDERS

**STATE**

**SPATIAL**
- Authority for Spatial Planning and Construction
- Ministry of Transport and Construction
- Magistrate of the Capital City of the SR
- Slovak Road Administration
- Geodesy, Cartography, and Cadastre Authority

**ECONOMIC**
- Ministry of Economy
- Ministry of Finance

**TECHNOLOGY**
- Statistical Office
- Ministry of Regional Development & Information
- Innovations of Bratislava (Inovácie mesta Bratislava)

**ENVIRONMENTAL**
- Ministry of Environment
- Ministry of Agriculture
- Slovak Green Building Council
- Institute for Environmental Policy (IEP)
- Slovak Environment Agency
- Slovak Hydrometeorological Institute (SHMU)

**SOCIAL**
- Ministry of Education, Science, Research, & Sport
- Implementation Unit (Implementacná Jednotka, IJ)
- Office of Labour, Social Affairs, & Family
- Ministry of Interior
- Slovak Chamber of Social Workers & Social Work
- Public Health Authority

**CULTURAL**
- Ministry of Culture
- Slovak Arts Council
- Slovak Convention Bureau
- Municipal Administration of Monument Care and Nature Conservation Office

**ACADEMIA**

**SPATIAL**
- Technical University of Košice (TUKE), Institute of Geodesy, Cartography, and GIS
- Slovak University of Technology (STU), Faculty of Architecture & Design (FAD)
- Comenius University, Faculty of Geography

**ECONOMIC**
- Technical University of Košice (TUKE), Faculty of Economics

**TECHNOLOGY**
- Technical University of Košice (TUKE), Faculty of Electrical Engineering and Informatics
- Slovak Academy of Science

**ENVIRONMENTAL**
- Technical University of Košice (TUKE), Faculty of Mining, Ecology, Process Control, and Geotechnologies

**SOCIAL**
- Technical University of Košice (TUKE), Faculty of Arts

**CULTURAL**
- Technical University of Košice (TUKE), Faculty of Arts

**Table 3.1** Key stakeholders from the 'four spheres of influence' in Slovakia.

## INDUSTRY

## CIVIL SOCIETY

**SPATIAL**
- Public Transport Company Slovakia (SR Railways, SR Lines)
- Real Estate Developers Slovakia
- Energy & Gas Companies
- Water Industries

**SPATIAL**
- Metropolitan Institute of Bratislava
- Open Street Map

**ECONOMIC**
- KPMG Slovakia
- National Bank of Slovakia (NBS)
- Slovenská Sporitelna

**ECONOMIC**
- Organisation for Economic, Co-op, & Development (OECD)

**TECHNOLOGY**
- ESRI
- Greehill
- Emerson
- Sova Group
- Telecommunication Organisations

**TECHNOLOGY**
- Association of Slovak Scientific & Tech Societies (ZSVTS)
- GLOBSEC

**ENVIRONMENTAL**
- Environmental Institute (EI)
- Waste Management & Recycling Companies Slovakia
- ENVI

**ENVIRONMENTAL**
- Greenpeace Slovensko
- International Institute for Applied Systems Analysis (IIASA)

**SOCIAL**
- Social Enterprises Slovakia

**SOCIAL**
- AKO
- 'Message for the Mayor' Team
- Green Foundation
- Creative Industries Košice (CIKE)

**CULTURAL**
- Slovak Tourist Board

**CULTURAL**
- Ethnographic Society Slovakia
- Creative Industries Košice (CIKE)

# CHAPTER 4.0

## ENABLING THE DIGITAL TWIN

**PART ONE: STAKEHOLDER ENGAGEMENT**

Stakeholder engagement, involving representatives from the 'four spheres of influence', was held to seek alignment and steer all stakeholders towards a common vision for Slovakia's NDT

**A COMMON PURPOSE OF THE DT OF SLOVAKIA**

'A centralised data platform across Slovakia to enable cross-sectoral, cross-regional collaborations and communications with increased data accessibility, data interoperability, and improved efficiency in a safe and cost-saving environment'.

**FUNCTION & IMPLEMENTATION OF THE DT**

| | |
|---|---|
| A centralised data platform to enable cross-sectoral, cross-regional collaborations and increased data interoperability | A connected ecosystem for making informed decisions regarding pilot projects, construction processes, and long-term planning |
| A user-friendly platform with clear aggregation hierarchy of data layers from the 'six-pillars' and data security protocols | 'Four spheres of influence' from the 'six-pillars', classified into data contributors and data consumers |
| Strong leadership to develop standardised systems, cultivate stakeholder collaborations, and build human and digital capacity | A purpose-driven site selection approach, taking the 'six-pillars' and the complexity of urban structures into account |

**PART TWO: STAKEHOLDER ENGAGEMENT**

Part Two of the stakeholder engagement scope was held to present Pomeroy Academy's DT Strategy in collaboration with the Authority for Spatial Planning and Construction: one that embraced and balanced stakeholders' insights with the practical side of Slovakia's NDT implementation, giving their voice to vision and turning their vision into reality

**POMEROY ACADEMY'S DIGITAL TWIN STRATEGY**

| Data layers encompassing the 'six pillars' | Theory of Change (ToC) | Information Management Framework (IMF) | Proof of Concepts (PoCs) & Scenario Planning |
|---|---|---|---|

**TAKING A STEP FORWARD**

| Promoting transparency in the process of PoCs and DT development | Calling for a change of mindset and the need for capacity building |
|---|---|

**Figure 4.1** The highlights from a two-part stakeholder engagement exercise in Bratislava, Slovakia to identify the key stakeholders and initiate their digital twinning journey.

# EXECUTIVE SUMMARY

The previous chapters have sought to shed light on the significance of involving stakeholders from the 'four spheres of influence' to ensure the success of DT development. This chapter elucidates a two-part stakeholder engagement exercise that took place in Bratislava, Slovakia, in order to identify the key stakeholders and initiate their digital twinning journey (Figure 4.1).

around leadership, IT infrastructure, cyber security, data formats, and algorithm robustness. Suggestions were also made by the stakeholders to resolve some of the highlighted concerns, forming the basis of purpose-to-impact plans for the DT strategy. These plans, substantiated through academic and desktop research, were then translated into a National Paradigm Shift framework.

## PART ONE HIGHLIGHTS

Part One of the stakeholder engagement aimed to align stakeholders towards a common vision for Slovakia's National DT (NDT). The stakeholders identified a purpose for the DT – 'a centralised data platform across Slovakia to enable cross-sectoral, cross-regional collaborations and communications with increased data accessibility, data interoperability, and improved efficiency in a safe and cost-saving environment'. With such impetus, the stakeholders specified relevant data and best practices for the DT, allowing Pomeroy Academy to validate data layers and indicators within the 'six-pillars' that formed the DT strategy for Slovakia. Concerns generally arose

## PART TWO HIGHLIGHTS

Part Two of the stakeholder engagement was held that built upon the previous engagement exercise. It was conducted with the aim to present Pomeroy Academy's DT strategy: one that integrated stakeholder perspectives with practical considerations for the NDT implementation. Conversations surrounding the DT strategy took place amongst the stakeholders, and were distilled into two key points required in developing the NDT:

1. Promoting transparency in the process of PoCs and DT development; and
2. Calling for a change of mindset and building capacity.

| | STAKEHOLDERS | PART ONE | PART TWO |
|---|---|---|---|
| STATE | • Regional capitals (Združenie K8) | 1 | - |
| | • Association of Towns and Communities of Slovakia (Združenie miest a obcí Slovenska) | 1 | - |
| | • Association of Towns of Slovakia (Únia miest Slovenska) | 2 | - |
| | • Metropolitan Institute of Bratislava (Metropolitný inštitút Bratislavy) | 2 | 1 |
| | • Creative Industry Košice (CIKE) | 1 | 1 |
| | • City of Bratislava | 1 | - |
| | • Association of Self-governing Regions (SK8) | - | 2 |
| | • Association of the capital city Bratislava and regional cities of the Slovak Republic (K8) | - | 1 |
| | • Union of towns and cities of Slovakia (UMS) | - | 2 |
| ACADEMIA | • Slovak University of Technology in Bratislava | 4 | - |
| | • Technical University of Košice | 3 | 1 |
| | • University of Žilina | 1 | - |
| | • Slovak University of Agriculture, Nitra | 2 | 2 |
| INDUSTRY | • Association of Construction Entrepreneurs of Slovakia (Zväz stavebných podnikateľov Slovenska) | 1 | - |
| | • Slovak Chamber of Civil Engineers (Slovenská komora stavebných inžinierov) | 1 | 1 |
| | • Institute of Urban Development (Inštitút urbánneho rozvoja) | 1 | 1 |
| | • Real Estate | 1 | - |
| | • Slovak Chamber of Architects (Slovenská komora architektov) | 2 | 1 |
| | • Energy Distributor | 1 | 4 |
| | • Slovenský plynárenský priemysel SPP (major energy supplier in Slovakia) | 1 | - |
| | • Telecommunication Industry | 1 | 2 |
| CIVIL SOCIETY | • Office of the Plenipotentiary of the Government of the Slovak Republic for the Development of Civil Society | 1 | - |
| | • Buildings for the Future | 1 | 1 |
| | • Office of the Plenipotentiary of the Slovak Government for National Minorities | 1 | - |
| | • Office of the Commissioner for Persons with Disabilities | - | 1 |

**Table 4.1** Number of attendees from the 'four spheres of influence' in stakeholder engagement Parts One and Two.

**1 SHORT LECTURE**
- REASONS FOR CREATING A DT PLATFORM
- DIFFERENT CONCEPTS OF DT
- KEY STAKEHOLDERS INVOLVED IN THE CO-CREATION OF DT PLATFORM
- KNOWLEDGE GAPS & CHALLENGES IN EXISTING DTS

**ROUND-TABLE DISCUSSION 2**

**PART 1**
FOCUSING ON FUTURE, BIG-PICTURE ASPIRATIONS

**PART 2**
WORKING BACKWARD WITH SPECIFICITY

**PART 3**
RECOGNISING INDIVIDUAL & COLLECTIVE BENEFITS

**PART 4**
IDENTIFYING KEY STAKEHOLDERS

**PART 5**
DETERMINING PURPOSE-DRIVEN TEST-BEDDING SITES

**PART 6**
PINNING DOWN BARRIERS TO CHANGE

**Figure 4.2** A two-step process to facilitate the collaborative process and develop contextual purpose-to-impact plans for Slovakia: short lectures as an introduction to DT and round-table discussions.

# PART ONE: STAKEHOLDER ENGAGEMENT

## PURPOSE-TO-IMPACT PLANS

It has been suggested that a purpose-driven DT is key to delivering outcome-focused solutions that bring benefits to the real world (Centre for Digital Built Britain, 2022c). The all-encompassing DT framework that encapsulates the 'six-pillars' highlights the complexity and relatedness amongst different domains in the co-creation and co-development of an NDT. Therefore, the Slovak government identified the need to translate sectoral and regional aspirations into a common purpose for the NDT through a collaborative environment amongst all relevant stakeholders. The collaborative process would form the basis of effective purpose-to-impact plans. This work adopted a two-step process to facilitate the collaborative process and develop contextual purpose-to-impact plans for Slovakia via (Figure 4.2):

1. Short lectures as an introduction to DT; and
2. Round-table discussions.

### Short Lecture

Considering the application of DTs for smart governance is arguably still in its infancy, with the short lecture aimed to establish a common ground amongst the stakeholders by bridging the gap between their existing background knowledge. This also allowed them to consider the gaps in existing DTs, which mirror the physical environment but contain little information on the socio-cultural aspects of the physical world.

### Round-table Discussion

Having established a common ground, the round-table discussion aspired to create dialogues between stakeholders from different stratum where everyone was on equal footing with equal influence (Bridgeman, 2010). Adapting from the existing framework by Craig and Snook (2014), which has been prominently used to define and distil purposes into impact plans to achieve concrete results, the round-table discussion

focused on the following six-key parts:

1. Focusing on future, big picture aspirations;
2. Working backward with specificity;
3. Recognising individual and collective benefits;
4. Identifying key stakeholders;
5. Determining purpose-driven test-bedding sites; and
6. Pinning down barriers to change.

### Part One: Focusing on Future, Big-picture Aspirations

Having a purpose is equivalent to having a sense of being navigated by meaningful intentions in the face of ever-changing circumstances and challenges. Part One aimed at providing the stakeholders with a common platform to discuss and identify their purpose for having a DT as a nation. This was conducted by 'mining' stories and commonalities involving the NDT, allowing the stakeholders to envision big-picture aspirations for the greater good of society.

### Part Two: Working Backward with Specificity

With Part One providing the overarching purpose and big-picture aspirations for the NDT, Part Two sought to reverse engineer the level of data that is critically relevant to the DT and its evaluation criteria. The socio-cultural aspect was also acknowledged as a crucial consideration. Facilitated by the 'card sorting' activity (Brent *et al.*, 2021), listing out the level of data and its criteria provided greater clarity for the foundation of the NDT and identified the necessary steps to ensure best practices are followed.

### Part Three: Recognising Individual and Collective Benefits

It is claimed that recognising the stimulation behind a purpose would significantly act as an incentive to achieve big goals (Craig and Snook, 2014). Having established the purpose and the basis that forms the NDT, Part Three prompted the stakeholders to ruminate on and explain the resultant benefits of having the DT as a nation.

### Part Four: Identifying Key Stakeholders & Relationships

Whilst Parts One to Three provided an emotional scaffolding to cultivate stakeholders' interests in the co-creation and co-development of the NDT, Part Four sought to identify key stakeholders and relationships needed to turn the DT implementation plan into reality. This list of key stakeholders and their interdisiplinary relationships would help to ensure the DT was implementable by bringing stakeholders from different domains on-board, based on their associated strengths and resources.

### Part Five: Determining Purpose-driven Test-bedding Sites

To put the ideas expanded from Parts One to Four into action, Part Five set the stakeholders' sights on identifying suitable sites to test-bed and validate concepts of the NDT in real-world settings. This offered the stakeholders an opportunity to discuss their site selection approaches and criteria, which should be driven by purpose(s).

### Part Six: Pinning down Barriers to Change

The implementation of an NDT inevitably necessitates changes in the modus operandi across different organisations, sectors, and regions in Slovakia. Part Six sought to empower the stakeholders to discuss possible ways of delivering the DT as a nation by identifying the changes required and associated barriers.

## STAKEHOLDER IDENTIFICATION

Stakeholder identification is of utmost importance to the entire stakeholder engagement process. This work involved a stakeholder analysis, partly based on methods by Jaansoo (2019), and identified a broad range of stakeholders at two different levels:

1. Across 'six pillars'; and
2. Across the 'four spheres of influence'.

During the initial level of stakeholder engagement, representatives and experts from Slovakia's six pillars were identified as potential stakeholders. The search process evaluated stakeholder characteristics, taking into account key factors by answering three questions to evaluate stakeholder influence and expertise related to the DT implementation plan:

1. Who are the stakeholders with the power to enable the DT implementation plan to achieve the anticipated impacts and outcomes, and who has the power to block them?
2. What is the domain knowledge that they can bring to the DT implementation plan?
3. How can their knowledge enforce the outputs of the DT implementation plan?

After identifying potential stakeholders among representatives and experts from Slovakia's six pillars, the next step involved profiling them to ensure a diverse range of stakeholders, embodying a spectrum of expertise, was represented. To foster effective collaboration, pre-existing trust and social ties were considered as key factors (Bodin et al., 2019). Therefore, relevant stakeholders with pre-existing networks with the Slovak government were also included. This approach aimed to create a rich and inclusive stakeholder engagement exercise, encouraging constructive contributions from a wide range of perspectives.

At the second level of stakeholder identification, the list of stakeholders identified from the first level was categorised into civil society, state, academia, and industry in order to ensure voices from every sphere would be included.

The stakeholder identification approach, as elaborated above, ultimately aimed to promote inclusivity and a diverse range of inputs in the development of the NDT for Slovakia. This advocated the quadripartite relationships of the 'four spheres of influence' in the DT development as elucidated in the previous chapters: one that reflects a paradigm shift from top-down, siloed, one-directional decision-making approaches to become a more deliberative, integrative, middle-out approach.

## STAKEHOLDER ENGAGEMENT EXERCISE

A public – private stakeholder engagement exercise with stakeholders representing the 'four spheres of influence' was conducted in-person in Bratislava. The exercise aimed to develop a shared vision for the NDT and establish a purpose-to-impact plan for Slovakia, whilst also gaining insights into stakeholders' perceptions toward the implementation of the DT platform. This would help to provide greater clarity to the anticipated potential of the NDT, identify barriers in existing work processes, as well as how the NDT would facilitate a more integrated approach for cross-sectoral and cross-regional collaborations. It would in turn contribute to Slovakia's transformation into a more sustainable, smart nation during its digital transformation.

To incorporate the above-mentioned two-step process, the engagement exercise started off with a short lecture that introduced DT applications for smart governance. This helped to create a shared understanding amongst the stakeholders by connecting their prior knowledge and experience. This was followed by a round-table discussion, where participants from the four spheres were organised into groups to exchange their ideas on the implementation of the DT for Slovakia, prompted by the six key parts highlighted for brainstorming. The six key parts were translated into six corresponding questions to facilitate the discussions amongst the stakeholders in ways that were essential to concretise the next steps for enabling the NDT. This allowed for the understanding of different perspectives to ultimately create a collaborative, cohesive DT (Figure 4.3). A total of 30 participants from the four spheres of influence partook in the engagement.

**SHORT LECTURE BY PROF. JASON POMEROY: INTRODUCTION TO DIGITAL TWINS**

The author delivered the lecture introducing the concepts of DT to the stakeholder groups. The lecture underscored the gaps in existing DT that are often mirrors of the physical environment, with little information on the socio-cultural aspects of our world.

**SIX PROMPTS FOR THINKING**

| | |
|---|---|
| Why do we need digital twins? Is there a business case / benefit to civil society, academia, state, & industry? | Who do you think the key stakeholders should be in the digital twin platform? |
| What would the digital twin be like? What level of data is to be collated & integrated into the digital twin platform? | Where should we locate the test bed within the city district / city and what is the optimal size of the test bed? |
| How will it benefit you? | How are we to deliver the digital twin platform and what are the barriers to change? |

Translated from the six key parts highlighted in the research methodology, six guiding questions were posed to engage participants and glean their perceptions and acceptance of having a DT in their country. Stakeholder groups were split into the 'four sphere of influence' to gain a multi-perspective understanding of public sentiment. Flipboards and sorting cards were provided to strengthen their understanding of Pomeroy's 'six-pillar framework' (Pomeroy, 2020a).

**DISTILLATION OF RESPONSES**

The results of the stakeholder exercise were photographed and translated into English for Pomeroy Academy to distill and frame key takeaways and observations to serve as onwards prompts for thinking and further enhance the DT Platform Strategy.

**Figure 4.3** Work flow of stakeholder engagement Part One.

# STATE

**FACILITATOR:** Jason Pomeroy

**Figure 4.4** Stakeholder engagement exercise with state representatives.

## ATTENDEES

| ORGANISATION | PAX |
|---|---|
| REGIONAL CAPITALS (ZDRUŽENIE K8) | 1 |
| ASSOCIATION OF TOWNS AND COMMUNITIES OF SLOVAKIA (ZDRUŽENIE MIEST A OBCÍ SLOVENSKA) | 1 |
| ASSOCIATION OF TOWNS OF SLOVAKIA (ÚNIA MIEST SLOVENSKA) | 2 |
| METROPOLITAN INSTITUTE OF BRATISLAVA (METROPOLITNÝ INŠTITÚT BRATISLAVY) | 2 |
| CREATIVE INDUSTRY KOŠICE | 1 |
| CITY OF BRATISLAVA | 1 |

**Table 4.2** Number of attendees from various state organisations at stakeholder engagement Part One.

**Q1. WHY DO WE NEED DIGITAL TWINS? IS THERE A BUSINESS CASE / BENEFIT TO CIVIL SOCIETY, ACADEMIA, STATE, & INDUSTRY?**

- Having a central platform, with a common data structure to integrate data across different regions, will allow for greater data accessibility and interoperability. This will facilitate cross-sectoral and cross-regional collaborations and communications.
- There is a need for greater data availability across Slovakia.

**Q2. WHAT WOULD THE DIGITAL TWIN BE LIKE? WHAT LEVEL OF DATA IS TO BE COLLATED & INTEGRATED INTO THE DIGITAL TWIN PLATFORM?**

- The DT should respond effectively and efficiently to changing operations in the physical twin in all aspects, with up-to-date and high-fidelity geo-spatial data serving as the foundation, accompanied by aggregated socio-demographic and geo-demographic data in consideration of data protection and privacy.
- Different levels of data availability and variances in data granularity are inevitable between areas or regions (e.g. cities vs. villages).

**Q3. HOW WILL IT BENEFIT YOU?**

- The DT is envisioned as a tool to establish a connected ecosystem of collaborations amongst municipalities, enabling proactive long-term planning with high-quality data and improved efficiency at a lower cost.

**Q4. WHO DO YOU THINK THE KEY STAKEHOLDERS SHOULD BE IN THE DIGITAL TWIN PLATFORM?**

- The DT is perceived as a cross-sectoral collaboration effort with key stakeholders involving the four spheres of influence – different levels of government (state, municipalities), academia, industries, and civil society like NGOs and information systems suppliers.

**Q5. WHERE SHOULD WE LOCATE THE TEST BED WITHIN THE CITY DISTRICT / CITY AND WHAT IS THE OPTIMAL SIZE OF THE TEST BED?**

- The test-bedding of the DT could be implemented in both urban and rural areas, taking into account the six pillars (spatial, economic, technological, environmental, social, and cultural).

**Q6. HOW ARE WE TO DELIVER THE DIGITAL TWIN PLATFORM AND WHAT ARE THE BARRIERS TO CHANGE?**

- Considering the need for greater data availability across Slovakia and cross-sectoral collaborations, a standardised system and sufficient capacity are imperative to be adopted by stakeholders who are wishing to be part of the DT platform in order to ensure data quality and fidelity.

# ACADEMIA

**FACILITATOR:** Daniela Hilčíková

**Figure 4.5** Stakeholder engagement exercise with representatives from academic institutions.

## ATTENDEES

| ORGANISATION | PAX |
|---|---|
| **SLOVAK UNIVERSITY OF TECHNOLOGY IN BRATISLAVA (SLOVENSKÁ TECHNICKÁ UNIVERZITA V BRATISLAVE):** | |
| • *FACULTY OF ARCHITECTURE AND DESIGN* <br> • *SPATIAL PLANNING DEPARTMENT* | *3* <br> *1* |
| **TECHNICAL UNIVERSITY OF KOŠICE (TECHNICKÁ UNIVERZITA V KOŠICIACH):** | |
| • *FACULTY OF CIVIL ENGINEERING* <br> • *DEPARTMENT OF ARCHITECTURE* | *2* <br> *1* |
| **UNIVERSITY OF ŽILINA:** | |
| • *FACULTY OF CIVIL ENGINEERING* | *1* |
| **SLOVAK UNIVERSITY OF AGRICULTURE, NITRA:** | |
| • *FACULTY OF HORTICULTURE AND LANDSCAPE ENGINEERING* | *2* |

**Table 4.3** Number of attendees from various academic institutions at stakeholder engagement Part One.

**Q1. WHY DO WE NEED DIGITAL TWINS? IS THERE A BUSINESS CASE / BENEFIT TO CIVIL SOCIETY, ACADEMIA, STATE, & INDUSTRY?**

- The need for a DT is mutually agreed upon owing to its great potential and benefit as a data unification platform, allowing different users and even the public to access up-to-date data. Data interoperability is key to ensuring large datasets are compliant with quality requirements for sharing across different sectors.

**Q2. WHAT WOULD THE DIGITAL TWIN BE LIKE? WHAT LEVEL OF DATA IS TO BE COLLATED & INTEGRATED INTO THE DIGITAL TWIN PLATFORM?**

- The DT is a central platform with data hierarchy (e.g. geo-spatial, climate, terrain, social) involving different stakeholders, with their access granted based on their roles, responsibilities and tasks.
- The need for responsive design to ensure optimal viewing and interactive experiences across different devices (e.g. PC, tablet, smart phone).
- The DT should increase data interoperability and models' level of detail (above and underground infrastructure) through data scanning.

**Q3. HOW WILL IT BENEFIT YOU?**

- The DT provides a safe and cost-saving environment for test-bedding new innovations without consequences on the physical twin, simulating scenarios for proactive strategic and urban planning. Other application domains that would benefit from a DT are education and tax collection.

**Q4. WHO DO YOU THINK THE KEY STAKEHOLDERS SHOULD BE IN THE DIGITAL TWIN PLATFORM?**

- While the key stakeholders involve the four spheres of influence – state, academia, industry, and civil society – it is important to identify the creators and data contributors (mainly the state sectors, academia, professionals from the IT sector and the field of planning and design, and the public) of the DT from the active users (an expanded list from the former, which also includes city operators, investors, and professionals from different domains).

**Q5. WHERE SHOULD WE LOCATE THE TEST BED WITHIN THE CITY DISTRICT / CITY AND WHAT IS THE OPTIMAL SIZE OF THE TEST BED?**

- Test-bedding and validation of the DT can be conducted based on the site selection approach – a fully complex city (i.e. average demography of the country, complex infrastructure, diversified socio-demographic including the ethnic minority communities, historical assets); or multiple sites (e.g. rapidly developing city, newly developed city).
- Getting ground support and participation from citizens and all relevant parties is critical.

**Q6. HOW ARE WE TO DELIVER THE DIGITAL TWIN PLATFORM AND WHAT ARE THE BARRIERS TO CHANGE?**

- The success of the DT needs a national framework and boundary-spanning collaboration to ensure project sustainability, in terms of stakeholder participation, finances, IT infrastructure, public awareness, and education.
- Having a GDPR in place is key to gain trust and support from the public.
- It is crucial to see the DT as a decision-making mechanism that balances human input and AI technology.

# INDUSTRY

**FACILITATOR:** Milota Sidorová

**Figure 4.6** Stakeholder engagement exercise with representatives from the industry sector.

## ATTENDEES

| ORGANISATION | PAX |
|---|---|
| ASSOCIATION OF CONSTRUCTION ENTREPRENEURS OF SLOVAKIA (ZVÄZ STAVEBNÝCH PODNIKATEĽOV SLOVENSKA) | 1 |
| SLOVAK CHAMBER OF CIVIL ENGINEERS (SLOVENSKÁ KOMORA STAVEBNÝCH INŽINIEROV) | 1 |
| INSTITUTE OF URBAN DEVELOPMENT (INŠTITÚT URBÁNNEHO ROZVOJA) | 1 |
| REAL ESTATE | 1 |
| SLOVAK CHAMBER OF ARCHITECTS (SLOVENSKÁ KOMORA ARCHITEKTOV) | 2 |
| ENERGY DISTRIBUTOR FOR THE WESTERN SLOVAKIA (ZÁPADOSLOVENSKÁ DISTRIBUČNÁ) | 1 |
| MAJOR ENERGY SUPPLIER IN SLOVAKIA (SLOVENSKÝ PLYNÁRENSKÝ PRIEMYSEL SPP) | 1 |
| TELECOMMUNICATION INDUSTRY | 1 |

**Table 4.4** Number of attendees from various industry sectors at stakeholder engagement Part One.

**Q1. WHY DO WE NEED DIGITAL TWINS? IS THERE A BUSINESS CASE / BENEFIT TO CIVIL SOCIETY, ACADEMIA, STATE, & INDUSTRY?**

- DT is seen as a centralised, open portal for unifying heterogeneous data sources, allowing for data sharing and improved efficiency.
- It helps to understand urban growth & develop urban planning strategies that respond to market trends for better economic planning of cities.
- However, there are skepticisms about the feasibility of a DT due to the costs required and the benefits (bound by research limitations) it could offer.

**Q2. WHAT WOULD THE DIGITAL TWIN BE LIKE? WHAT LEVEL OF DATA IS TO BE COLLATED & INTEGRATED INTO THE DIGITAL TWIN PLATFORM?**

- State to specify data priority & requirements for data format (e.g. scale, purposes), fidelity, and level of detail.
- Reasonable timeline should be given for mapping of infrastructure data, noting the limitations and challenges in mapping underground structures.
- It is important to ensure user-friendly UIUX, data security & cybersecurity, as well as a structured way to grant access rights (based on users' respective purposes and given tasks).

**Q3. HOW WILL IT BENEFIT YOU?**

- Stakeholders from industry welcome the DT and would like to be part of the platform, as it will provide them access to data that they do not own currently as architects. Having such a platform with a wealth of data will allow for improved efficiency in the planning and construction processes.

**Q4. WHO DO YOU THINK THE KEY STAKEHOLDERS SHOULD BE IN THE DIGITAL TWIN PLATFORM?**

- State: Municipalities and state government; Slovak Hydrometeorological Institute; Geodesy, Cartography and Cadastre Authority; Financial Administrator
- Industry: Investors, builders, users of building production, city service providers and suppliers (e.g. utility, networks), and designers.
- Academia: Researchers and scientists
- Civil Society: NGOs

**Q5. WHERE SHOULD WE LOCATE THE TEST BED WITHIN THE CITY DISTRICT/CITY AND WHAT IS THE OPTIMAL SIZE OF THE TEST BED?**

- The test-bedding of the DT would be ideal in regional cities with different types of urban structures and buildings. This will include the underground infrastructure of the cities, keeping in mind the level of detail needed. On the other hand, sprawl suburbia is worth considering so comparison of the test-bedding outcomes can be drawn between cities and suburbia.

**Q6. HOW ARE WE TO DELIVER THE DIGITAL TWIN PLATFORM AND WHAT ARE THE BARRIERS TO CHANGE?**

- The state's competency determines long-term stakeholder collaboration to provide HQ data (underground structures should be tested as PoC) disregarding government changes.
- DT should be phased with agile procurement, maintained by data and tech experts.
- User-friendly UIUX is key for data segregation for predictive modelling.
- Digital education initiatives are needed to re-educate different professions.

# CIVIL SOCIETY

**FACILITATOR:** Katarina Brestovanská

**Figure 4.7** Stakeholder engagement exercise with representatives from the civil society organisations.

## ATTENDEES

| ORGANISATION | PAX |
|---|---|
| OFFICE OF THE PLENIPOTENTIARY OF THE GOVERNMENT OF THE SLOVAK REPUBLIC FOR THE DEVELOPMENT OF CIVIL SOCIETY | 1 |
| BUILDINGS FOR THE FUTURE | 1 |
| OFFICE OF THE PLENIPOTENTIARY OF THE SLOVAK GOVERNMENT FOR NATIONAL MINORITIES | 1 |

**Table 4.5** Number of attendees from various civil society organisations at stakeholder engagement Part One.

## Q1. WHY DO WE NEED DIGITAL TWINS? IS THERE A BUSINESS CASE / BENEFIT TO CIVIL SOCIETY, ACADEMIA, STATE, & INDUSTRY?

- Having a central platform to store and integrate multi-source datasets, which are currently siloed, in a machine-readable format that is accessible to the public.
- There is a need for a common data platform to expand outlook and improve transparency across different sectors and organisations, allowing different stakeholders to communicate ideas and develop holistic solutions that solicit inputs from all possible relevant professions.

## Q2. WHAT WOULD THE DIGITAL TWIN BE LIKE? WHAT LEVEL OF DATA IS TO BE COLLATED & INTEGRATED INTO THE DIGITAL TWIN PLATFORM?

- In addition to integrating the available data, it is essential to have a DT that encompasses datasets from all six pillars. This is particularly crucial for socio-cultural practices and socio-spatial behaviours, which are vital in informing social development and meeting the needs of various groups, including minorities. Currently, these elements are separated from other data in the urban living environment's development process.

## Q3. HOW WILL IT BENEFIT YOU?

- A DT platform will support civil society in creating well-informed initiatives and engaging in more meaningful pilot projects by considering various aspects like history and culture. This will contribute to the country's future plans, such as development, innovation, and sustainability.
- A data-driven decision-making mechanism is required to enhance the credibility of the decision-making body, promote transparency, and build trust within the state and society.

## Q4. WHO DO YOU THINK THE KEY STAKEHOLDERS SHOULD BE IN THE DIGITAL TWIN PLATFORM?

- The need to involve representatives from the six pillars in the process
- The necessity of identifying local government representatives, i.e. The Chamber of NGOs (Komora MVO), who can nominate NGO representatives, provide support to civil society, and recognise the value of collaborating with NGOs.

## Q5. WHERE SHOULD WE LOCATE THE TEST BED WITHIN THE CITY DISTRICT / CITY AND WHAT IS THE OPTIMAL SIZE OF THE TEST BED?

- The site selection for test-bedding of the DT highly depends on the purpose(s) of testing. For comprehensive concept testing, regional cities (e.g. Bratislava, Trnava) with optimal size and progressive local government would be ideal. On the other hand, to test the problem-solving capability of a DT for a particular issue, areas with rapid development or transformation (e.g. Horná Nitra) would be an ideal choice.

## Q6. HOW ARE WE TO DELIVER THE DIGITAL TWIN PLATFORM AND WHAT ARE THE BARRIERS TO CHANGE?

- A strong technological infrastructure is crucial for a successful DT to ensure secure data sharing among relevant parties who understand its benefits. This requires coordination and communication among all stakeholders, with visionary authorities leading public – private collaborations supported by the central government (Úrad).
- Defining the DT with a realistic vision that can be financially supported to motivate and inspire confidence in stakeholders and citizens.

# OBSERVATIONS & PROMPTS FOR THINKING

**A centralised data platform to enable cross-sectoral, cross-regional collaborations and increase data interoperability**

A DT is acknowledged by the four stakeholder spheres as a centralised platform for unifying data, enhancing accessibility and interoperability throughout Slovakia. Made publicly accessible, the integrated DT approach fosters collaborations across different sectors, organisations, and regions with improved efficiency. Additionally, a DT provides a safe and cost-saving environment for test-bedding new innovations and simulating what-if scenarios without consequences on the physical twin.

**A user-friendly platform with clear aggregation hierarchy of data layers from the 'six-pillars' and data security protocols**

A DTs feasibility can be undermined by stakeholders, data security protocol, and the amount of data involved. IT infrastructure concerns can also arise, calling for a user-friendly platform with a clear data aggregation hierarchy and high modularity for better system reconfigurability. For instance, historical and current data of the physical world can evaluate performance of the urban environment to-date; and with other pre-defined factors, simulate data in the virtual world for future projections.

**Strong leadership to develop standardised systems, cultivate stakeholder collaborations, and build human and digital capacity**

The DT implementation requires strong leadership and collaboration, given the number of stakeholders involved and the socio-technological changes required. A national implementation plan with clear vision, coordination, and goals prioritisation is essential, alongside proactive engagement with stakeholders. An Information Management Framework (IMF) is crucial to guide data collection efforts in terms of format and detail level. This will facilitate conversations between stakeholders, ensure alignment, and channel efforts in the right direction for public benefit.

**A connected ecosystem for making informed decisions regarding pilot projects, construction processes, and long-term planning**

Working in incremental steps, based on prioritised goals and available resources, may be a more feasible approach to DT implementation. This allows for expansion over time and enhanced informed decision making for pilot projects, evaluated based on data availability, model fidelity, and national planning priorities to define the platform's PoCs. The PoCs should not be tied to a particular pillar but equitable across – spatial, economic, technological, environmental, social, and cultural pillars – due to the interdependence of all data sets in mirroring the physical twin's ecosystem.

**Four spheres of influence from the 'six pillars', classified into data contributors and data consumers**

The DTs fidelity depends on data accumulation and model creation. This requires more thought in optimising data collection efforts at scale, involving the 'four spheres of influence' from the 'six pillars'. This should be supported by interdisciplinary data experts to provide technical advice for data contributors and consumers to streamline data in ways that can ensure meaningful analytics to the DT platform. This enriches the platform with more high-quality data, increasing capabilities of AI technology, embedded in the DT, for more accurate simulations and forecasting models over time.

**A purpose-driven site selection approach, taking the 'six pillars' and the complexity of urban structures into account**

It further appears that there is no one-size-fits-all approach to identify an optimal site for test-bedding of the DT. This will require conversations between stakeholders to identify the specific purpose(s) of the test-bedding – whether it is to test the comprehensive concepts of the DT or to test its capacity in solving real-world (physical) problems of any particular area.

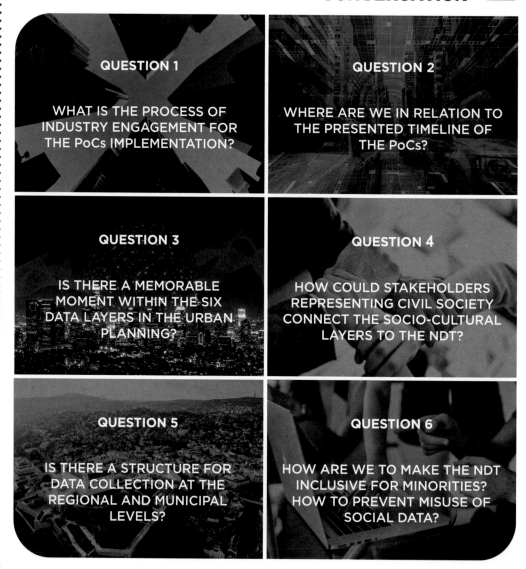

**1 SHORT LECTURE**
- DATA LAYERS ENCOMPASSING THE 'SIX PILLARS'
- THEORY OF CHANGE (ToC)
- INFORMATION MANAGEMENT FRAMEWORK
- PROOF OF CONCEPTS (PoCs) & SCENARIO PLANNING

**FISH-BOWL CONVERSATION 2**

**QUESTION 1**
WHAT IS THE PROCESS OF INDUSTRY ENGAGEMENT FOR THE PoCs IMPLEMENTATION?

**QUESTION 2**
WHERE ARE WE IN RELATION TO THE PRESENTED TIMELINE OF THE PoCs?

**QUESTION 3**
IS THERE A MEMORABLE MOMENT WITHIN THE SIX DATA LAYERS IN THE URBAN PLANNING?

**QUESTION 4**
HOW COULD STAKEHOLDERS REPRESENTING CIVIL SOCIETY CONNECT THE SOCIO-CULTURAL LAYERS TO THE NDT?

**QUESTION 5**
IS THERE A STRUCTURE FOR DATA COLLECTION AT THE REGIONAL AND MUNICIPAL LEVELS?

**QUESTION 6**
HOW ARE WE TO MAKE THE NDT INCLUSIVE FOR MINORITIES? HOW TO PREVENT MISUSE OF SOCIAL DATA?

**Figure 4.8** A two-step process to facilitate stakeholder engagement Part Two: short lectures to present Pomeroy Academy's DT Strategy and fish-bowl conversation.

# PART TWO STAKEHOLDER ENGAGEMENT

## STAKEHOLDER ENGAGEMENT EXERCISE

Following the Part One stakeholder engagement exercise, Part Two of the stakeholder engagement was held in person, in Bratislava. The ultimate goal of this stakeholder engagement exercise was to present Pomeroy Academy's DT Strategy, developed in collaboration with the Authority for Spatial Planning and Construction of the Slovak Republic. The DT aimed to balance stakeholders' insights with Slovakia's National DT (NDT) implementation, giving their voice to vision and turning their vision into reality. To this end, stakeholders (representatives from the 'four spheres of influence') from the last engagement were reinvited to this engagement exercise. A total of 22 (out of the original 30) stakeholders partook in this engagement exercise.

Creating a familiar environment for the engagement exercise was key to ensure that stakeholders felt comfortable and confident in participating. This led to a more productive and meaningful engagement that involved a short lecture and fish-bowl conversation (Figure 4.8). During the short lecture given by the author, an overview of the NDT strategy was provided. This strategy encompassed the data layers within the six pillars (as elaborated in Chapter Three) that form the NDT of Slovakia, and a National Paradigm Shift framework (which is further explained in Chapters Five and Six) developed using stakeholders' insights from the last engagement session. The National Paradigm Shift framework consists of:

1. Theory of Change (ToC): the socio-technological changes required for the four spheres of influence involved in the co-creation of the NDT for Slovakia;
2. The Information Management Framework: a standardised documentation to outline appropriate standards and protocols that facilitate data collection and data exchange, as

well as data interoperability and integration at a national level; and
3. Proof of Concept (PoCs) and Scenario Planning: the PoCs, identified by the Slovak government, augmented with the data layers encapsulating the 'six pillars' to demonstrate the potential of the NDT in facilitating the work flow involving the 'four spheres of influence'.

The short lecture concluded with a presentation on the development of the Information System (IS) 'myUrbium': an IT system developed by the Authority for Spatial Planning and Construction to ensure a common data environment that provides gradually scaled functionality of electronisation and digitisation of services by analysing inputs from 3D national models. This presentation enabled stakeholders to have a holistic view of how the NDT strategy, presented by Pomeroy Academy, was translated into practical applications that manifested in six PoCs as an initial stage.

A fish-bowl conversation, facilitated by a representative from the Authority for Spatial Planning and Construction, followed immediately after the short lecture to encourage an open discussion amongst the stakeholders in response to the DT strategy and the IS 'myUrbium'. The fish-bowl conversation was organised in such a way that the inner circle of stakeholders sat facing each other, while the outer circle observed the conversation. The stakeholders in the inner circle were given specific topics to discuss and share their thoughts, while the outer circle observed. The outer circle was also invited to join the conversation if the topics were relevant to them. This conversation allowed the stakeholders to have better clarity on the NDT strategy and PoCs implementation, and to share their thoughts on the topics discussed.

# ATTENDEES FROM THE FOUR SPHERES

## STATE

| ORGANISATION | PAX |
| --- | --- |
| ASSOCIATION OF SELF-GOVERNING REGIONS (SK8) | 2 |
| ASSOCIATION OF THE CAPITAL CITY BRATISLAVA AND REGIONAL CITIES OF THE SLOVAK REPUBLIC (K8) | 1 |
| UNION OF TOWNS AND CITIES OF SLOVAKIA (UMS) | 2 |
| CREATIVE INDUSTRY KOŠICE (CIKE) | 1 |
| METROPOLITAN INSTITUTE OF BRATISLAVA (MIB) | 1 |

## INDUSTRY

| ORGANISATION | PAX |
| --- | --- |
| SLOVAK CHAMBER OF CIVIL ENGINEERS (SKSI) | 1 |
| INSTITUTE OF URBAN DEVELOPMENT (IUR) | 1 |
| SLOVAK CHAMBER OF ARCHITECTS (SKA) | 1 |
| ENERGY DISTRIBUTORS | 4 |
| TELECOM COMPANIES | 2 |

## ACADEMIA

| ORGANISATION | PAX |
| --- | --- |
| TECHNICAL UNIVERSITY OF KOŠICE, FACULTY OF ENGINEERING | 1 |
| UNIVERSITY OF ŽILINA, FACULTY OF ENGINEERING | 1 |
| SLOVAK UNIVERSITY OF AGRICULTURE, FACULTY OF HORTICULTURE AND LANDSCAPE ENGINEERING | 2 |

## CIVIL SOCIETY

| ORGANISATION | PAX |
| --- | --- |
| BUILDINGS FOR FUTURE | 1 |
| OFFICE OF THE COMMISSIONER FOR PERSONS WITH DISABILITIES | 1 |

**Table 4.6** Number of attendees from the 'four spheres of influence' at stakeholder engagement Part Two.

### Q1. WHAT IS THE PROCESS OF INDUSTRY ENGAGEMENT FOR THE PoCs IMPLEMENTATION?

- The presentation by the Technical University of Košice (TUKE) provided stakeholders with a better understanding of the development team responsible for PoCs implementation and presented job opportunities for data experts. To build trust among stakeholders, the Authority for Spatial Planning and Construction and TUKE should improve transparency and communication regarding PoCs implementation.

### Q2. WHERE ARE WE IN RELATION TO THE PRESENTED TIMELINE OF THE PoCs?

- It was made clear that currently the development team is at the data cleaning stage and is working closely with data experts from across the country. The team meets regularly and is exploring ways to integrate decrees related to construction and spatial planning into the project's PoCs.

### Q3. IS THERE A MEMORABLE MOMENT WITHIN THE SIX DATA LAYERS IN URBAN PLANNING?

- It was observed that the stakeholders seemed to be more concerned with what is feasible to be realised in the near future, but had overlooked the importance of having a vision of the optimal potential of a NDT. It was, thus, important to help the stakeholders visualise how each of the six pillars complement one another in the holistic context of urban governance and management through a dynamic DT that goes beyond spatial and temporal dimensions.

### Q4. HOW COULD STAKEHOLDERS REPRESENTING CIVIL SOCIETY CONNECT THE SOCIO-CULTURAL LAYERS TO THE NDT?

- While the benefits of integrating social and cultural data layers into the DT were recognised, the feasibility of achieving this objective would remain a challenge due to the Slovak citizens' low trust in the judiciary (validated with the report shared by OECD [2021]). More still needs to be done in order to seek alignment in exploring the upcoming data layers and PoCs that could be integrated into the DT.

### Q5. IS THERE A STRUCTURE FOR DATA COLLECTION AT THE REGIONAL AND MUNICIPAL LEVELS?

- The need for a generalised format, as well as level of detail (LOD), to facilitate participation in the PoCs and DT implementation project was discussed. As only 5% of digital capacity is currently being used, the NDT was also perceived as a potential educational tool for digital transformation, and hopefully to increase digital capacity.

### Q6. HOW ARE WE TO MAKE THE NDT INCLUSIVE FOR MINORITIES? HOW TO PREVENT MISUSE OF SOCIAL DATA?

- Debates continue over the adoption of technology and the NDT, with some hesitant and others eager to embrace change. To ensure successful implementation, it's important to assess public and stakeholder sentiment and readiness for change, and develop educational initiatives to promote a growth mindset. Ultimately, the benefits of PoCs should outweigh any concerns about potential risks and negative consequences.

# OBSERVATIONS & PROMPTS FOR THINKING

### Promoting transparency in the process of PoCs and DT development

DT technology is indeed a rapidly advancing field that offers benefit in urban governance and management. However, one of the biggest challenges facing digital twin technology is the lack of a standard data format for these models.

There were a number of stakeholders that expressed their interest in joining the digital twinning journey with the Authority for Spatial Planning and Construction and the Technical University of Košice (TUKE). But without a common format made available to them, it becomes difficult for the interested stakeholders to be able to efficiently contribute to the PoCs and the implementation of the NDT.

As different stakeholders continue the data collection effort as part of their organisational duties, it would seem necessary for the development team from TUKE to share a certain data format with collaborating parties. This would allow the testing of the data format, the NDT, and PoCs implementation plan; especially as more stakeholders will be involved eventually and over a protracted period of time.

Alternatively, the development team from TUKE could also identify missing information or challenges that they encountered. This could be circulated amongst the stakeholders who would potentially be able to contribute and facilitate the development of the PoCs and NDT as a nation. It would seem essential to explore and concretise ways to include more stakeholders to collaborate effectively, paving the way for even greater innovation.

### Calling for a change of mindset and the need for capacity building

The DT technology has revolutionised the way different disciplines operate and innovate, but to fully reap its benefits, it requires a change of mindset. The stakeholder engagement revealed that while some were excited about the digital twinning journey, others had yet to embrace the positive transformation that can be brought forth by the DT technology. To fully embrace the potential of DT technology and ensure its implementation, it would seem essential for the Authority for Spatial Planning and Construction to identify suitable and open-minded stakeholders as early innovators, collaborators, and adopters of the PoCs and NDT.

The Authority for Spatial Planning and Construction could also identify potential partners to co-create different initiatives for capacity building. This could include training on the use of software platforms, data analysis, and integration with other technologies, allowing organisations and individuals to visualise the value of digital twin technology and even to be equipped with the necessary skills to implement and utilise this powerful technology. This would help to build their confidence and trust in the DT technology over time.

# CHAPTER 9.0
## A NATIONAL PARADIGM SHIFT

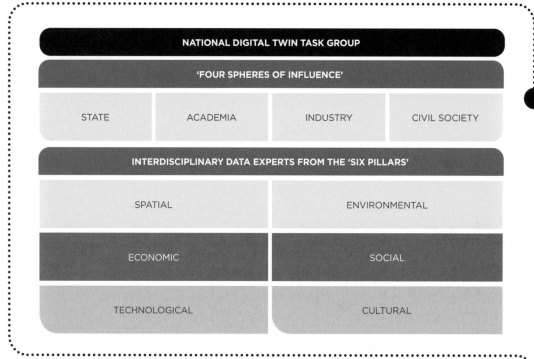

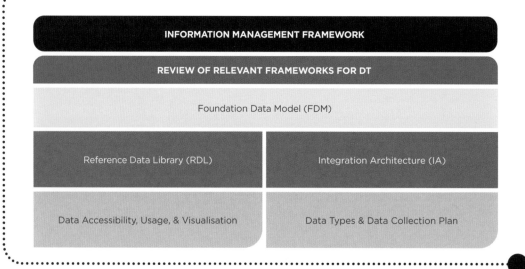

**Figure 5.1** The socio-technological changes involved to ensure the success of an NDT implementation plan, including initiating a Theory of Change (ToC) and developing an Information Management Framework.

# EXECUTIVE SUMMARY

Established as a tool for smart governance, the National Digital Twin (NDT) aims to provide quality information and a harmonised, collaborative digital environment that will facilitate and enhance informed decision-making and planning processes. These processes often involve cross-sectoral, cross-organisational, and cross-regional interventions to improve infrastructure and the public services provided to the citizens. Given the multitude of stakeholders and scale of interventions involved, this necessitates strong leadership to develop an NDT implementation plan with a clear vision, as well as a precise methodology in coordination, goals prioritisation, and resources optimisation.

Proactive coordination and continuous engagement is a key step to seek alignment amongst all relevant stakeholders who wish to be part of the NDT. It also helps to steer efforts in the right direction (Centre for Digital Built Britain, 2022c): guided with the same core values to create an NDT for public benefit in perpetuity, regardless of government changes. Considering that the required long-term commitment could potentially outlive changes in government, the leadership of an NDT Implementation Plan should not be tied to political systems but led by a dedicated NDT Task Group with representatives from each sphere of influence, i.e. state, industry, academia, and civil society.

The NDT Task Group should ideally comprise of interdisciplinary data experts (possibly by nominated leaders drawn from the 'six pillars'), as they can, to the best of their knowledge, provide technical advice on the required datasets (e.g., level of detail) that would contribute to meaningful analytics of the DT. This will help to ensure collective knowledge is united and diverse voices of experts are heard while plotting the NDT Implementation Plan. Furthermore, it provides new avenues and synergies for collaborations to support a more comprehensive implementation plan.

To this end, socio-technological changes are inevitable to ensure the success of an NDT Implementation Plan. With the effective leadership of an NDT Task Group, these changes include initiating a Theory of Change (ToC) and developing an Information Management Framework (IMF), which can be derived based on the research methodology as follows (Figure 5.1).

## 1. Theory of Change (ToC)

At the core of Slovakia's NDT, an initial Theory of Change (ToC) was developed by triangulating the review on relevant ToC documents and the strategies and priorities outlined for the Digital Transformation of Slovakia 2030 (Digital Skills and Jobs Platform, 2022), as well as the feedback received from the stakeholder engagement exercise held in September 2022. The ToC identified the socio-technological changes required for the four spheres of influence involved in the co-creation of the NDT, as well as other anticipated changes that would occur progressively over time to achieve Slovakia 2030 with the facilitation of the NDT.

## 2. Information Management Framework (IMF)

An Information Management Framework (IMF) was deemed important as a reference to outline the appropriate standards and protocols that will facilitate data collection and data exchange, as well as data interoperability and integration at a national level. Relevant frameworks were reviewed to develop an IMF with the objective to place Slovakia in a global context with respect to digital twinning for smart governance.

# THEORY OF CHANGE

The concept of a Theory of Change (ToC) is well established in international development for project and impact planning, emerging as a need for stakeholders to execute initiatives in the context of an increasingly complex society. The concept of ToC provides stakeholders with a platform to develop a shared understanding of how a desired change might come about. This can be achieved by defining a shared vision and then reverse engineering to implement changes that need to happen for a particular vision to be adopted (Maru *et al.*, 2018; Peta, 2018; Taplin *et al.*, 2013).

In a similar vein, a ToC was a key tool for the Slovak NDT Task Group to articulate potential changes and interventions that were required by each sphere of influence; as well as to show how different interventions could create compound impacts to achieve the NDT Implementation Plan. This was made possible by holding regular workshop sessions amongst the NDT Task Group in order to co-develop a ToC based on contextual relevance.

By triangulating the ToC from the Centre for Digital Built Britain (2022c), the strategies and priorities outlined for Digital Transformation of Slovakia 2030 (Digital Skills and Jobs Platform, 2022), and the feedback from the stakeholder engagement exercise held in September 2022 (Figure 5.2), an initial ToC was proposed that sought to address the respective changes required by each sphere of influence (Table 5.1).

It is intended that similar stakeholder engagement exercises will be run on a regular basis, so that the ToC can be updated based on fresh perspectives regarding the NDT, as well as how changes can be brought about to realise any new initiatives, ideas, or innovations.

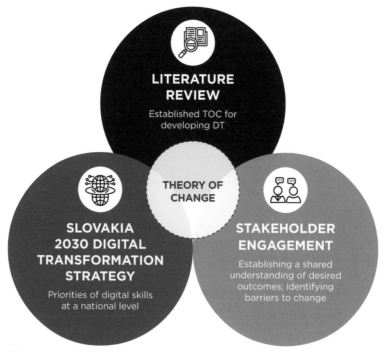

**Figure 5.2** The multiple sources applied in deriving the initial Theory of Change for Slovakia.

# KEY TAKEAWAYS

## STATE

- Articulating a clear vision and developing a national implementation plan
- Forming a National Digital Twin (NDT) Task Group with representatives from each sphere of influence to coordinate and seek alignment amongst key players and stakeholders who wish to be part of NDT
- Setting up a robust IT infrastructure with greater capacity whilst maintaining high cyber security and General Data Protection Regulation (GDPR)
- Building up a technical support team, supported by interdisciplinary data experts
- Developing and launching an Information Management Framework (IMF) to articulate specific data priority and format requirements (e.g. scale, purposes, file format, line / point / polygon data), ensuring data exchange, interoperability, and integration
- Reviewing the Theory of Change on a regular basis and updating it over time
- Evaluating the DTs progress on a regular basis; reviewing and discussing the results with key players and stakeholders to determine any changes needed
- Reviewing policies in place and establishing governance to support the required changes and NDT implementation plan
- Preparing IT infrastructure to communicate and link to similar efforts in DT implementation that are taking place globally

## ACADEMIA

- Reviewing learning pathways and curricula of school systems, from early childhood education through to tertiary education; to promote the use of digital technologies (educational platforms) and enhance digital competences amongst students
- Enhancing collaborations between academia, industry, and state to advance and ensure relevance of education systems and training in digital skills that are transferable to the DT
- Developing a set of initial assumptions and robust algorithms for validating quantitative simulation models and running what-if scenarios on the DT
- Establishing and validating new scientific methodologies in studying specific subject(s) through data modelling
- Creating new knowledge pathways; test-bedding of new innovations based on open data on the DT

**Table 5.1** An initial ToC proposed to address the respective changes required by each sphere of influence in Slovakia.

## INDUSTRY

- Assessing change readiness and identifying roles and skills needed, as well as capability gaps in the existing workforce
- Supporting education initiatives on advanced digital skills; re-educating different professions and bringing them up to the level of expertise required to adapt and adjust to the digital landscape while performing their existing tasks through the digital twin (e.g. architects and planners are shifting from CAD to BIM and GIS)
- Enhancing business processes and upskilling their workforce
- Adopting the use of BIM and CIM; recognising the value of secure and resilient data sharing across boundaries
- Built environment consultants and related service providers, such as architects, planners, contractors, and developers, to start mapping out the existing buildings and infrastructure according to the Information Management Framework (IMF) identified by the state

## CIVIL SOCIETY

- Partaking in crowd-sourced data programmes to support the state's effort in data gathering at a national level
- Developing better-informed initiatives and pilot projects based on open data and sense making with the DT
- Supporting and adapting to revised learning paths and school systems in the integration of digital technologies
- Embracing the culture of systemic lifelong learning where the existing workforce is supported by digital education initiatives on upskilling throughout industries and occupations

# INFORMATION MANAGEMENT FRAMEWORK

## COMPONENTS OF INFORMATION MANAGEMENT FRAMEWORK

To establish an inclusive NDT, it is necessary to lay socio-technological groundwork that fosters a shared understanding across Slovakia's eight regions. The adoption of an Information Management Framework (IMF) is crucial in achieving this goal, as it provides accessible technical and non-technical standards, guidance, and shared resources that facilitate seamless information exchange within the NDT. The IMF also aims to promote information coordination, consistency, and maturity across diverse sectors, organisations, and regions in Slovakia.

Specifically, the IMF outlines extensive standards and protocols for various elements, including common data models, reference data, and universal data formalisms. Therefore, the IMF plays a pivotal role in ensuring that high-quality information is compatible and presented in a consistent format, making it easier to share and link data and models across national boundaries. This, in turn, enables more informed decision-making and the discovery of valuable insights for the nation, now and into the future.

The success of the NDT depends on the quality of the information it relies on. As the Centre for Digital Built Britain (2020) suggests, preceeding efforts are necessary to ensure that the information meets certain quality standards, such as consistency, clarity, and availability; and to support greater data exchange, interoperability, and integration. This can be governed by a well-established IMF, comprising three key resources:

1. Foundation Data Model (FDM): 'the grammar of the language', which entails a consistent, crystalline understanding of what makes up the DT technology ecosystems;

2. Reference Data Library (RDL): 'the words of the language' that define the specific set of classes and properties used for describing a DT; and

3. Integration Architecture (IA): the procedures that facilitate the controlled exchange of information.

To enhance collaboration between the 'four spheres of influence' in Slovakia, the NDT Task Group could expand its IMF beyond the three key resources suggested. Specifically, the framework could address Data Accessibility, Usage, and Visualisation, as well as Data Types and Collection Plan. The former recognises the interrelated nature of data accessibility, usage, and visualisation within the NDT, and provides guidance for achieving a balance between accessibility and security. The latter defines the various characteristics of the heterogeneous data that the NDT handles, and includes a template for a data collection plan to guide the NDT Task Group in aligning data capturing approaches and update frequency at a national level. The addition of these two components addressed the key concerns that arose from the stakeholder engagement exercise that was held in September 2022. These key concerns included: cyber security, data accessibility, UIUX design, system reconfigurability, ensuring high-quality data, and diversifying data collection effort at scale. In essence, the IMF for Slovakia comprises:

1. Foundation Data Model (FDM);
2. Reference Data Library (RDL);
3. Integration Architecture (IA);
4. Data accessibility, usage, and visualisation; and
5. Data types and data collection plan.

Ultimately, having an IMF with these five components will support greater data exchange, interoperability, and integration within a secure and user-friendly digital environment (Figure 5.3). These five components are further explained in the following sections.

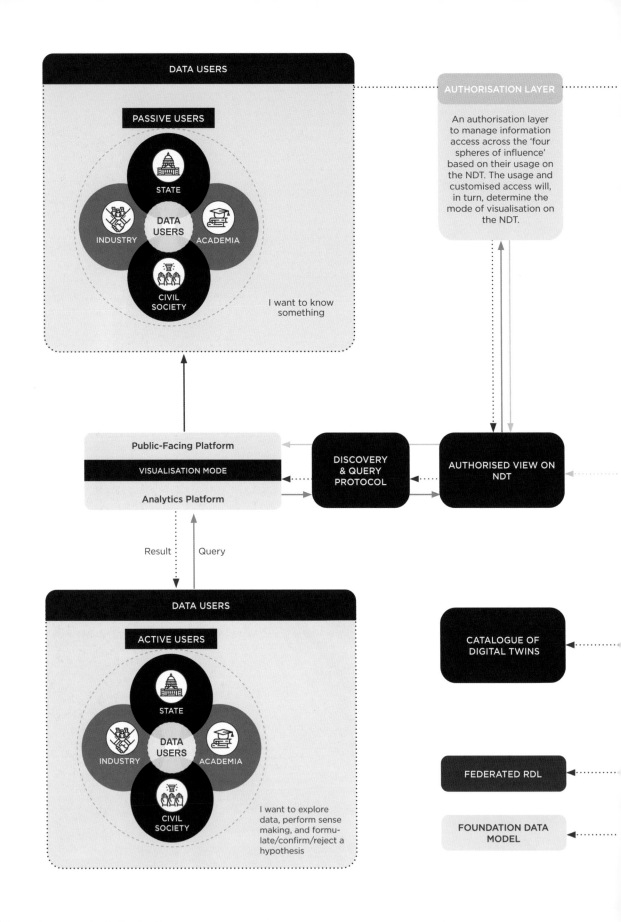

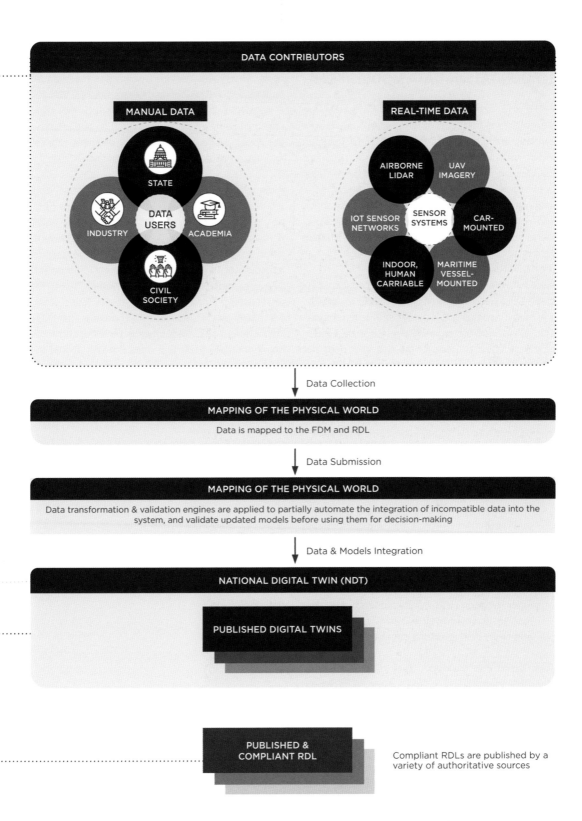

**Figure 5.3** Conceptual view of the NDT for Slovakia – an NDT enabled by an Information Management Framework.

# 1. FOUNDATION DATA MODEL (FDM)

A DT is a real-time digital representation of the physical world that reflects the continuous two-way dynamic mapping and bi-directional links between the physical world and its virtual replica (Stanford Engineering, 2020). The physical world is inevitably made up of complex relationships, in which these relationships are captured in predominantly static and real-time data that has often failed to depict the intricate webs of interactions between different entities.

Moreover, the data that captures these relationships may be acquired by different organisations or systems and stored according to different data requirements. This is because the organisation or source system may have intended uses for the data that does not fully align with the requirements of other systems. As a result, acquiring, integrating, and storing data on a DT remains a challenging task (Lu, Q. *et al.*, 2020; Mavrokapnidis *et al.*, 2021).

Ensuring the robustness and sustainability of a DTs entire life cycle requires addressing two important components related to data integration:

1. The complex relationships in the physical world must be translated into a machine-interpretable format when creating the virtual representation; and
2. Incompatibility issues arising from differences in the conceptual understanding of relationships, held between data and models, must be resolved to ensure data extensibility, modularity, and cross-domain linking capabilities.

This called for the NDT Task Group, working alongside interdisciplinary data experts, to develop a Foundation Data Model (FDM) that was contextually relevant to Slovakia.

The FDM serves as a foundational, ontological model to establish a consistent and clear understanding of what constitutes the world of DTs by using common terms and definitions to formally describe them, as well as the relationships held within and between DTs, models, datasets, and their physical twins. These relationships encompass methods for aggregating and validating model inputs and outputs, especially in situations where there may be modelling gaps or uncertainties in areas such as actuality and possibility; scale and granularity; and time, space, and place (Centre for Digital Built Britain, 2020).

Although there are various ontology-based data models – such as Industry Foundation Classes (IFC) and Brick Schema – designed to represent the entire domain of smart buildings, these models (software) seem to primarily concentrate on the operational aspects of the built environment (hardware) (Mavrokapnidis *et al.*, 2021), rather than the relationships between the soft assets found within the social world (heartware). Therefore, the NDT Task Group could work towards developing a more comprehensive FDM that does not only model the relationships of the operational aspects of hardware but also accounts for socially constructed items such as socio-cultural practices and social norms found within the heartware of the social world (Figure 5.4).

Establishing an FDM to ensure consistent information within Slovakia's context was a valuable time- and cost-efficient asset. This was especially important when collecting information from a multitude of stakeholders and domains at national scale. With an FDM in place, little to no effort was required for translation when data was received. It therefore permitted immediate use of the received data, allowing for accurate data integration, rapid evaluations, faster response times, and enhanced decision-making.

## TIME, SPACE, & PLACE

- How does the ontology deal with time and space-time?
- How does the ontology deal with places, locations, and shapes?
- How should the NDT aggregate models that operate at very different tempos – from seconds, to hours, to days?
- How do we describe and capture change over time?
- How do we model future operations to assess the impact of planned changes, without disturbing the current operating model?

## ACTUALITY & POSSIBILITY

- How does the ontology deal with uncertainty, such as where multiple data sets give conflicting stories on the behaviour of a network?
- How do we handle uncertainty? How should we best manage the difference between 'measurement uncertainty', 'variability within a class', 'variation over time', etc.?
- How can a lack of reliability be taken into account when some models, on one hand, are derived based on known understanding and some, on the other hand, are based on maximising goodness-of-fit from models?

## SCALE & GRANULARITY

- How does the ontology deal with scale, resolution, and granularity?
- How does the ontology deal with internal variance in the granularity level of the DT between areas and buildings from different centuries?
- How do we aggregate models, particularly in circumstances where there may be modelling gaps? How do we deal with missing information or unconnected assets?

## QUALITIES, ARTEFACTS, & SOCIALLY CONSTRUCTED ENTITIES

- How does the ontology deal with qualities and other qualitative attributes?
- How does the ontology deal with artefacts (e.g. engineered items) and socially constructed items like socio-economic, socio-cultural practices, time-tested rituals, social interactions, social norms, history, democracy, politics, human rights, ethics?
- How do we model social concepts related to ownership, rights, legislation, and regulation? What are the permitted uses of the model and any licence or usage constraints?

**Figure 5.4** A Foundational Data Model (FDM) that models the relationships of the operational aspects of hardware and accounts for socio-cultural practices and social norms found within the heartware of the social world (Source: adapted from Centre for Digital Built Britain, 2020).

## 2. REFERENCE DATA LIBRARY (RDL)

Just as it is important to have an FDM to establish 'grammar of the language', the need for a Reference Data Library (RDL) is also a recognised component to outline the 'words of the language' for the DT. While the FDM aims to provide a clear understanding of core concepts at a higher level (for instance, what constitutes a 'city'), the RDL ensures the consistent use of words at the sub-category level to describe what a 'city' entails (such as buildings, road networks, utilities, sanitation, and people) (Centre for Digital Built Britain, 2020).

The RDL specifies the taxonomies and vocabularies, as well as classifications and properties of things, used across DTs. The RDL enables the sharing of high-quality data with enhanced interoperability that provides a common reference for stakeholders who want to exchange data as part of Slovakia's NDT. This ensures consistency in taxonomies and classifications for mapping and interpreting each other's data. It is worth noting that the FDM must guide the design of each RDL to achieve consistency. The FDM, with the RDL being designed subject to it, should facilitate the development of components for the IMF without requiring all the necessary information to be identified upfront. As the scope expands, both the model and data can be expanded accordingly in time.

Therefore, it would seem essential to acknowledge that the RDL is not an isolated resource that the IMF uses to promote consistency, but rather an interconnected ecosystem of libraries that rely on established definitions and adhere to community-wide practices. The RDL sits alongside the FDM: developed according to Slovakia's contextual relevance, for managing information quality. By adhering to methodologies and standards, a high level of consistency can be achieved across a wide range of subjects. As a result, two individuals who independently model the same concept are likely to produce similar outcomes.

Established by the Open Geospatial Consortium (OGC), CityGML (Geography Markup Language) 3.0 has been widely adopted as a standardised information model and file format. Not only does CityGML represent geometric (geographical and topological) appearances of 3D city objects, it also outlines the common reference for the representation of taxonomies, as well as the semantic and thematic properties (Open Geospatial Consortium Inc., 2008). The CityGML will, therefore, facilitate data collection, aggregation, and integration of different types of datasets under the spatial layers (e.g. building, land use, vegetation, transportation, water body), laying the foundation of the NDT for Slovakia.

The NDT should have the capacity to support different granularity levels of detail (LOD) (Table 5.2) between areas, considering that century-old buildings may not have the same level of detail as the newer buildings, which receive more frequent updates (Lehtola et al., 2022). In the case of the NDT for Slovakia, the foundation established by geo-referenced spatial layers and 3D city objects enables the lowest levels of granularity to aggregate data layers from other pillars, such as social, cultural, technological, economic, and environmental. These data layers can be populated and geo-tagged accordingly on the DTs, which will become richer over time as more data is collected.

Nevertheless, it is important to note that CityGML currently possesses the common reference only for geographical and topological properties, specifically the spatial pillar. It underscores the pressing need for the NDT Task Group to further explore and refine the RDL, augmented by the common reference for the other pillars – economic, technological, environmental, social, and cultural – based on the contextual relevance of Slovakia. This will eventually steer national data collection and data logging efforts using standardised representations of classifications.

| | LOD0 | LOD1 | LOD2 | LOD3 | LOD4 |
|---|---|---|---|---|---|
| **MODEL SCALE DESCRIPTION** | Regional, landscape | City, region | City districts, projects | Architectural models (outside), landmark | Architectural models (interior) |
| **CLASS OF ACCURACY** | Lowest | Low | Middle | High | Very high |
| **ABSOLUTE 3D POINT ACCURACY (POSITION/ HEIGHT)** | Lower than LOD1 | 5/5m | 2/2m | 0.5/0.5m | 0.2/0.2m |
| **GENERALISATION** | Maximal generalisation (classification of land use) | Object blocks as generalised features; > 6*6m/3m | Objects as generalised features; > 4*4m/2m | Objects as real features; > 2*2m/1m | Constructive elements and openings are represented |
| **BUILDING INSTALLATIONS** | - | - | - | Representative exterior effects | Real object form |
| **ROOF FORM/ STRUCTURE** | No | Flat | Roof type and orientation | Real object form | Real object form |
| **ROOF OVERHANGING PARTS** | - | - | n.a. | n.a. | Yes |
| **CITY FURNITURE** | - | Important objects | Prototypes | Real object form | Real object form |
| **SOLITARY VEGETATION OBJECT** | - | Important objects | Prototypes, higher 6m | Prototypes, higher 2m | Prototypes, real object form |
| **PLANT COVER** | - | >50*50m | >5*5m | <LOD2 | <LOD2 |

**Table 5.2** The graphical illustration of the five levels of detail (LOD) defined by CityGML (Source: Photos on Unsplash by USGS, 2020; Charlie Deets, 2018; Miguel Ibáñez, 2017; Lorenzo Gerosa, 2023) and their accuracy requirements (Source: after Albert *et al.* 2003, cited in Open Geospatial Consortium Inc., 2008).

# 3. INTEGRATION ARCHITECTURE (IA)

One of the significant benefits of having an NDT for Slovakia is being able to use it as 'a centralised data platform to enable cross-sectoral, cross-regional collaborations and communications with increased data accessibility, data interoperability, and improved efficiency in a safe and cost-saving environment'. With this in mind, it was vital to design and develop the NDT with this perspective. While the FDM and RDL establish the 'grammar and words of the language' respectively, an Integration Architecture (IA) specifies the protocols needed to manage data sharing flexibly, securely, and resiliently. To develop a comprehensive NDT for Slovakia, the NDT Task Group had to consider various aspects, including:

1. Catalogue & Discovery of DTs;
1. Data/Model Modularisation & Service-oriented Architecture (SOA);
1. Data Transformation & Validation; and
1. Security & Authorised Access.

Figure 5.5 illustrates a proposed methodological design in the development of the NDT in Slovakia.

## Catalogue & Discovery of DTs

A DT catalogue is an inventory of DT datasets. With discovery and query protocols in place, a DT catalogue enables efficient retrieval of DTs, allowing for querying of twins and assets managed by different owners. This subsequently makes way for linking different DTs through the IA for enhanced decision-making (Centre for Digital Built Britain, 2020).

## Data/Model Modularisation & Service-oriented Architecture (SOA)

The aggregation hierarchy of data, functionality, and model within the NDT should be supported by a high level of modularity and loosely coupled architectural components for better system reconfigurability (Kruger, Human and Basson, 2022; Segovia and Garcia-Alfaro, 2022). For instance, historical and current data of the physical world can be used to evaluate performance to-date; but together with other pre-defined factors these data sets can be simulated in the virtual world for future projections.

In the review of service-oriented architectures (SOA) in related literature , Lu *et al.*, (2020) noted that the architecture developed for smart cities and big data analytics is often restricted to specific applications and lacks interaction with human users. They suggest that future research should propose more user-centred architectures. Seebacher *et al.* (2017) goes further to highlight three pillars to improve visual analytics and similarity search, in which the three pillars can be adopted here to support heterogeneous environments (e.g. multi-function and large amount of data). These pillars are:

1. Data: Paying particular attention to data pre-processing and aggregation is crucial to prevent errors from propagating throughout the system and adversely affecting the quality of the results.
2. Task/Application: NDT applications vary with user expertise, including obtaining updates through visualisation, exploring data for hypotheses, and examining data to confirm or reject an existing hypothesis.
3. Users: Users set requirements, which are often intricate and ambiguous, while exploring data or setting various scenarios within the NDT. Thus, designing an SOA that considers user expertise levels and their applications is vital.

Hence, understanding the users, their goals, and the conditions under which they use the NDT is crucial.

## Data Transformation & Validation

The received data or models from multiple stakeholders are not always available in formats that are fully compatible with the foundational ontology used in the NDT. A data transformation and validation engine helps to address this issue by partially automating the integration of incompatible data into the platform, and run automated validation before the models are used in decision-making.

## Security & Authorised Access

The security of the NDT can be enhanced by implementing an authorisation layer to manage information access across the 'four spheres of influence' based on their usage within the NDT and other predefined attributes.

## SYSTEM PROPERTIES

### OBJECTIVES & FUNCTIONAL REQUIREMENTS

Condition
Monitoring

Dynamic
Scheduling

Quality
Control

Predictive
Maintenance

Deterministic
Simulation

Stochastic
Simulation

### PROCESS PLANS & SYSTEM REQUIREMENTS

Functions to Include
& Implement

Model
Types

Data Flow Components
Communications

Stakeholders
& Roles

Constraints, Limitations,
& Uncertainties

Hardware & Software
Requirements

### ARCHITECTURE

| | | |
|---|---|---|
| Define interactions between physical world (historical & current data) & virtual world (simulated data) | Define system layer, functional components and data layers | Identify data exchange & dependencies between services (condition monitoring, predictive maintenance, dynamic scheduling) |
| Define processes (behaviours / state of physical world items / procedure) & interfaces | Define user's data accessibility, usage & visualisation interfaces | Define data transformation & validation engines |

**Figure 5.5** The proposed methodological design for the development of the NDT of Slovakia.

# DATA ACCESSIBILITY, USAGE & VISUALISATION

An important observation was gleaned from the stakeholder engagement exercise held in September 2022: security and access are key concerns of the NDT. The NDT should ensure that all data and functions are secure from unintended use; but it should also be accessible to those who desire it in order to execute their respective tasks. The pressing need to strike a balance between the two draws special attention to evaluating the potential usage of the NDT, which will subsequently determine data accessibility, and the NDTs visual design. The tripartite relationship between usage, data accessibility, and visualisation is illustrated in Figure 5.6, with each category containing three different aspects:

1. **Usage:** passive use vs. active use;
2. **Data accessibility:** open access vs. secure access; and
3. **Visualisation:** public-facing platform vs. analytics platform.

## Usage & Data Accessibility

Table 5.3 demonstrates examples of potential usage, data accessibility, and visualisation for the NDT of Slovakia. Given the range of data to be accessed and the potential usage of the NDT by various stakeholders, the security of the NDT can be enhanced by adopting the 'attribute-based access control (ABAC)'. ABAC allows for fine-grained access to data based on matching attributes of the data with the stakeholders' profiles (Hu *et al.*, 2015).

An example of ABAC would be allowing users who are type=industry and have department=engineering status to access the infrastructure maintenance system during work hours and within the same time zone as to where the NDT is hosted. Another aspect of data accessibility, regardless of open access or secure access, is to consider the conditions under which the data can be used – i.e., online only or downloadable (Centre for Digital Built Britain, 2021).

## Visualisation

As a public-facing platform, it is recommended that the NDT should be made available through a web browser that is perpetually accessible 24/7 on the user's platform of choice, such as desktop, tablet, and/or mobile devices (Esri, 2021). Having a user-tagging feature adds value to the NDT, as it allows stakeholders (particularly the public) to geo-tag real-life problems and provide feedback in the NDT model; and even contribute (geo)data to the relevant government department or NDT ecosystem (White *et al.*, 2021). The visualisation experience, depending on the usage, can also be enhanced by augmented reality, virtual reality, and even mixed reality (Chalmers University of Technology, 2021). For an analytics platform, one of the key components lies in the interactivity between data, task, and user (Seebacher *et al.*, 2017). The platform should be designed to fuse (geo)analytics with data (granted on special access) and intelligence work flows, allowing for visualisation of information through intuitive analysis charts and analysis maps (Tunçer and You, 2017).

Lehtola *et al.* (2022) goes further to outline the cartographic visualisation considerations related to DTs, which include:

1. **Symbolisation** of how things are presented for the viewer;
2. **Scale** of models: whether to simulate the real, embodied experience, or at a smaller scale;
3. **Perspective** of which the models are presented to the viewer;
4. **Interface** usability that involves panning, zooming, and rotating abilities for the viewer; and
5. **Bring Your Own Device (BYOD)** compatibility to ensure a diversity of devices are able to participate in visualising the 3D DT.

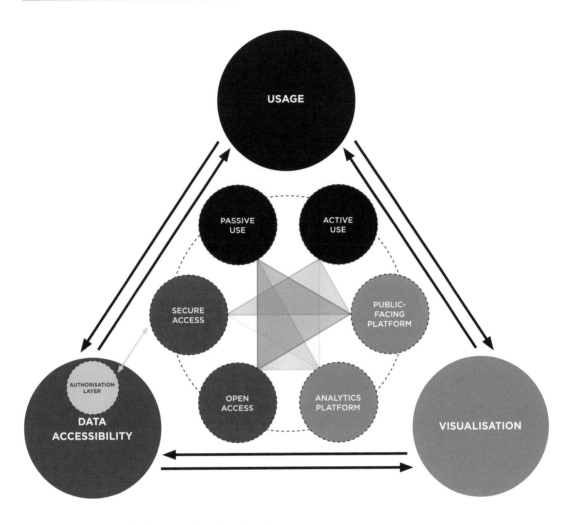

The above diagram depicts the dynamic, tripartite relationship amongst three elements: the potential usage of the NDT by diverse stakeholders, the data accessibility in the NDT, and the visualisation of the NDT (determined by the first two elements). Each component encompasses two distinct dimensions:

1. Usage: Passive use vs Active use;
2. Data Accessibility: Open Access vs Secure Access; and
3. Visualisation: Public-Facing Platform vs Analytics Platform.

**Figure 5.6** The tripartite relationship between usage, visualisation, and data accessibility for the NDT of Slovakia.

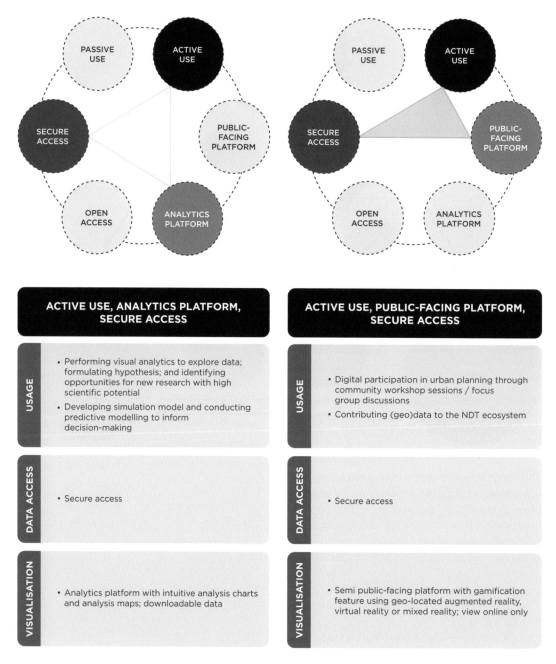

**Table 5.3** Examples of potential usage, data accessibility, and visualisation design for the NDT of Slovakia.

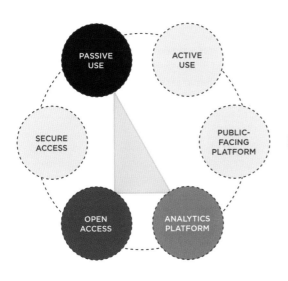

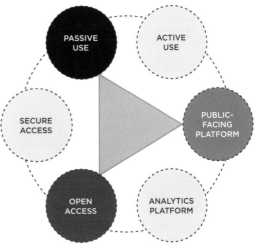

## PASSIVE USE, ANALYTICS PLATFORM, OPEN ACCESS

**USAGE**

- Generating insights into developing better-informed decisions, initiatives, and pilot projects based on open data and sense making on the NDT (e.g. property value analysis)
- Visualising results from scientific research / simulation models (e.g. environmental hazards, daylight, and shadow casting)

**DATA ACCESS**

- Open access

**VISUALISATION**

- Semi analytics platform with intuitive analysis charts and analysis maps; view online only

## PASSIVE USE, PUBLIC-FACING PLATFORM, OPEN ACCESS

**USAGE**

- Having access to municipal, regional, national information (e.g. job openings, upcoming developments & activities, improvement and construction work status, disaster alerts)
- Sending feedback / voting on newly proposed development, geo-tagging real-life problems; seeking municipal assistance

**DATA ACCESS**

- Open access

**VISUALISATION**

- Public-facing platform with user-tagging feature; view online only

# DATA TYPES & DATA COLLECTION PLAN

Besides ensuring the quality of data, it is imperative to understand the characteristics of the data that an NDT deals with. This data may be multi-temporal, multi-scale, multi-dimensional, multi-source, and heterogeneous; 'big' and 'small' and both quantitative and qualitative (Tunçer and You, 2017).

Some data may be collected from physical entities using different sensor systems. This could include both static attribute data (e.g. urban infrastructure; topological features) and dynamic condition data (e.g. real-time transport tracking data; social network data containing geo-information about events, places, or opinions). Some (synthetic) data is generated from virtual models based on simulation results (e.g. virtual population for predictive analysis; virtual image or video for autonomous car's vision

algorithms training) (Qi et al., 2021). Some may be user-volunteered data (e.g. indoor, human carriable sensor; Global Positioning System (GPS) location data retrieved from phone data; health data retrieved from relevant public mobile applications) that contributes to the bottom-up formation of publicly available databases in the NDT ecosystem (Mark, 2012). See Figure 5.7 for examples of big vs. small and quantitative vs. qualitative data.

Not only does this mixed-method complement the long-established sources (e.g. surveys or interviews) that are often costly and labour intensive, it also leads to innovative ways of urban governance through urban analysis and evidence-based planning (Reades et al., 2007; Tunçer and You, 2017).

**Manual Data VS Real-time Data**

There are two categories of data: i.e. real-time data and manual data. Real-time data relies on

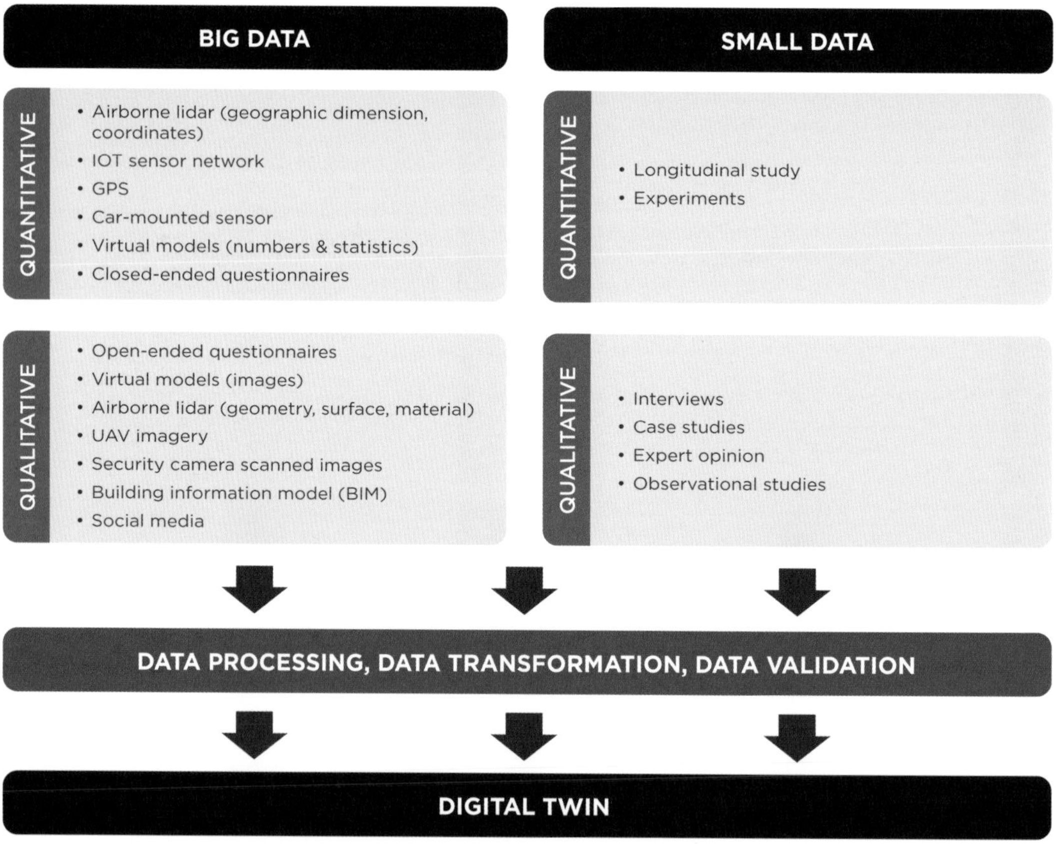

**BIG DATA**

QUANTITATIVE
- Airborne lidar (geographic dimension, coordinates)
- IOT sensor network
- GPS
- Car-mounted sensor
- Virtual models (numbers & statistics)
- Closed-ended questionnaires

QUALITATIVE
- Open-ended questionnaires
- Virtual models (images)
- Airborne lidar (geometry, surface, material)
- UAV imagery
- Security camera scanned images
- Building information model (BIM)
- Social media

**SMALL DATA**

QUANTITATIVE
- Longitudinal study
- Experiments

QUALITATIVE
- Interviews
- Case studies
- Expert opinion
- Observational studies

**DATA PROCESSING, DATA TRANSFORMATION, DATA VALIDATION**

**DIGITAL TWIN**

Figure 5.7 The charactheristics of NDT data.

technologies for data gathering, such as deployment of sensor systems and Artificial intelligence (AI) algorithms, whilst manual data mostly requires human interventions to facilitate data-generating processes (Figure 5.8).

## Real-time Data

Real-time data is often preferred because the automated data collection effort is relatively more time- and cost-efficient. Its automation capabilities also prove to be valuable in performing end-to-end data management – from (spatial, technological, and environmental) data collection, to data transformation (compatibility and validity checks) and data integration on the DT system (Lehtola *et al.*, 2022; Esri, 2021).

## Manual Data

Although the collection of manual data is deemed to be more arduous and costly, the values that manual data has to offer should not be overlooked. Manual data offers a means to capture intangible (social, cultural, and economic) concepts or even generate non-existent information. Through humans' tacit knowledge and procedural techniques, the descriptive concepts and information can be quantified and translated into a machine-readable format for further analysis. For instance, survey questionnaires have been widely adopted to collect behavioural and perception data on quality of life (Bowling *et al.*, 2013; Ventegodt, Merrick, and Andersen, 2003), traffic risks and pedestrian safety (Hongsranagon *et al.*, 2011; Mukherjee and Mitra, 2019), and so on. The application of synthetic data generated from virtual models are well recognised for its potential to enhance statistical modelling in different domains, such as building energy consumption and rainfall prediction (Jamalinia *et al.*, 2020; Reddy and Claridge, 1994), to name a few.

Therefore, the benefits of having both real-time and manual data within the NDT platform are manifold – not only will the NDT emulate the physical entities and assets based on real-time data, but it will also simulate the intangible concepts and predict future events in the physical ecosystems. This invariably offers a more holistic understanding of the physical twin.

Table 5.4 guided the NDT Task Group on data collection. It aligned data capturing approaches, updated frequency, scale of data collection, and potential stakeholders involved (top-down, middle-out, or bottom-up approach).

**AIRBORNE LIDAR**

**CCTV**

**QUALITATIVE SURVEYS**

**BIM MODELS**

**Figure 5.8** Mixed-use of both manual and real-time data to facilitate data-generating processes (Source: Photo on Unsplash by Mitch Nielsen, 2016; Brock Wegner, 2021; Scott Graham, 2015; Evgeniy Surzhan, 2021).

## REAL-TIME DATA (NON-EXHAUSTIVE)

| SENSOR SYSTEMS | POTENTIAL APPLICATION(S) | UPDATE FREQUENCY | SCALE | DATA COLLECTION APPROACH |
|---|---|---|---|---|
| **AIRBORNE LIDAR** | • Collecting accurate and dense topographic data at very high speed | • 2-3 years | • City-wide | • Top-down |
| **UAV IMAGERY** | • Mapping of geometrical, environmental, and topographic properties<br>• Mapping, reconstructing, and monitoring canopy structure with 3D point cloud data estimated from UAV imagery | • Monthly | • Local flight path | • Middle-out (State, Academia, Industry) |
| **CAR-MOUNTED** | • Collecting road-related data such as road surface conditions, as well as data related to the positions and volumes of pedestrians and bicycles | - | • Driven streets | • Middle-out (State, Academia, Industry) |
| **MARITIME VESSEL-MOUNTED** | • Collecting wind data for the possible design of an offshore wind farm, determining size and placement of wind turbines | - | • Steamed channels | • Middle-out (State & Industry) |
| **INDOOR, HUMAN CARRIABLE** | • Evaluating quantity and quality of movements (human activity recognition) corresponding with indoor localisation<br>• Crowd-sensing and determining congestion status, noise levels, hotspots for indoor air pollution, etc. | • On need only | • Local | • Middle-out (State, Academia, Industry, Civil Society) |
| **IOT SENSOR NETWORK** | • Monitoring and managing traffic and transportation systems, power plants, utilities, water supply networks, waste management, crime detection, information systems, etc. | • Online | • Local | • Middle-out (State, Academia, Industry) |
| **IMAGE SENSORS (USED IN SECURITY CAMERAS)** | • Providing surveillance; capturing HQ images for image analysis; collecting real-time information related to crowds, classification of vehicles, traffic volume, etc. in specific areas | • Varied based on goals – reducing response times, decreasing crime rates, improving the availability of parking, etc. | • City-wide, local (test-bedding site) | • Top-down |
| **GPS PHONE TRACKERS** | • Collecting location and time information | - | • City-wide, local (test-bedding site) | • Middle-out (State, Academia, Industry, Civil Society) |

**Table 5.4a** Real-time data: a data collection template to guide the NDT Task Group in aligning data-capturing effort.

## MANUAL DATA (NON-EXHAUSTIVE)

| COLLECTION INSTRUMENT | POTENTIAL APPLICATION(S) | UPDATE FREQUENCY | SCALE | DATA COLLECTION APPROACH |
|---|---|---|---|---|
| QUESTIONNAIRES | • Collecting information on census; quantifying subjective experiences, perceptions, attitudes, opinion | • Annually (census); as and when required | • National (census); local | • Top-down |
| INTERVIEWS | • Developing bottom-up framework and parameters for collecting citizen-centric data (e.g. quality of life, inequalities, public services, civil society support for democracy) | • 2–3 years | • City-wide, local (test-bedding site) | • Middle-out (State, Academia, Civil Society) |
| BUILDING INFORMATION MODEL (BIM) | • Designing, planning, creating, and managing building information on a construction project throughout its whole life cycle | • As and when required | • City-wide, local (test-bedding site) | • Middle-out (State & Industry) |
| SOCIAL MEDIA DATA | • Collecting emotional and behavioural data with reference to certain places, subjects, etc. | • As and when required | • City-wide, local (test-bedding site) | • Middle-out (State, Academia, Industry, Civil Society) |
| VIRTUAL MODELS | • Generating synthetic data based on simulation results (e.g. virtual population for predictive analysis; virtual image or video for autonomous car's vision algorithms training) | • As and when required | • City-wide, local (test-bedding site) | • Middle-out (State, Academia, Industry) |

**Table 5.4b** Manual data: a data collection template to guide the NDT Task Group in aligning data capturing effort.

# CHAPTER 6.0

## IMPLEMENTING THE DIGITAL TWIN

City network internet, 2021 © Photo by Gerd Altmann on Pixabay

# EXECUTIVE SUMMARY

In the previous chapters, we covered the categorisation of data layers governed by the 'six-pillar' framework (Pomeroy, 2020a, p. 2–3); the process of gathering collective inputs from relevant stakeholders; and socio-technological changes involved in establishing a Theory of Change (ToC) and an Information Management Framework (IMF). This chapter articulates the practical steps to turn these strategic plans into operational implementation for Slovakia's DT journey. Working collaboratively with the Authority for Spatial Planning and Construction, this articulation was essential to enable the Slovak government to go beyond mere recognition of the significance of having a National Digital Twin (NDT). It legitimised the strategic plans and brought them to the point of implementation effectively supported by smart governance in Slovakia.

The operational implementation of the NDT involved translating strategic plans formulated in the previous chapters into actionable tasks, delegating responsibilities, and executing on objectives to achieve desired outcomes. The transition from strategic planning to operational implementation was seen as a crucial phase that significantly impacted the success of the NDT.

With this in mind, it was important to approach this transition as a dynamic and iterative process, rather than a linear one that ended with implementation. In other words, this transition was conceived as a circular process that required constant monitoring and improvement, regularly reviewing and discussing the tangible results achieved, and using this information to determine if any changes are needed to optimise the implementation process and outcomes.

With the goal of translating strategic plans into operational implementation for Slovakia, the following agenda was set in action:

## 1. Proof of Concepts (PoCs) & Scenario Planning

Six PoCs were initially identified by the Slovak government to test the envisaged functions and verify the feasibility of the 3D DT conceptual model. These PoCs were integrated into Scenario Planning, augmented with the data layers encapsulated in the 'six-pillar' framework in order to demonstrate the feasibility of the NDT in facilitating the work flow involving the 'four spheres of influence', namely state, industry, academia, and civil society (Pomeroy, 2020b, p. 201–202). The showcase of both PoCs and Scenario Planning demonstrates the NDTs aims in optimising and making the work flow friendly for diverse stakeholders from cross-sectoral and cross-regional backgrounds in Slovakia.

## 2. Monitoring & Evaluation (M&E) Plan

The Monitoring and Evaluation (M&E) Plan outlines systematic procedures to track and monitor progress, as well as to quantify impacts of the NDT implementation strategy in Slovakia. Through academic research on existing evaluation frameworks for digital transformation and smart city development, a recurring pattern was discovered where the evaluation aspects often cover the socio-technological changes as a result of digital maturity and intensity, as well as the policy environment that can affect these changes. This work adopted a two-step M&E plan for Slovakia:

1. Evaluation Indicators for the Impacts of the NDT and Digital Transformation; and
2. Effectiveness of Stakeholder Collaborations.

Whilst the former can be measured by using a modified smart city audit framework, the latter adopts a mixed-method approach, including semi-structured interviews, non-participant observations, and survey questionnaires.

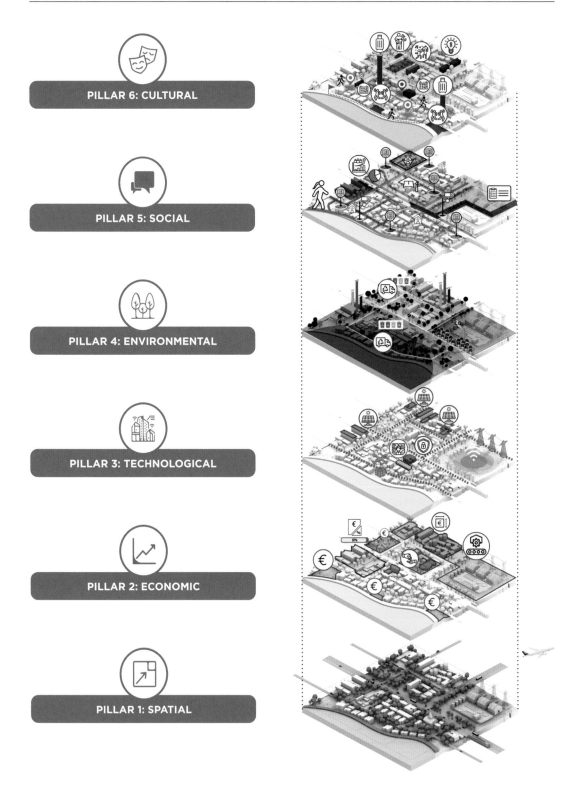

**PILLAR 6: CULTURAL**

**PILLAR 5: SOCIAL**

**PILLAR 4: ENVIRONMENTAL**

**PILLAR 3: TECHNOLOGICAL**

**PILLAR 2: ECONOMIC**

**PILLAR 1: SPATIAL**

**Figure 6.1** Representational image of 3D city information models of Slovakia, proposed by Pomeroy Academy.

# PROOF OF CONCEPTS & SCENARIO PLANNING

## PROOF OF CONCEPTS (PoCs)

It has been suggested that the most established approach to realising a DT is to start from the use of a 3D city information model (Lehtola *et al.*, 2022; Schrotter and Hürzeler, 2020). Chapter Three demonstrated a 'six-pillar' framework (Pomeroy, 2020a, p. 2–3) that can facilitate the organisation and categorisation of data, in which the data can be used to describe the conditions of the physical environment and form the 3D city information model of Slovakia (Figure 6.1). This section discusses the additional properties that can help to shift the 3D city information model from an information content perspective to a connected NDT, as well as the envisaged scenario that can be brought forth by implementing the NDT.

There should be a widely shared understanding that the NDT will not be a large, single model of the entire built and natural environment for Slovakia. Rather, it consists of multiple constituent DTs integrated together with shared data, presented in consistent formats for data interoperability (Centre for Digital Built Britain, 2022a; Lehtola *et al.*, 2022). In view of the new legislation on spatial planning and construction, the Authority for Spatial Planning and Construction has identified six Proof of Concepts (PoCs), which include:

1. PoC 1: Dendrology;
2. PoC 2: Smart Zone Plan;
3. PoC 3: Construction Notice;
4. PoC 4: Building an Apartment;
5. PoC 5: Monitoring of Water Pipe Leaks; and
6. PoC 6: Road Construction Project (Authority for Spatial Planning and Construction of the Slovak Republic, 2022).

These PoCs specifically target the spatial pillar, which serves as the foundation for the NDT in order to provide essential geo-spatial information and context, and facilitate end-to-end business processes related to applying and issuing spatial planning permits and building permits, including integrated Strategic Environmental Assessment (SEA) and Environmental Impact Assessment (EIA).

## SCENARIO PLANNING

As the data layers become more comprehensive over time, the NDT should aim to expand upon the initial PoCs and endeavour to comprehensively capture all the data pillars (i.e. spatial, economic, technological, environmental, social, and cultural) (Figure 6.2). This holistic approach will truly reflect the ecosystem of the physical twin, encompassing the hardware, software, and heartware of the built environments in Slovakia. By expanding the data layers and capturing all data pillars, the NDT will enable a broader range of stakeholders to leverage its insights for intelligent, informed decision-making.

The Scenario Planning section in the following pages demonstrates a compelling case where the work flow incorporates the 'four spheres of influence' (Pomeroy, 2020b, p. 201–202) – from industry to state, academia, and civil society – all of which are seamlessly optimised and made user friendly through the implementation of the proposed NDT. The work flow of each sphere is elucidated with accompanying diagrams and a step-by-step approach with reference to the specific data layers required. This comprehensive overview vividly illustrates how the NDT empowers the 'four spheres of influence' to effectively execute their respective desired task(s), thereby fostering a collaborative and synergistic approach towards leveraging the benefits of the NDT across various stakeholders.

# PROOF OF CONCEPT

## POC 1: DENDROLOGY

**3D TREE MODELS CONSTRUCTED BY LIDAR, RBG, AND SPECTRAL IMAGING**

Real-time precision forestry through tree inventory and analysis, tree condition monitoring, and risk detection

## POC 2: SMART ZONE PLAN

**3D TERRITORIAL MODEL BUILT BASED ON LIDAR, PHOTOGRAMMETRY, AND GEOPHYSICAL SCANNING**

Scan zoning plans and construction objectives within the territory, examining their compatibility with the proposed regulation of the functional and spatial arrangement of the territory

## POC 3: CONSTRUCTION NOTICE

**BIM MODELS OF BUILDINGS (UNDER CONSTRUCTION)**

Supervise construction status of buildings; give real-time updates on the projects' status; report on stopping conditions based on automated detection should any construction conflicts occur

## POC 4: BUILDING AN APARTMENT

**3D MODELS OF PROPOSED PROJECT(S)**

Perform real-time scanning of construction submissions; report status of construction permit process and stopping conditions should any construction conflicts occur

## POC 5: MONITORING OF WATER PIPE LEAKS

**3D MODELS OF UNDERGROUND INFRASTRUCTURE CONSTRUCTED WITH LIDAR AND GEOPHYSICAL SCANNING**

Detect compatibility of infrastructure with proposed regulation of the functional and spatial arrangement of the territory; inform predictive maintenance

## POC 6: ROAD CONSTRUCTION PROJECT

**BIM MODELS OF ROAD CONSTRUCTION PROJECT(S)**

A monitoring tool to supervise construction status and report on stopping conditions should any construction conflicts occur

**Figure 6.2** Highlighting the need for the NDT of Slovakia to expand upon the initial PoCs and endeavour to comprehensively capture all the data pillars.

# SCENARIO PLANNING

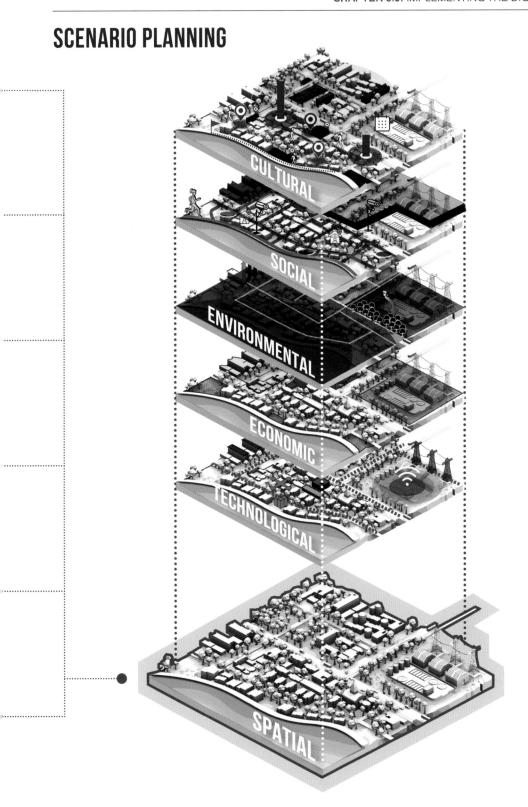

# SCENARIO PLANNING

## INDUSTRY
### *JOZEF*

Meet Jozef, a developer. Jozef is wanting to build a mixed-use development by the Danube River that is adjacent to a port. He takes the digital twin model to scout for a suitable plot of land that will yield high returns on investment. He switches on the spatial (1), economic, and environmental layers, which reveal the planning constraints, permitted land uses (2), and environmental conditions (3) respectively. Jozef thinks proximity to the Danube offers transportation as well as revenue benefits from riverfront food and beverage facilities (4). Jozef plans to also sell river facing views at a premium with large terraces. So he uses the digital twin model to run a property value analysis and is satisfied with the forecasted gross development value. He tries to push for greater Floor Area Ratio (5) (FAR) by building a tower with a series of planted sky terraces, which he believes would appeal to a youthful, middle-income demographic (6) taken from the social component of the digital twin data.

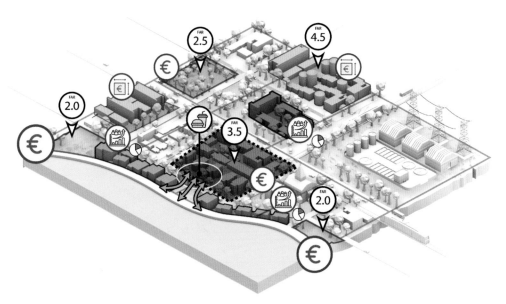

**Figure 6.3** A data model that illustrates the essential data layers needed to support the work flow of a representative from the industry sphere.

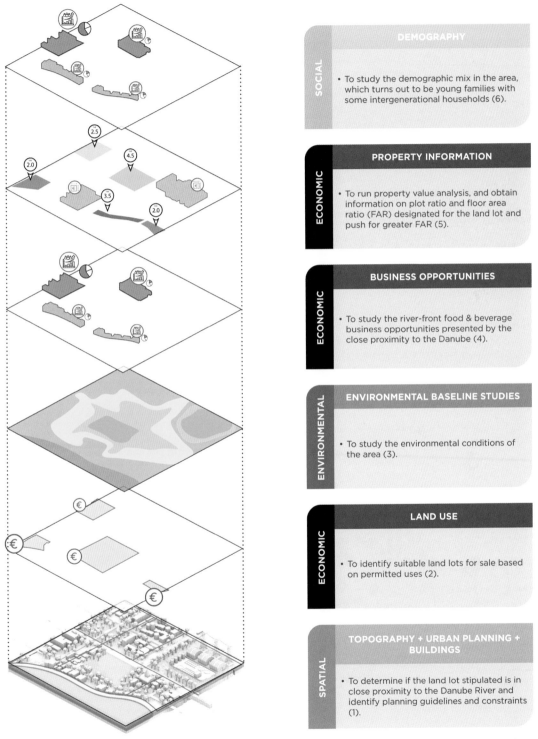

**DEMOGRAPHY**

SOCIAL

- To study the demographic mix in the area, which turns out to be young families with some intergenerational households (6).

**PROPERTY INFORMATION**

ECONOMIC

- To run property value analysis, and obtain information on plot ratio and floor area ratio (FAR) designated for the land lot and push for greater FAR (5).

**BUSINESS OPPORTUNITIES**

ECONOMIC

- To study the river-front food & beverage business opportunities presented by the close proximity to the Danube (4).

**ENVIRONMENTAL BASELINE STUDIES**

ENVIRONMENTAL

- To study the environmental conditions of the area (3).

**LAND USE**

ECONOMIC

- To identify suitable land lots for sale based on permitted uses (2).

**TOPOGRAPHY + URBAN PLANNING + BUILDINGS**

SPATIAL

- To determine if the land lot stipulated is in close proximity to the Danube River and identify planning guidelines and constraints (1).

**Figure 6.4** An exploded axonometric view of the necessary data layers to facilitate the work flow of a representative from the industry sphere.

# SCENARIO PLANNING

## STATE
### *LUKAS*

Meet Lukas, an officer from the Authority for Spatial Planning and Construction. Lukas receives the schematic design of the development from Jozef. Whilst the basic planning parameters can be checked via algorithms (1), the more borderline elements are checked with his colleagues. Firstly, Lukas runs the Smart Zone Plan advanced analytics (PoC2: Smart Zone Plan) to assess if Jozef's proposed scheme is in line with the proposed regulation of the functional and spatial arrangement of the territory (2). Next, Lukas continues to run an environmental impact assessment (3) as well as cross-checks the borderline design components with the planning regulations and realises that the scheme is not fully-compliant. Not only will the tower cast shadow over the adjacent public plaza (4), the proposal seeks to use cross-laminated timber construction that necessitates further fire-safety research (5). Lukas engages with Laura in an online portal to find the right solution for the plot and also suggests an opportunity to engage in further research if the project could be used as a 'living lab'. At this point in time, Jozef is able to check the real-time status of his construction plan submission (6) (PoC4: Building an Apartment). He is informed of the 'stop work order' and that his proposed scheme would require further research.

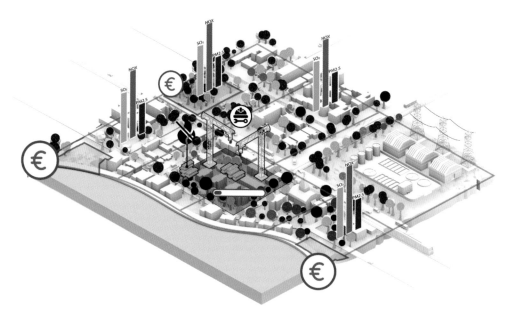

**Figure 6.5** A data model that illustrates the essential data layers needed to support the work flow of a representative from the state sphere.

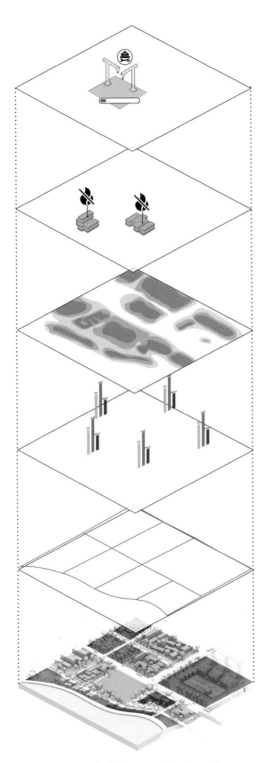

**URBAN PLANNING**

SPATIAL

- Jozef to check the real-time status of his construction plan submission (PoC4: Building an Apartment) (6).

**BUILDINGS**

SPATIAL

- To examine the construction materials and techniques of the proposed scheme – it seeks to use cross-laminated timber construction that necessitates further fire-safety research (5).

**ENVIRONMENTAL BASELINE STUDIES**

ENVIRONMENTAL

- To run an environmental impact assessment based on Jozef's proposed scheme. It is discovered that the proposed scheme will cast shadow over the adjacent public plaza (4).

**POLLUTION**

ENVIRONMENTAL

- To run an environmental impact assessment based on Jozef's proposed scheme to examine the pollution it could potentially cause to the surroundings (3).

**URBAN PLANNING**

SPATIAL

- To assess if Jozef's proposed scheme is in line with the proposed regulation of the functional and spatial arrangement of the territory (PoC2: Smart Zone Plan) (2).

**LAND USE**

ECONOMIC

- To assess if Jozef's proposed scheme is in line with the permitted land use(s) of the territory (PoC2: Smart Zone Plan) (1).

**Figure 6.6** An exploded axonometric view of the necessary data layers to facilitate the work flow of a representative from the state sphere.

# SCENARIO PLANNING

## ACADEMIA
### *LAURA*

Meet Laura, who runs a research lab in the Faculty of Architecture and Design at the local university. Lukas invites Laura as a pre-qualified academic advisor to test the feasibility of cross-laminated timber construction and the environmental benefits of the vertical urban greenery to the sky terraces. The researchers use the environmental, technological, and spatial layers of the digital twin to identify the carbon footprint (1) of the proposed form of construction, as well as considering its fire safety (2). They also consider how the green terraces offer environmental benefit, by running dendrology analysis (PoC1: Dendrology) and suggesting appropriate tree species to aid flood mitigation (3). The vertical urban greenery (4) to the sky terraces turns out to be in the right place given orientation, and the other components required to maintain the vertical urban greenery (regulating temperature, humidity) (5) can be conveniently monitored and optimised on the dashboard of the digital twin (6).

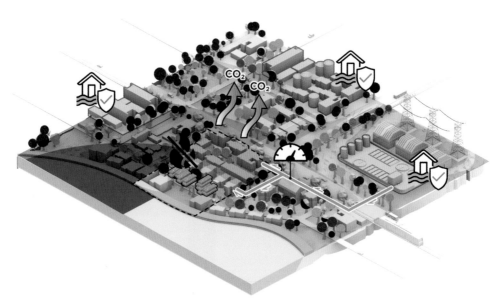

**Figure 6.7** A data model that illustrates the essential data layers needed to support the work flow of a representative from the academic sphere.

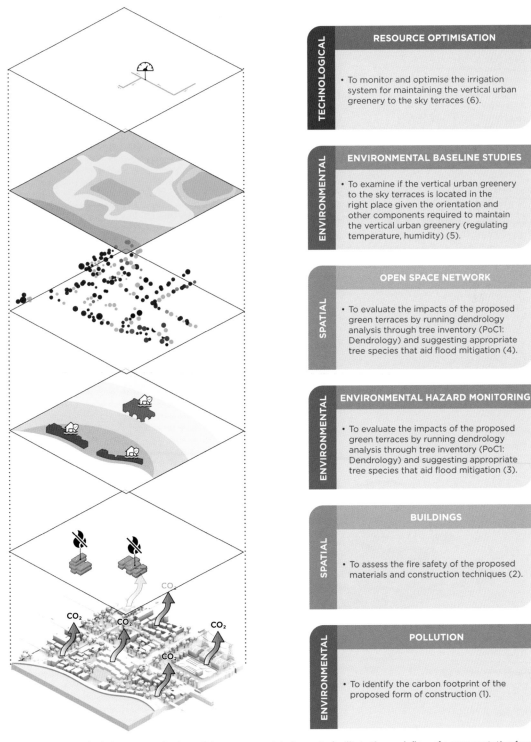

**RESOURCE OPTIMISATION**

TECHNOLOGICAL

- To monitor and optimise the irrigation system for maintaining the vertical urban greenery to the sky terraces (6).

**ENVIRONMENTAL BASELINE STUDIES**

ENVIRONMENTAL

- To examine if the vertical urban greenery to the sky terraces is located in the right place given the orientation and other components required to maintain the vertical urban greenery (regulating temperature, humidity) (5).

**OPEN SPACE NETWORK**

SPATIAL

- To evaluate the impacts of the proposed green terraces by running dendrology analysis through tree inventory (PoC1: Dendrology) and suggesting appropriate tree species that aid flood mitigation (4).

**ENVIRONMENTAL HAZARD MONITORING**

ENVIRONMENTAL

- To evaluate the impacts of the proposed green terraces by running dendrology analysis through tree inventory (PoC1: Dendrology) and suggesting appropriate tree species that aid flood mitigation (3).

**BUILDINGS**

SPATIAL

- To assess the fire safety of the proposed materials and construction techniques (2).

**POLLUTION**

ENVIRONMENTAL

- To identify the carbon footprint of the proposed form of construction (1).

**Figure 6.8** An exploded axonometric view of the necessary data layers to facilitate the work flow of a representative from the academic sphere.

# SCENARIO PLANNING

## INDUSTRY + STATE + ACADEMIA
### *JOZEF, LUKAS, & LAURA*

Jozef, Lukas, and Laura identify benefits in the research and believe the development plot can be designated as a 'living-lab' to test further ideas (1) that may inform the planning and building legislation (2). The adjacent public plaza, and its connection to the proposed food and beverage board walk, provides an opportunity to test flood and urban heat island mitigating strategies, as well as heightened pedestrian access. Switching on the environmental, spatial, and social layers, it becomes apparent that the layout of the food and beverage outlets can be better positioned to capture passing footfall – made apparent by pedestrian modelling data (3). The model reveals hotter areas of the plazas (4) that can be planted with trees (5) to reduce temperatures. Flood surge data also suggests the provision of landscaped areas to reduce flood risk (6).

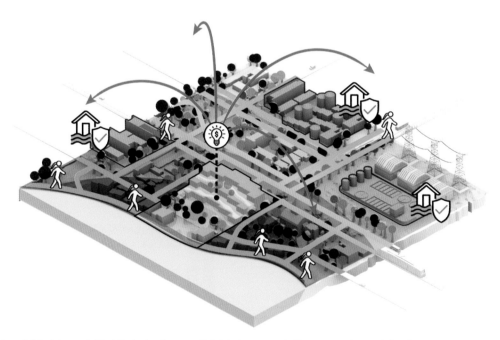

**Figure 6.9** A data model that illustrates the essential data layers needed to support the work flow between representatives from the state, industry, and academic spheres.

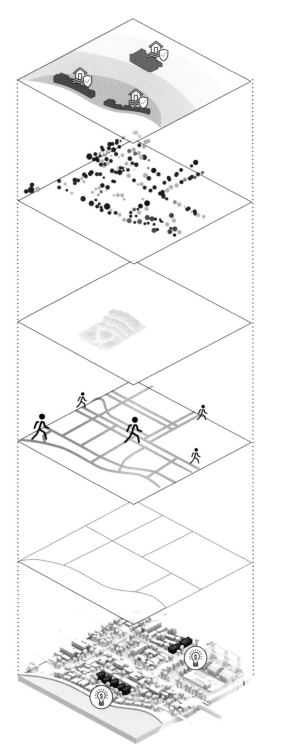

**ENVIRONMENTAL**

## ENVIRONMENTAL HAZARD MONITORING

- To run flood simulation model based on flood surge data and determine whether the provision of landscaped areas help to reduce flood risk (6).

**ENVIRONMENTAL**

## ENVIRONMENTAL BASELINE STUDIES

- To suggest tree planting at those identified areas to reduce temperatures (5).

**ENVIRONMENTAL**

## ENVIRONMENTAL BASELINE STUDIES

- To identify the hotter areas of the proposed scheme (4).

**SOCIAL**

## SOCIAL INFRASTRUCTURE

- To run pedestrian modelling simulation using pedestrian movement data to evaluate if the location of the food and beverage outlets have been optimised in consideration of pedestrian access (3).

**SPATIAL**

## URBAN PLANNING

- To provide evidence-based results from the 'living-lab' to inform the planning and building legislation (2).

**CULTURAL**

## CULTURE OF INNOVATION

- To set Jozef's proposed scheme as a 'living-lab' to test further ideas (1).

**Figure 6.10** An exploded axonometric view of the necessary data layers to facilitate the work flow between representatives from the state, industry, and academic spheres.

# SCENARIO PLANNING

## CIVIL SOCIETY
### *MIKOLÁS & XÉNIA*

Meet Mikolás and Xénia, an aspirational young couple living in the city with a baby on the way. They have been tracking the progress of the research, made friendly through a digital portal that allows the community to understand the status of construction permits (1) (PoC4: Building an Apartment) and also ongoing research (2) that offers greater environmental protection. They look at the proposed scheme that has been submitted for planning and assess it in relation to its relative proximity to community centres (3), educational institutions, and park spaces (4), as well as the demographic composition in the area (5). They are delighted to see that the social layer yields data suggesting young families with some intergenerational households live in the vicinity, and has good access to public amenities. This proves ideal for the couple who make a more informed purchase. Elated with their purchase and expecting their new house with great pleasure, Mikolás and Xénia use the digital twin to keep track of the construction notice in real time (6) (PoC3: Construction Notice).

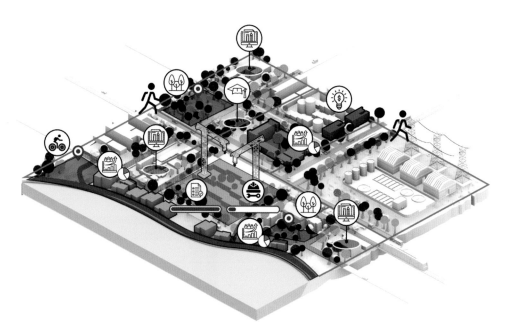

**Figure 6.11** A data model that illustrates the essential data layers needed to support the work flow of representatives from civil society.

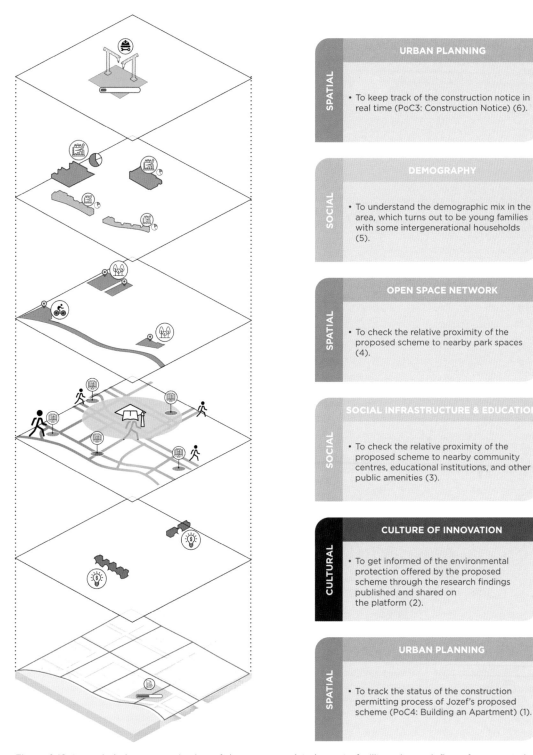

**URBAN PLANNING**

SPATIAL

- To keep track of the construction notice in real time (PoC3: Construction Notice) (6).

**DEMOGRAPHY**

SOCIAL

- To understand the demographic mix in the area, which turns out to be young families with some intergenerational households (5).

**OPEN SPACE NETWORK**

SPATIAL

- To check the relative proximity of the proposed scheme to nearby park spaces (4).

**SOCIAL INFRASTRUCTURE & EDUCATION**

SOCIAL

- To check the relative proximity of the proposed scheme to nearby community centres, educational institutions, and other public amenities (3).

**CULTURE OF INNOVATION**

CULTURAL

- To get informed of the environmental protection offered by the proposed scheme through the research findings published and shared on the platform (2).

**URBAN PLANNING**

SPATIAL

- To track the status of the construction permitting process of Jozef's proposed scheme (PoC4: Building an Apartment) (1).

**Figure 6.12** An exploded axonometric view of the necessary data layers to facilitate the work flow of representatives from civil society.

# SCENARIO PLANNING

## INDUSTRY + STATE
### *CONTRACTORS & LUKAS*

As soon as the proposed scheme has been constructed and people start moving in, the building information model made available on the digital twin has been a useful tool for monitoring and improving the performance of the mixed-use development. For instance, the monitoring of underground ducting, made possible via a dashboard on the digital twin, allows Lukas's colleagues to work with the relevant contractors to optimise predictive maintenance schedules and prevent any potential infrastructure anomalies, e.g. water pipe leaking (1) (PoC5: Monitoring of Water Pipe Leaks). With great development comes great investment opportunities and high volume of traffic. This calls for a road planning strategy and road construction project to be made to improve the traffic flow in that area, with the whole construction process being monitored on the digital twin (2) (PoC6: Road Construction Project).

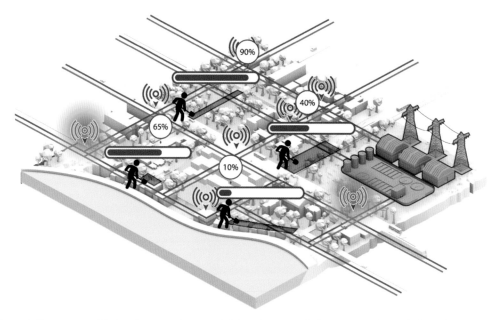

**Figure 6.13** A data model that illustrates the essential data layers needed to support the work flow of representatives from the industry and state spheres.

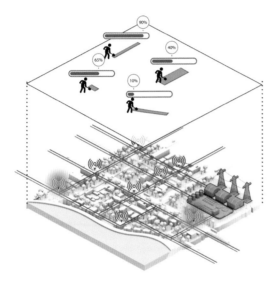

**MOBILITY INFRASTRUCTURE**

SPATIAL

- To monitor status of road construction projects (PoC6: Road Construction Project) (2).

**MONITORING, OPERATIONS, & MAINTENANCE**

TECHNOLOGICAL

- To monitor underground ducting and optimise predictive maintenance schedules, preventing any potential infrastructure anomalies, e.g. water pipe leaking (PoC5: Monitoring of Water Pipe Leaks) (1).

**Figure 6.14** An exploded axonometric view of the necessary data layers to facilitate the work flow of representatives from the industry and state spheres.

# SCENARIO PLANNING

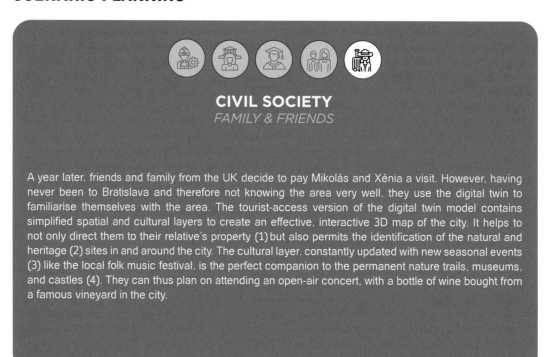

## CIVIL SOCIETY
### *FAMILY & FRIENDS*

A year later, friends and family from the UK decide to pay Mikolás and Xénia a visit. However, having never been to Bratislava and therefore not knowing the area very well, they use the digital twin to familiarise themselves with the area. The tourist-access version of the digital twin model contains simplified spatial and cultural layers to create an effective, interactive 3D map of the city. It helps to not only direct them to their relative's property (1) but also permits the identification of the natural and heritage (2) sites in and around the city. The cultural layer, constantly updated with new seasonal events (3) like the local folk music festival, is the perfect companion to the permanent nature trails, museums, and castles (4). They can thus plan on attending an open-air concert, with a bottle of wine bought from a famous vineyard in the city.

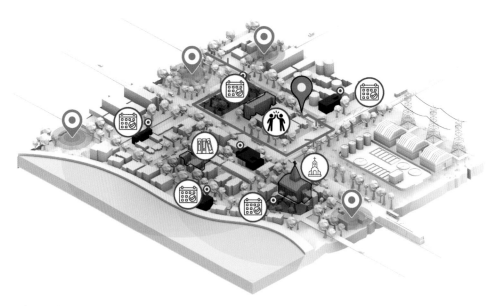

**Figure 6.15** A data model that illustrates the essential data layers needed to support the work flow of representatives from the civil society sphere.

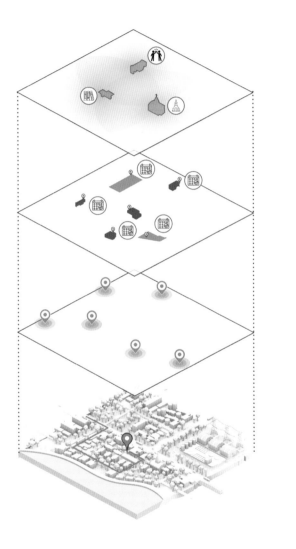

### CIVIC AMENITIES & FACILITIES

CULTURAL

• To identify the museums and castles in and around the city (4).

### CALENDAR OF CULTURAL EVENTS

CULTURAL

• To explore upcoming seasonal events, concerts, and festivals during the time of visit (3).

### LANDMARKS OF NATIONAL IMPORTANCE

CULTURAL

• To explore the natural and heritage sites in and around the city, e.g. vineyard, nature trails (2).

### BUILDINGS

SPATIAL

• To locate and navigate the way through to Mikolás and Xénia's property (1).

**Figure 6.16** An exploded axonometric view of the necessary data layers to facilitate the work flow of representatives from the civil society sphere.

# MONITORING & EVALUATION PLAN

When realising a DT technology at a national scale, the evaluation and monitoring of its success is as important as the implementation plan that enables it. The different benefits of DT have been extensively discussed in previous studies (Centre for Digital Built Britain, 2022b; Singh *et al.*, 2021). However, the quantified impacts of DTs have proven to be elusive. This necessitates the need for a Monitoring and Evaluation (M&E) Plan to outline systemic procedures and track the progress of the NDTs implementation in Slovakia.

For the purpose of this study, evaluation methods used to measure digital transformation and smart city practices were applicable due to the following reasons:

1. Slovakia is in the midst of a national digital transformation;
2. The concurrence of the digital transformation and the NDT implementation would create reciprocal impacts that could form the basis of augmenting smart city practices; and
3. There are limited studies conducted on the M&E Plan for DT technologies.

Such reasons implied that a holistic evaluation approach would be required to assess the multi-faceted impacts brought forth by both the NDT implementation and digital transformation in Slovakia.

Following an in-depth study of the collective practices of existing digital transformation and smart city / nation assessments (Table 6.1), a recurring pattern was discovered where the evaluation aspects often cover the technological changes as a result of digital maturity and intensity, as well as the governance and policy models that can affect these changes. Therefore, a two-step process was adopted to develop a comprehensive M&E plan for Slovakia (Figure 6.17):

1. Evaluation Indicators for the Impacts of NDT and Digital Transformation; and
2. Effectiveness of Stakeholder Collaborations.

The M&E plan allowed the Slovak government and the NDT Task Group to report on measurable changes brought forth by the NDT.

## EVALUATION INDICATORS FOR THE IMPACTS OF THE NDT & DIGITAL TRANSFORMATION

Indicators that assess the changes brought forth by the NDT in the context of the smart city movement and digital transformation, such as:

1. The key changes in areas where NDT is applied to (e.g. PoCs), and its contribution towards the smart city movement and digital transformation
2. The digital policy in place and its relevance in supporting the required changes for enabling the NDT

## EFFECTIVENESS OF STAKEHOLDER COLLABORATIONS

Indicators that measure the effectiveness of stakeholder collaborations, e.g. outputs of stakeholders vs. impacts created

**Figure 6.17** A two-step process adopted to develop a comprehensive M&E plan for Slovakia.

| FRAMEWORK/ AUTHOR(S) | DESCRIPTIONS OF FRAMEWORK | EVALUATION ASPECTS | METHODS |
|---|---|---|---|
| **Indicator Framework for Quantitative Measurement of Change in Darwin** (Williams, Meharg, and Muster, 2020) | Track changes in Darwin with respect to liveability, sustainability, and resilience | • Effectiveness of collaboration within organisation<br>• Key changes in Darwin (e.g. green cover, thermal comfort, policy environment) | • Identifying relevant UN Sustainable Development Goals<br>• Cross-referencing other relevant indicator frameworks<br>• Filtering on the basis of redundancy / indispensability |
| **Measuring the Digital Transformation** (Organisation for Economic Co-operation and Development, 2019) | To offer policymakers and analysts key indicators in different dimensions, providing detail and nuance, and link to relevant policy levers and generating deeper insights into how economies are performing along those dimensions | • Digital maturity and digital intensity in various areas (education, innovation, trade, economic, social outcomes)<br>• Current digital policy issues | • Mapping indicators against current digital policy issues |
| **National Digital Strategy Comprehensiveness** (Gierten and Lesher, 2022) | To measure national digital strategy comprehensiveness, providing insights into the potential of a country's national digital strategy to coordinate the policies needed to make digital transformation work for growth and well-being | • The framework consists of seven overarching dimensions: Access, Use, Innovation, Jobs, Society, Trust, Market Openness | • Bringing together 38 specific policy domains under the seven dimensions<br>• Mapping policy measures from respective documents to the policy domains using a scoring system with pre-defined criteria |
| **Qualitative Evaluation of a National Digital Health Transformation Program in England** (Cresswell et al., 2021) | To explore mechanisms that support or inhibit the exchange of inter-organisational digital transformation knowledge | • Effectiveness of inter-organisational digital transformation knowledge in different forms of convergence between groups<br>• Policy interventions | • Semi-structured interviews with relevant stakeholders<br>• Non-participant observations of knowledge transfer activities through attending meetings, workshops, and conference<br>• Documentary analysis of policy documents |
| **Smart Cities Evaluation – A Survey of Performance and Sustainability Indicators** (Petrova-Antonova and Ilieva, 2018) | To identify Smart City Indicators (SCIs) that can be adopted by planning authorities | • Actual performance of smart activity or initiative.<br>• Exploration of SCIs according to six thematic areas: Smart Nature, Smart Living, Smart Mobility, Smart Governance, Smart People, and Smart Economy<br>• Conditions for building relationships between stakeholders | • Systematic review of SCIs<br>• Filtering literature according to predefined inclusion and exclusion criteria<br>• Identifying 1152 SCIs and categorising them into the six thematic areas |
| **Smart Framework for Smart Cities Management in Europes** (Vanlı and Marsap, 2018) | To develop a conceptual framework for Smart City (SC) projects management | • Effectiveness of project management practices covering practices in: smart planning, smart organising, smart leading, smart controlling, and project success<br>• Impacts of smart management practices on project success according to cost, quality, time, sustainability, and the created value to all stakeholders (e.g. new knowledge generated) | • Conducting literature review of relevant contents about SC concepts, frameworks, critical success factors, and challenges<br>• Finalising an SC Projects Management Framework by identifying positive correlation between smart practices and project success through statistical analysis (data collected from questionnaire) |

**Table 6.1** The collective practices of existing digital transformation assessments.

# 1. EVALUATION INDICATORS FOR THE IMPACTS OF THE NDT & DIGITAL TRANSFORMATION

The Smart City (SC) Audit Matrix developed by Pomeroy Studio and Academy was adopted as the evaluation indicators to assess the changes brought forth by the NDT in the context of the smart city movement and its digital transformation in Slovakia. The SC Audit Matrix was a two-step process of aggregating and categorising.

At the aggregation step, six smart city indices were used. The key indicators within these smart city indices invariably covered a diverse range of sustainability, smart technology, and governance-related assessment criteria that were then weighted and aggregated together, along with their sub-indicators that would cover more detailed considerations. For instance, the broader key indicator of smart surveillance ostensibly had sub-categories that reflect coverage of digital surveillance cameras, population registered with a public safety alert system, and so on. The resultant aggregation of key indicators and sub-key indicators formed the basis from which the indices for the SC Audit could be created.

The process of aggregation effectively acted as a filter for the next step of categorisation. This followed Pomeroy's 'six-pillar' framework (Pomeroy, 2020a, p. 2–3) that formed the broad prompts for thinking on the creation of smart and sustainable environments where digital transformation and the NDT can effectively transpire (Figure 6.18).

By way of assessment across key indicators, a scoring system was formulated based on two further dimensions:

1. Strategy; and
2. Execution.

The Strategy dimension assessed Slovakia's smart city programme, including its position, vision, goals, and objectives. The Execution dimension assessed the city's burgeoning and actual achievements, from initial projects to realised deployment of innovative technologies and services.

Each dimension was further split into five evaluation categories (Figure 6.19). The evaluation categories for the Strategy dimension were as follows:

1. Not applicable;
2. Non existent;
3. Established business case;
4. Diagnostics / feasibility;
5. Vision / outlined proposals; and
6. Ratified strategy.

The evaluation categories used for assessing the Execution dimension were categorised as follows:

1. Prototype / test-bedding;
2. Initial implementation;
3. Commissioning and testing;
4. Full implementation; and
5. Operational.

The above criteria paved the way for assessing Slovakia across a broad range of indicators, which went beyond the general foci of technologically and economically driven indicators often found in SC frameworks.

As the NDT for Slovakia evolves over time, the SC Audit Matrix will serve as a tool for evaluating two crucial aspects:

1. Component 1 | Key changes of the NDT: The first component involves assessing the significant changes brought about by the application of the NDT and its contribution towards the advancement of smart city initiatives and digital transformation.
2. Component 2 | Digital Policy: The second component focuses on evaluating the existing digital policies in place; their relevance in supporting the necessary NDT changes and facilitating digital transformation in the Slovak Republic.

The utilisation of the SC Audit Matrix to provide a detailed evaluation process for these two components is further elaborated in the following pages.

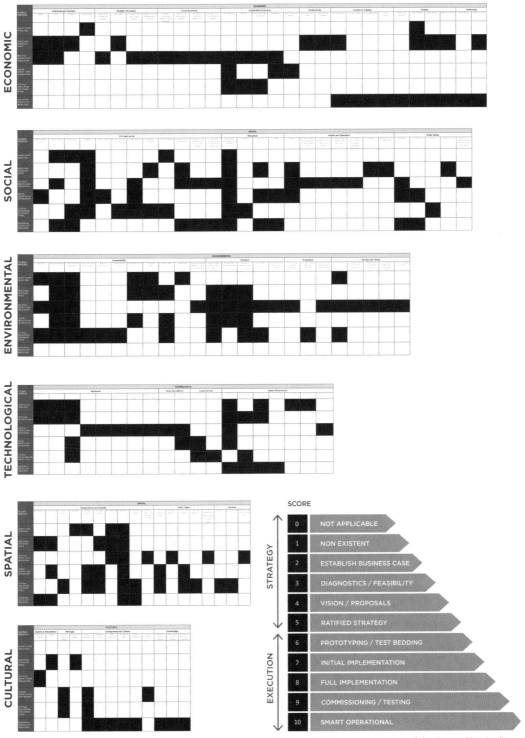

**Figure 6.18** The Global Frameworks of Smart City Indices aggregated and categorised into Pomeroy's 'six-pillar' framework.

**Figure 6.19** The scoring system of the Smart City Audit Matrix.

SCORE

| | STRATEGY | |
|---|---|---|
| 0 | | NOT APPLICABLE |
| 1 | | NON EXISTENT |
| 2 | | ESTABLISH BUSINESS CASE |
| 3 | | DIAGNOSTICS / FEASIBILITY |
| 4 | | VISION / PROPOSALS |
| 5 | | RATIFIED STRATEGY |
| 6 | EXECUTION | PROTOTYPING / TEST BEDDING |
| 7 | | INITIAL IMPLEMENTATION |
| 8 | | FULL IMPLEMENTATION |
| 9 | | COMMISSIONING / TESTING |
| 10 | | SMART OPERATIONAL |

## Component 1 | Key Changes of the NDT

It is worth noting that the DT Framework (data layers and indicators discussed in Chapter Three) and the SC Audit Matrix (indicators and sub-indicators) were both categorised into Pomeroy's 'six-pillar' framework (Pomeroy, 2020a, p. 2–3). Therefore, the parallel makes it possible to establish links between the PoCs and the SC Audit Matrix by performing a two-level mapping exercise.

Referring to Figure 6.20 using PoC 1: Dendrology as an example, the first level involves mapping each of the PoCs (left column) to the DT Framework (middle column) based on the data domain(s) required to execute the respective PoC. This effectively sieves out the relevant indicators from the framework for the next level of mapping.

At the second level, each of the relevant indicators identified from the previous exercise is mapped to the sub-indicators stipulated in the SC Audit Matrix (right column). After establishing the links, the key changes of the respective PoC can be measured based on the scoring system designed in the SC Audit Matrix.

## Component 2 | Digital Policy

The evaluation of Component 2 begins with the compilation of a unique policy database. This database contains information regarding Slovakia's digital policy measures, including digital transformation and coordination visions, strategies, and policies. All information in this database should consist of verbatim text from the identified strategy and policy documents, labelled with its provenance. Similarly, a mapping exercise is required to establish the explicit links between the digital policy measures and the sub-indicators in the SC Audit Matrix. This is followed by quantifiably measuring the relevance of the digital policy in supporting the NDT implementation and its digital transformation, by using the scoring system in place.

The evaluations of both Components 1 and 2 should be conducted at various time intervals (e.g. once every three years) to assess if the initial PoCs have led to higher scores and accelerated the smart city movement in Slovakia over time. This evaluation method essentially enables the Slovak government to quantify the impacts of the NDT, and to review the tangible results to determine any changes needed.

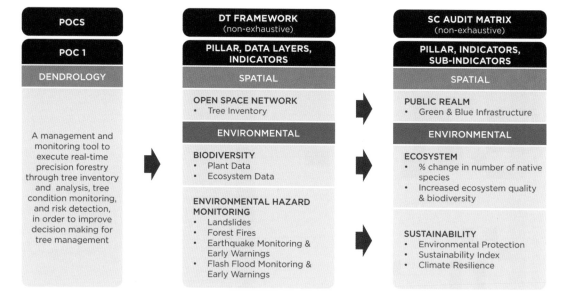

**Figure 6.20** The two-level mapping exercise for the evaluation of key changes brought forth by the NDT in the context of digital transformation and smart city movement in Slovakia.

## 2. EFFECTIVENESS OF STAKEHOLDER COLLABORATIONS

Stakeholder collaboration is indispensable in the NDT implementation plan, as it enables joint problem-solving for challenges beyond individual capabilities (Gray, 1985). The dynamics and complexity level change with the entry or exit of each stakeholder in the project (Hamdan, Andersen, and de Boer, 2021), emphasising the importance of regularly measuring the collaboration's effectiveness amongst the 'four spheres of influence' (Pomeroy, 2020b, p. 201–202) in the NDT implementation plan.

It is also imperative to take into account that stakeholder collaboration is not a singular event but an ongoing, iterative process throughout the digital twinning journey for data sharing and exchange, model integration, consensus building, and decision-making. Therefore, it is crucial to not only identify the factors that impact the compound inputs and outputs in jointly delivering the NDT, but also to evaluate the collaboration's effectiveness in promoting collective learning and knowledge exchange with a people-focused approach (Cresswell *et al.*, 2021; Kusters *et al.*, 2018).

Summarising from a literature review on stakeholder collaboration evaluation, Woodland and Hutton (2012) developed a Collaboration Evaluation and Improvement (CEIF) Framework with five entry points:

1. Operationalising the construct of collaboration;
2. Identifying and then mapping communities of practice;
3. Monitoring stage / stages of development;
4. Assessing levels of integration; and
5. Assessing cycles of inquiry.

Vanlı and Marsap (2018) proposed four practices, from a smart city project management perspective, to quantitatively measure success in cross-organisational collaborations, including:

1. Smart planning;
2. Smart organising;
3. Smart leading; and
4. Smart controlling.

Considering the aforementioned, further research is needed to develop a contextual framework for evaluating stakeholder collaborations throughout the NDT Implementation Plan. It was recommended to adopt a mixed-method approach framework (Figure 6.21), involving qualitative methods like semi-structured interviews and observations of meetings, and quantitative methods like survey questionnaires, designed around the extant literature on stakeholder collaboration.

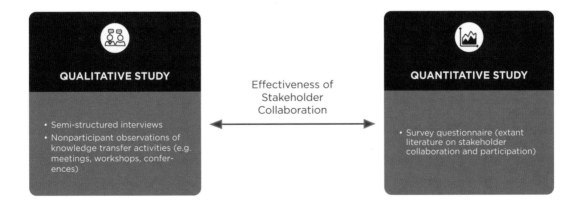

**Figure 6.21** Mixed-method approach for evaluating the effectiveness of stakeholder collaborations in Slovakia.

# CONCLUSION

Animal
Laborans

Homo Faber

# CONCLUSION

The theoretical physicist J. Robert Oppenheimer once said during an interview that examined the impact of atomic theory: 'when you see something that is technically sweet, you go ahead and do it; and argue about what to do about it only after you have had your technical success. That is how it was with the atomic bomb' (Oppenheimer, 1953). Since time memorial, we have often seen our innovations transcribed to paper and subsequently become physical reality. Sometimes, such utopian visions may have remained on paper. Other times, the pressing needs of civil society or state would have seen the execution of those visions in a hastened form: the imperatives of rapidly 'going ahead and doing it' outweighing the careful consideration of the consequences of one's actions.

The philosopher Hannah Arendt postulated that mankind falls into two categories in this regard: Homo Faber (the working man 'who thinks') may be content in postulating better built environment outcomes without physically realising the end product of a building, a district, or a city. Animal Laborans (the labourer 'who does') may be content with not giving careful thought to the consequences of physically realising the end product of the very same (Pomeroy, 2016). Oppenheimer postulated and executed his plan, but was unable to fully appreciate that the consequences of his scientific brilliance would be the first weapon of mass destruction that would kill more people in a single explosion than the accumulated battles of the previous 100 years (Sennett, 2009).

We have witnessed the cataclysmic effects of 'going ahead and doing it' too many times, and our built environment bears the scars of 'trial and error' and 'build now and fix later'. Buildings, districts, and even complete cities assume functions that fail to materialise, given a lack of evidence as to how the people will function within them; or solutions that are climatically and culturally dysfunctional to the place that they are meant to serve (Hall, 2002; Sudjic, 2005). Even the most celebrated of architects run

the risk of trying to predict better social outcomes but fail to understand that the 'hardware' of an architectural solution can be undermined by the 'heartware' of socio-political factors. The architect Minoru Yamasaki's Pruitt Igoe housing development in St Louis, Missouri, whilst initially heralded as a breakthrough in urban renewal, would eventually become a symbol of the failure of public-policy planning and social housing (Pomeroy, 2014).

With the realisation that we cannot solve our urban challenges through the 'hardware' of a built environment solution alone, the temptation, in our digitally-enabled age, is to turn to 'software' as the panacea to our woes. Songdo, the ubiquitous first generation smart city, may have been heralded as the epicentre for north Asian economic growth, but its deployment of sensors to capture big data and enhance the operational efficiencies of the city arguably 'senses' too late (Pomeroy, 2020b). The city was built on reclaimed land and the hardware of the built environment was already in place before sensors could make sense of the city's systems and thus inform of the weaknesses in its 'hardware'. The 'software' was certainly an enabler of retroactive solutions and decision-making in order to improve the built environments' efficiencies. But what this book has sought to consider is the role of 'software' (and in particular, the DT) as an enabler to test, shape, and hone the built environment before solutions become physical reality.

We have seen from the case studies presented in Chapter Two that cities and their municipalities are increasingly turning to DTs as a tool in which its system can sense, analyse, predict, and make informed decisions in the interests of improving the operability of the city it serves. In their current guise, DTs for cities tend to be tools of the state, with the active participation of ICT industry partners and occasionally academic institutions who act as enablers of proof-of-concepts for commercial and academic interests respectively.

From the case studies we can see the DT has often been used as a means to test retro-fitted ideas and innovations; or they may, in the case of vacant sites, be used to test various urban scenarios before becoming the physical reality within the city. The complexity of the DT models can be seen to vary across the case studies; though the commonality lies in their ability to be a predominantly spatial model, with greater regard to solving municipal 'hardware' issues. A lesser regard has been given to the socio-cultural and economic dynamics, which we have referred to in this book as the 'heartware'.

Yet the cities in which mankind has an enduring relationship, have 'heartware' at their core. Cities have been the product of social convergence since the first settlements: our monthly festivals, our weekly political rallies, our daily religious rituals, and our hourly commercial transactions being testimony to how we converge at various times to form our bonds of association within the physical realm. Cities have grown out of such convergences and become symbols of economic prosperity, power, knowledge, and culture, and accordingly have been a source of both attraction and seduction for people to migrate to them. Cities are our 'theatres' for our time-specific performances and interactions: the street and the square being the stage set for society's 'actors' to converge and 'play'. Such convergences and transactions between people and place, coupled with centuries of industrial, technological, and now digital advancement have seen our urban habitats transform from being cities of spaces, to cities of objects (Koetter and Rowe, 1979) to now networks of digitalised cities that need not rely on one's physical presence to be able to transact (Sassen, 2002).

In short, our physical cities have thrived through the 'heartware' of civil society to turn spaces into places. In *Civic Realism*, the academic Peter G. Rowe highlights how successful public spaces are forged from the healthy tensions between civil society and state and their social interactions. He references the Campo in Siena: a public space created by the resident five noble families that worked collectively to create a forum for trade, political rallies, sermons, and festivals – one of which exists today in the form of the Palio (Rowe, 1999). The rival families

would hold each other accountable; come together to create their own administrative corporation to manage, maintain, and police the square; and celebrate their rivalries through the famous horse race that has become as ubiquitous a symbol of the city as its clock tower. If the clock tower and square are symbolic of the 'hardware', then the Palio, and its yearly ability to converge civil society and state in celebration, is the 'heartware'.

Just as a city comes to life through the social-cultural and political practices of its people, then the next generation of DT platforms require greater considerations to capture the 'heartware' of our cities to be used as a positive enabling tool to create more sustainable built environments. As we have seen in this book, the NDT for Slovakia sought to build upon a spatial model to include further economic, technological, environmental, social, and cultural pillars of data. It recognises the importance of capturing a more holistic picture of a nation if it is to be a truly virtual representation. Just as it is recognised that 'Rome was not built in a day', neither can the digital counterpart. As the complexion of our cities change according to socio-economic pressure, spatial contestation, technological advancement, climatic cataclysm, or cultural migration over time, the future DT models will need to continually evolve and adapt to the changing nature of the physical world.

As the NDT of Slovakia continues to be built upon the foundations of spatial, technological, and environmental data gleaned from state, industry, and academic sources, the crowd-sourcing of social, economic, and cultural data, consensually drawn from the behavioural patterns of civil society as an empowered fourth sphere of influence alongside the predetermined three, will hopefully engender a greater democratisation of data and lead to a more useful DT for all spheres of influence to appreciate. After all, whilst medieval Siena may have been forged through the healthy tensions of civil society and state, the more contemporary evolution of Amsterdam as a third generation smart city clearly demonstrates how the active engagement of not just civil society groups and state agencies but also academic institutions and corporations can all work collectively and collaboratively to solve the urban challenges for which they are beset. The Amsterdam Metropolitan Solutions Institute (AMS) is a case in point where the four spheres of influence have successfully implemented transformative projects for the greater good of the city (Pomeroy, 2020b).

The DT of the future is not without its challenges and draws me back to the beginning of this conclusion. If we consider how the vibrancy of our cities can be in part attributed to a social spontaneity (i.e., the ability to create neutral spaces that citizens contest; and for the creators to not necessarily appreciate the social consequences until after their completion), then something must be said for the 'trial and error' that can nurture new adaptive approaches for civil society to inhabit a city's street, square, or quarter. The South Bank Arts Complex, the brutalist structure on the banks of the river Thames, was characterised by concrete undercrofts and overground plazas that were neglected for years, only to be appropriated later by a subculture of skateboarders and graffiti artists who found a use for the contested space alongside pop-up second-hand book stalls (Pomeroy, 2014). Would the South Bank Arts Complex look the way it does today had there been the ability to use big data and a DT to predict the use of these spaces by its occasional occupants?

Assuming, therefore, that the DT captures the appropriate socio-cultural and economic data to allow for the predictive element of how the undercroft will be used (for instance, a conversion into a food and beverage destination that has displaced the sub-cultural elements), has the DT exercised a greater socio-cultural purpose through data to allow us to make informed decisions; or has it unwittingly undermined a cultural sustainability by making us over prescriptive in the future use of the space and deny the undercroft opportunities for social spontaneity and diversity? Herein lies the risk: whilst there may be the will to use socio-cultural data to shape the spaces of the future, could the DT potentially be used as a tool to implicitly control social behaviour that eradicates the unpredictable and the chaotic and leads to a sanitised public realm? This is why a four sphere approach to the DTs governance is essential to ensure an inclusive built environment

where everyone contributes to a common good and is represented.

In an age where machine learning can use algorithms to design the places in which we live, work, play, and learn, the DTs strength lies in being an enabler for better decision making. As we have considered at the start of this book, astronautics and lunar landings cannot rely on just DT simulations, ground control support, and space vehicles for a successful mission. An astronaut's training, judgement, and 'heartware' form an integral part of any lunar missions' operational system.

Similarly, the DT for a city, district, or neighbourhood is unlikely to provide all the answers to our urban challenges through 'software' alone; and neither can we expect the creation of more urban infrastructural 'hardware' to do so either. But the due acknowledgement and integration of civil society's socio-cultural and economic data, which can represent the 'heartware' of a place, plays an integral part in mapping our virtual selves in a similar way to how our physical selves shape the realities of the places we live. The symbiotic relationship between the 'hardware' of the 'physical' world, the 'software' of the 'virtual' world, and the 'heartware' of the 'social' world should thus allow us to conceive and create more sustainable built environments in the future.

Page 214: (Top left) Animal Laborans, 2023 © Pomeroy Academy; (Top right) Homo Faber, 2023 © Pomeroy Academy; (Bottom left) Detroit Ruins, 2018 © Photo by Daniel Lincoln on Unsplash; (Bottom right) Archigram's "Walking Cities" by Ron Herron in 1964, 2020 © Designing Buildings Ltd.

# GLOSSARY

### Attribute-based Access Control (ABAC)

Refers to an authorisation strategy that defines access control policies based on specific attributes.

### Building Information Modelling (BIM)

Refers to the process of creating and managing information throughout the whole life cycle of a built asset. It also serves as a digital representation of a physical built asset and its functional characteristics. It is commonly used as a tool to link professionals involved in the architecture, engineering, and construction (AEC) industry, supporting them to improve outcomes in building and construction.

### CityGML (Geography Markup Language)

Refers to an open standardised data model and exchange format to store digital three-dimensional (3D) models of cities and landscapes.

### Computer-Aided Design (CAD)

Refers to the use of computer-based software to aid in design processes. It can be used to create two-dimensional (2D) drawings (e.g. plan, section, elevation) and three-dimensional (3D) isometric drawings.

### Data Layer

Refers to a common data framework and virtual layer where data can be processed and organised accordingly, providing users with data interoperability and access to a list of indicators used to measure the respective data layer.

### Digital Twin (DT)

Refers to a virtual, dynamic, three-dimensional representation of the real world – including physical objects and systems between social, economic, and digital infrastructure, as well as the natural environment.

### Foundation Data Model (FDM)

Refers to an ontological model to establish a consistent understanding of what constitutes the world of DTs by using common terms and definitions to formally describe them, as well as the relationships held within and between DTs, models, datasets, and their physical twins.

### 'Four Spheres of Influence'

Refers to the four stakeholder spheres – state, industry, academia, and civil society – that are acknowledged as equally important contributors throughout the Digital Twin development process.

### Geographic Information Systems (GIS)

Refers to a computer system with a database containing geographic data. Combined with software tools, it displays geographically referenced information, as well as managing, analysing, and visualising those information.

### Indicator

Refers to a list of indices used as the statistical measure to represent the different complementary aspects of the respective data layer. Each indicator can be operationalised by relevant datasets. For instance, the 'micro-mobility infrastructure' indicator can be operationalised by datasets such as micro-mobility road networks, locations of charging stations, locations of docking areas, etc.

### Information Management Framework (IMF)

Refers to a built environment information management landscape and data environment, which will adequately define parties, processes, information, protocols, and technology to support the National Digital Twin implementation plan.

### Information System (IS) 'myUrbium'

Refers to the programme containing projects for the delivery and operation of IS (information system) spatial planning and construction (IS SPC).

# GLOSSARY

**Integration Architecture (IA)**

Refers to a set of principles, protocols, and re-deployable architectural patterns composed of functional components for the creation of a digital twin platform in order to govern the sharing and linking of data and models securely and conveniently.

**Middle-out Approach**

Refer to the combination of both bottom-up and top-down approaches, and the influence of further spheres of influence beyond state (top-down) and civil society (bottom-up).

**National Digital Twin (NDT)**

Refers to an ecosystem of connected twins that can all communicate to each other and understand each other by secure data sharing, model integration, and consensus building, with the ultimate goal to enable informed decision-making for better outcomes for the built environment at different scales (local, regional, national).

**Non-participant Observation**

Refers to a field observation involving observing participants without actively participating in a particular event.

**Open Geospatial Consortium (OGC)**

Refers to an international voluntary consensus standards organisation that is driven to make geo-spatial (geographical) information and services FAIR – Findable, Accessible, Interoperable, and Reusable.

**Open Government**

Refers to a culture of governance based on innovative and sustainable public policies and practices inspired by the principles of transparency, accountability, and participation that fosters democracy and inclusive growth.

**Proof of Concepts (PoCs)**

Refers to the pre-defined objectives in the Information System (IS) 'myUrbium' programme, including: 1) The creation of a digital twin model in the selected territory of one city with the possibility of testing methodological approaches and implementation procedures; and 2) Designing, implementing, testing, and evaluating the implementation through a set of sub-projects (i.e. Dendrology, Smart Zone Plan, Construction Notice, Building an Apartment, Monitoring of Water Pipe Leaks, and Road Construction Project).

**Reference Data Library (RDL)**

Refers to the particular common set of taxonomies, vocabularies, classes, and properties of things used to describe the digital twin platform.

**'Six Pillars'**

Refers to a sustainability framework that can be used to guide the data categorisation of digital twin data layers. The six pillars – i.e., spatial, economic, technological, environmental, social, and cultural – represent key pillars that are relevant in the context of digital twin technology.

**Synthetic Data**

Refers to information that is artificially generated (using virtual models, algorithms) rather than produced by real-world events.

**Theory of Change (ToC)**

Refers to a methodology based on a diagram to illustrate how and why a desired change is expected to happen in a particular context.

**Urban Heat Island (UHI)**

Refers to the phenomenon of higher temperatures in urban areas compared to surrounding rural areas due to human activities and infrastructure.

# IMAGE CREDITS

# IMAGE CREDITS

# IMAGE CREDITS

**Page 48**    Penarth Marina from above, 2017 © Photo by Steffan Mitchell on Unsplash

**Page 52**    Toronto Financial Ditstrict, 2017 © Photo by Davi Rezende on Unsplash

**Page 53**    Decision Taking, 2022 © Icon by Design Cirle on The Noun Project; (Icon) Sense Making, 2020 © Icon by Gregor Cresnar on The Noun Project; (Icon) Data Management, 2015 © Icon by Cassandra Cappello on The Noun Project; Spatial, 2021 © Icon by Vectplus on The Noun Project; Economic, 2018 © Icon by Darshana Girkar on The Noun Project; Technology, 2020 © Icon by Linector on The Noun Project; Environmental, 2022 © Icon by Gung Yoga on The Noun Project; Social, 2017 © Icon by Iconsphere on The Noun Project; Cultural, 2022 © Icon by Umer Younas on The Noun Project; Post-decision, 2020 © Icon by Ricardo Job-Reese on The Noun Project; Multiple data sources, 2019 © Icon by H Alberto Gongora on The Noun Project

**Page 55, 56, & 106**    Representational image of Virtual Singapore, 2016 © Google Earth

**Page 57**    Jurong East Station, Singapore, 2020 © Photo by Shawnanggg on Unsplash

**Page 59**    Screenshot shows the semantic 3D modelling and visualisation in VSg, 2016 © National Research Foundation (2:37); Screenshot shows the analysis of potential for solar energy production in VSg © National Research Foundation (3:59)

**Page 54, 62, & 106**    Digital Twin Smart City of the Docklands area, Dublin, Ireland © Reprinted from Cities, vol. 110, White, G. *et al.*, A digital twin smart city for citizen feedback, p. 103069, Copyright

(2021), with permission from Elsevier.

**Page 63**    The Docklands area, Dublin, Ireland, 2022 © Google Maps

**Page 65**    Layers required to develop a digital twin smart city for the Docklands area in Dublin, Ireland © Reprinted from Cities, vol. 110, White, G. *et al.*, A digital twin smart city for citizen feedback, p. 103066, Copyright (2021), with permission from Elsevier.

**Page 55, 68, & 106**    Representational image of Digital Twin city of the Xiong'an new area, China, 2023 © Pomeroy Academy

**Page 69**    West facade of Xiong'an Railway Station, Xiong'an New Area, North China's Hebei province, 2020 © Photo by N509FZ on Wikimedia Commons

**Page 71**    (Image) Overview of work on Xiong'an New Area Digital Twin city, 2021 © after Chen, Lai, and Zhang; Green Efficient Energy, 2019 © Icon by IronSV on The Noun Project; Smart, Public Security, 2015 © Icon by Gerardo Martín Martínez on The Noun Project; Social Connectivity, 2022 © Icon by Supalerk Laipawat on The Noun Project; Future Mobility, 2022 © Icon by Foxyard Studio on The Noun Project; Future City Scenarios, 2018 © Icon by Mohkamil on The Noun Project

**Page 55, 74, & 106**    3D city model of PLATEAU, Japan, 2023 © Ministry of Land, Infrastructure, Transport and Tourism website (https://www.mlit.go.jp/plateau/about/)

**Page 75**    Aerial view of the Shiba-koen district of Minato, Tokyo, Japan, 2022 © Google Earth

# IMAGE CREDITS

**Page 77**   Use cases for activity monitoring, disaster management, and smart planning, 2023 © Ministry of Land, Infrastructure, Transport and Tourism website (https://www.mlit.go.jp/plateau/use-case/)

**Page 55, 80, & 106**   Screenshot shows the 3D Darwin's Digital Twin platform, 2023 © CSIRO, Darwin Living Lab, Australia

**Page 81**   Basemap of 3D Darwin, 2023 © CSIRO, Darwin Living Lab, Australia

**Page 83**   Schematic of spatial layers of different types of datasets, the foundation of Digital Twin for Darwin © Reprinted from Journal of Cleaner Production, vol. 265, Schandl, H. *et al.*, A spatiotemporal urban metabolism model for the Canberra suburb of Braddon in Australia, p. 121772, Copyright (2020), with permission from Elsevier; AirRater, a mobile app for citizens to learn how air quality affects health, and to improve symptoms management, 2023 © AirRater (https://airrater.org/); Monitor your Environment, 2022 © Icon by Gung Yoga on The Noun Project; Track you Symptoms, 2017 © Icon by Arafat Uddin on The Noun Project; Help Manage Health, 2019 © Icon by Akhmad Taufiq on The Noun Project

**Page 54, 86, & 106**   Screenshot shows the digital 3D Model of Boston, Massachusetts, USA, 2023 © Boston Planning & Development Agency GIS Lab

**Page 87**   Downtown Boston, Massachusetts, USA, 2022 © Google Earth

**Page 89**   Visualising shadow casting of Downtown Boston around 4pm in fall, 2023 © Boston Planning & Development Agency GIS Lab;

Flood modelling showing the entire city of Boston and areas prone to flooding, 2023 © Boston Planning & Development Agency GIS Lab

**Page 54, 92, & 106**   Screenshot shows the digital 3D web application/digital twin of Tallinn, Estonia, 2023 © Estonian Land Board

**Page 93**   Downtown Tallinn, Estonia, 2019 © Photo by Jaanus Jagomäg on Unsplash

**Page 95**   (Top) A dynamic layer of green infrastructure that enables analysis of the interplay between the built and natural environment in GreenTwins, 2023 © Pomeroy Academy; (Bottom Left) vision of the CityHUB for participatory processes using VR, 2021 © Fabian Dembski / High-Performance Computing Center Stuttgart; (Bottom right) The Urban Tempo App for the simulation and visualisation of seasonal and temporal change showing the effect of the environment to the urban atmosphere, 2021 © Lauri Lemmenlehti

**Page 54, 98, & 106**   Representational image of Qatar's new initiative TASMU platform to enhance the digital economy, 2021 © GCC Business News

**Page 99**   The Pearl-Qatar, Doha, Qatar, 2022 © Photo by Visit Qatar on Unsplash

**Page 101**   (Top) A diagram showing the five strategic sectors to be enhanced by the TASMU platform, 2021 © World Summit Awards & 2022 © TASMU Digital Valley; (Bottom) Cross-sectoral use cases categorised into the five strategic sectors – Transport, 2022 © Photo by Ross Sneddon on Unsplash; Logistic, 2017 © Photo

# IMAGE CREDITS

by Frank McKenna on Unsplash; Environment, 2021 © Photo by Katrien Van Crombrugghe on Unsplash; Healthcare, 2019 © Photo by National Cancer Institute on Unsplash; Sports, 2017 © Photo by Thomas Serer on Unsplash

**Page 110**    (Top left, top section) Bratislava, 2021 © Photo by Martin Katler on Unsplash; (Top right, top section) Prešov, 2009 © Photo by Ing.Mgr. Jozef Kotulic on Wikimedia Commons; (Bottom left, top section) Košice, 2019 © Photo by Mohammed Thoufik on Unsplash; (Bottom right, top section) Trencín, 2018 © Photo by Repkovatatiana on Pixabay; (Top left, bottom section) Banská Bystrica, 2021 © Photo by Dušan Veverkolog on Unsplash; (Top right, bottom section) Nitra, 2022 © Photo by Adrian Regeci on Unsplash; (Bottom left, bottom section) Trnava, 2021 © Photo by Trnava University on Unsplash; (Bottom right, bottom section) Žilina, 2021 © Photo by Frantisek Duris on Unsplash

**Page 112**    Gulf of Mexico, United States, 2015 © Photo by NASA on Unsplash

**Page 132, 164, 168, & 169**    State, 2019 © Icon by Vectors Point on The Noun Project; Academia, 2016 © Icon by Nikita Kozin on The Noun Project

**Page 133, 165, 168, & 169**    Industry, 2019 © Icon by Kon Kapp on The Noun Project; Civil Society, 2018 © Icon by Nithinan Tatah on The Noun Project

**Page 138**    Part 1, Focusing on future, big-picture aspirations, 2021 © Photo by Davi Rezende on Unsplash; Part 2, Working backward with specificity, 2019 © Photo by Tumisu on Pixabay; Part 3, Recognising individual & collective benefits, 2018 © Photo

by Freestocks on Unsplash; Part 4, Idenftifying key stakeholders, 2020 © Photo by Krakenimages on Unsplash; Part 5, Determining purpose-driven, test-bedding sites, 2021 © Photo by Martin Katler on Unsplash; Part 6, Pinning down barriers to change, 2018 © Photo by Mimi Thian on Unsplash

**Page 152**    Question 1, What is the process of industry engagement for the PoCs implementation, 2021 © Photo by Davi Rezende on Unsplash; Question 2, Where are we in relation to the presented timeline of the PoCs, 2019 © Photo by Geralt by Pixabay; Question 3, What is the memorable moment of the six data layers in urban planning, 2019 © Photo by Tumisu by Pixabay; Question 4, How could stakeholders representing civil society connect the socio-cultural layers to the NDT, 2020 © Photo by Krakenimages on Unsplash; Question 5, Is there a structure for data collection at the regional and municipal levels, 2021 © Photo by Martin Katler on Unsplash; Question 6, How are we to make the NDT inclusive for minorities? How to prevent misuse of social data, 2018 © Photo by Mimi Thian on Unsplash

**Page 162**    Literature review, 2019 © Icon by Eucalyp on The Noun Project; Stakeholder engagement, 2017 © Icon by IconTrack on The Noun Project; Slovakia 2030 Digital Transformation strategy, 2022 © Icon by Studio 365 on The Noun Project

**Page 163**    All hands on deck, 2021 © Photo by Hannah Busing on Unsplash

**Page 167**    Dubai, United Arab Emirates, 2017 © Photo by Daniel Zacatenco on Unsplash

# IMAGE CREDITS

**Page 171**  Time, Space & Place, 2017 © Icon by Tomasz Pasternak on The Noun Project; Actuality & Possibility, 2023 © Icon by Nadia Zilfah on The Noun Project; Scale & Granularity, 2021 © Icon by Vectplus on The Noun Project; Qualities, Artefacts & Socially Constructed Entities, 2023 © Icon by Feri Ulan Taufiq on The Noun Project

**Page 173**  LOD0, 2020 © Photo by USGS on Unsplash; LOD1, 2018 © Photo by Charlie Deets on Unsplash; LOD2, 2017 © Photo by Miguel Ibáñez on Unsplash; LOD4, 2023 © Photo by Lorenzo Gerosa on Unsplash

**Page 175**  Condition monitoring, 2022 © Icon by Arif Arisandi on The Noun Project; Dynamic scheduling, 2017 © Icon by Aneeque Ahmed on The Noun Project; Quality control, 2022 © Icon by Verry Poernomo on The Noun Project; Predictive maintenance, 2019 © Icon by Round Icons on The Noun Project; Deterministic simulation, 2017 © Icon by Arafat Uddin on The Noun Project; Stochastic simulation, 2015 © Icon by OliM on The Noun Project; Functions to include & implement, 2019 © Icon by Flatart on The Noun Project; Model types, 2019 © Icon by Adrien Coquet on The Noun Project; Data flow components communications, 2022 © Icon by Icelloid on The Noun Project; Stakeholders & roles, 2018 © Icon by Nithinan Tatah on The Noun Project; Constraints, limitations & uncertainties, 2022 © Icon by Kamin Ginkaew on The Noun Project; Hardware & software requirements, 2022 © Icon by KonKapp on The Noun Project

**Page 181**  Airborne LiDar, 2016 © Photo by Mitch Nielsen on Unsplash; CCTV, 2021 © Photo by Brock Wegner on Unsplash; Qualitative surveys, 2015 © Photo by Scott Graham on Unsplash; BIM models, 2021 © Photo by Evgeniy Surzhan on Unsplash

**Page 186**  City network internet, 2021 © Photo by Geralt on Pixabay

**Page 188**  Spatial, 2021 © Icon by Vectplus on The Noun Project; Economic, 2018 © Icon by Darshana Girkar on The Noun Project; Technological, 2020 © Icon by Linector on The Noun Project; Environmental, 2022 © Icon by Gung Yoga on The Noun Project; Social, 2017 © Icon by Iconsphere on The Noun Project; Cultural, 2022 © Icon by Umer Younas on The Noun Project

**Page 192–204**  Industry sector, 2020 © Icon by sripfoto on The Noun Project; State, 2021 © Icon by Studio 365 on The Noun Project; Academia, 2018 © Icon by Binpodo on The Noun Project; Civil society (couple), 2019 © Icon by Webtechops LLP on The Noun Project; Civil society (traveller), 2019 © Icon by Monkik on The Noun Project

**Page 211**  Qualitative study, 2017 © Icon by IconTrack on The Noun Project; Quantitative study, 2017 © Icon by Arafat Uddin on The Noun Project

**Page 214**  (top left) *Animal Laborans*, 2023 © Pomeroy Academy; (top right) Homo Faber, 2023 © Pomeroy Academy; (bottom left) Detroit Ruins, 2018 © Photo by Daniel Lincoln on Unsplash; (bottom right) Archigram's 'Walking Cities' by Ron Herron in 1964, 2020 © Designing Buildings Ltd (https://www.designingbuildings.co.uk/wiki/Archigram)

# BIBLIOGRAPHY

# BIBLIOGRAPHY

Abe, E. and Fitzgerald, R. (1995) 'Japanese economic success: timing, culture, and organisational capability', *Business History*, 37(2), pp. 1–31. doi: https://doi.org/10.1080/00076799500000053

Agrest, D. (1980) 'The city as the place of representation', *Design Quarterly*, 113/114, pp. 8–13. doi: https://doi.org/10.2307/4091024

AirRater (2023) *AirRater*. Available at: https://airrater.org/

Al-Ammari, B. and Romanowski, M. (2016) 'The impact of globalisation on society and culture in Qatar', *Social Sciences & Humanities*, 24(3), pp. 1535–1556.

Albert, J., Bachmann, M., and Hellmeier, A. (2003) 'Zielgruppen und Anwendungen für Digitale Stadtmodelle und Digitale Geländemodelle. Erhebungen im Rahmen der SIG 3D der GDI NRW' [in German only]. Available at: https://docplayer.org/20358349-Zielgruppen-und-anwendungen-fuer-digitale-stadtmodelle-und-digitale-gelaendemodelle.html

Allen, B.D. (2021) 'Digital twins and living models at NASA', *Digital Twin Summit* [Virtual], 3 November. Available at: https://ntrs.nasa.gov/api/citations/20210023699/downloads/ASME%20Digital%20Twin%20Summit%20Keynote_final.pdf

Authority for Spatial Planning and Construction of the Slovak Republic (2022) *Applications of the digital 3D model of the Slovak Republic territory in selected industries*.

Basiago, A.D. (1995) 'Methods of defining "sustainability"', *Sustainable Development*, 3(3), pp. 109–119. doi: https://doi.org/10.1002/sd.3460030302

Batty, M. (2018) 'Digital twins', *Environment and Planning B: Urban Analytics and City Science*, 45(5), pp. 817–820. doi: https://doi.org/10.1177/2399808318796416

Benson, M.H. and Craig, R.K. (2014) 'The end of sustainability', *Society & Natural Resources*, 27(7), pp. 777–782. doi: https://doi.org/10.1080/08941920.2014.901467

Bhavnani, S.P. and Sitapati, A.M. (2019) 'Virtual care 2.0: a vision for the future of data-driven technology-enabled healthcare', *Current Treatment Options in Cardiovascular Medicine*, 21(21). doi: https://doi.org/10.1007/s11936-019-0727-2

Bodin, Ö. *et al.* (2019) 'Working at the "speed of trust": pre-existing and emerging social ties in wildfire responder networks in Sweden and Canada', *Regional Environmental Change*, 19(8), pp. 2353–2364. doi: https://doi.org/10.1007/s10113-019-01546-z

Booth, C. (1889) 'Descriptive map of London poverty', London: British Library. Available at: https://www.bl.uk/collection-items/charles-booths-london-poverty-map

Bowling, A. *et al.* (2013) 'A short measure of quality of life in older age: the performance of the brief older people's quality of life questionnaire (OPQOL-brief)', *Archives of gerontology and geriatrics*, 56(1), pp. 181–187. doi: https://doi.org/10.1016/j.archger.2012.08.012

Brent, R. *et al.* (2021) 'Who tells your story? A card-sort activity for eliciting authentic narratives', *International Journal of Qualitative Methods*, 20, p. 16094069211053104. doi: https://doi.org/10.1177/16094069211053104

Bridgeman, P.A. (2010) 'Round table discussion: an effective public engagement strategy', *North American Association of Christians in Social Work Convention*, Raleigh-Durham, NC, 11–14 November. Available at: https://www.nacsw.org/Publications/Proceedings2010/BridgemanPRoundTable.pdf

Brundtland, G.H. (1987) *Report of the World Commission on environment and development: our common future*. United Nations. Available at: https://sustainabledevelopment.un.org/content/documents/5987our-common-future.pdf

# BIBLIOGRAPHY

Bruynseels, K., Santoni de Sio, F., and Van den Hoven, J. (2018) 'Digital twins in health care: Ethical implications of an emerging engineering paradigm', *Frontiers in Genetics*, 9(31). doi: https://doi.org/10.3389/fgene.2018.00031

Centre for Digital Built Britain (2020) *The pathway towards an Information Management Framework – a 'commons' for Digital Built Britain*. Cambridge: Centre for Digital Built Britain. doi: https://doi.org/10.17863/CAM.52659

Centre for Digital Built Britain (2021) *National Digital Twin: Integration Architecture pattern and principles*. Cambridge: Centre for Digital Built Britain. doi: https://doi.org/10.17863/CAM.68207

Centre for Digital Built Britain (2022a) *Gemini Papers: what are connected digital twins*. Cambridge: Centre for Digital Built Britain. doi: https://doi.org/10.17863/CAM.82194

Centre for Digital Built Britain (2022b) *Gemini Papers: why connected digital twins*. Cambridge: Centre for Digital Built Britain. doi: https://doi.org/10.17863/CAM.82237

Centre for Digital Built Britain (2022c) *Gemini Papers: how to enable an ecosystem of connected digital twins*. Cambridge: Centre for Digital Built Britain. doi: https://doi.org/10.17863/CAM.82193

Chalmers University of Technology (2021) *Twinable: a multiscale design interaction and visualization approach using mixed realities*. Available at: https://dtcc.chalmers.se/twinable/

Charitonidou, M. (2022) 'Urban scale digital twins in data-driven society: challenging digital universalism in urban planning decision-making', *International Journal of Architectural Computing*, 20(2), pp. 238–253. doi: https://doi.org/10.1177/14780771211070005

Chen, Y., Lai, N., and Zhang, X. (2021) *China's city of the future: Xiong'an New Area. Global Innovation Report*. Available at: https://www.hitachi.com/rev/archive/2021/r2021_01/pdf/gir.pdf

China Briefing (2019) 'Xiong'an New Area: President Xi's dream city', *China Briefing*, 26 March. Available at: https://www.china-briefing.com/news/xiongan-new-area-beijing-tianjin-hebei/

Coates, P. *et al.* (2010) 'The changing perception in the artefacts used in the design practice through BIM adoption', *CIB 2010 World Congress Proceedings*. University of Salford, pp. 1037–1048. Available at: http://eprints.hud.ac.uk/id/eprint/25938

Commonwealth Scientific and Industrial Research Organisation (2021a) *Urban monitor*. Available at: https://www.csiro.au/en/research/technology-space/data/urban-monitor

Commonwealth Scientific and Industrial Research Organisation (2021b) *AirRater app helps outdoor workers beat the Darwin heat*. Available at: https://blog.csiro.au/airrater-app-darwin/

Craig, N. and Snook, S.A. (2014) 'From purpose to impact', *Harvard Business Review*. Available at: https://hbr.org/2014/05/from-purpose-to-impact

Cresswell, K. *et al.* (2021) 'Interorganisational knowledge sharing to establish digital health learning ecosystems: qualitative evaluation of a National Digital Health Transformation Program in England', *Journal of Medical Internet Research*, 23(8), p. e23372. doi: https://doi.org/10.2196/23372

Dassault Systèmes (2015) *Virtual Singapore and the economy of the digital twin*. Available at: https://blogs.3ds.com/perspectives/virtual-singapore-and-the-economy-of-the-digital-twin/

# BIBLIOGRAPHY

Delices, P. (2010) 'The Digital Economy', *Journal of International Affairs* 64 (1), pp. 225–226.

Dembski, F. (2021) *GreenTwins Tallinn and Helsinki: digital twins for more democratic, resilient and greener cities.* Available at: https://fabiandembski. com/2021/05/28/greentwins-tallinn-and-helsinki-digital-twins-for-more-democratic-resilient-and-greener-cities/

Deng, T., Zhang, K., and Shen, Z.-J. (Max) (2021) 'A systematic review of a digital twin city: a new pattern of urban governance toward smart cities', *Journal of Management Science and Engineering*, 6(2), pp. 125–134. doi: https://doi.org/10.1016/j.jmse.2021.03.003

Deniz, G.O. (2018) 'Emerging CAD and BIM trends in the AEC education: an analysis from students' perspective', *Journal of Information Technology in Construction*, 23, pp. 138–156. Available at: https://www.itcon.org/paper/2018/7

Deren, L., Wenbo, Y., and Zhenfeng, S. (2021) 'Smart city based on digital twins', *Computational Urban Science*, 1(1), pp. 1–11. doi: https://doi.org/10.1007/s43762-021-00005-y

Digital Skills and Jobs Platform (2022) *Slovakia - 2030 Digital Transformation Strategy.* Available at: https://digital-skills-jobs.europa.eu/en/actions/national-initiatives/national-strategies/slovakia-2030-digital-transformation-strategy

Dushkova, D. *et al.* (2021) 'Cultural ecosystem services of urban green spaces. How and what people value in urban nature?', in Vasenev, V. *et al.* (ed.) *Advanced technologies for sustainable development of urban green infrastructure.* Springer International Publishing, pp. 292–318. doi: https://doi.org/10.1007/978-3-030-75285-9_28

Elshenawy, A.A. (2017) 'Globalization's effect on Qatari culture', *Journal of Cultural Studies*, 2(1), pp. 6–17.

Esri (2018) *Meet Boston's digital twin.* Available at: https://www.esri.com/about/newsroom/blog/3d-gis-boston-digital-twin/

Esri (2021) *ArcGIS: the foundation for digital twins.* California: Esri. Available at: https://www.esri.com/en-us/lg/industry/infrastructure/arcgis-the-foundation-for-digital-twins

European Commission (2022) *Digital Economy and Society Index (DESI) 2022: Slovakia.* Available at: https://ec.europa.eu/newsroom/dae/redirection/document/88712

Fan, C. *et al.* (2021) 'Disaster city digital twin: a vision for integrating artificial and human intelligence for disaster management', *International Journal of Information Management*, 56. doi: https://doi.org/10.1016/j.ijinfomgt.2019.102049

FinEst Centre (n.d.) *Tallinn-Helsinki dynamic green information model.* Available at: https://www.finestcentre.eu/greentwins

Ford, D.N. and Wolf, C.M. (2020) 'Smart cities with digital twin systems for disaster management', *Journal of Management in Engineering*, 36(4). doi: https://doi.org/10.1061/(ASCE)ME.1943-5479.0000779

Foucault, M. (1970) *The order of things: an archaeology of the human sciences.* New York: Pantheon.

Fuldauer, E. (2019) *Smarter cities are born with digital twins.* Available at: https://tomorrow.city/a/smarter-cities-are-born-with-digital-twins#:~{}:text=In%20 the%20realm%20of%20smart,movement%20of%20 people%20and%20vehicles

GE Healthcare Partners (2023) *GE healthcare command centres.* Available at: https://www.gehccommandcenter.com/digital-twin

# BIBLIOGRAPHY

Gierten, D. and Lesher, M. (2022) 'Assessing national digital strategies and their governance', *OECD Digital Economy Papers*, 324. Paris: OECD Publishing. doi: https://doi.org/10.1787/baffceca-en.

Glaessgen, E.H. and Stargel, D. (2012) 'The digital twin paradigm for future NASA and U.S. Air Force vehicles', *53rd Structures, Structural Dynamics, and Materials Conference: special session on the digital twin*, Honolulu, HI, 23–26 April. doi: https://doi.org/10.2514/6.2012-1818

Gobeawan, L. *et al.* (2018) 'Modelling trees for Virtual Singapore: from data acquisition to CityGML models', *The International Archives of the Photogrammetry, Remote Sensing and Spatial Information Sciences*, pp. 55–62. doi: https://doi.org/10.5194/isprs-archives-XLII-4-W10-55-2018

Gray, B. (1985) 'Conditions facilitating interorganisational collaboration', *Human relations*, 38(10), pp. 911–936. doi: https://doi.org/10.1177/001872678503801001

Grieves, M. (2006) *Product lifecycle management: driving the next generation of lean thinking.* New York: McGraw-Hill Education.

Grieves, M. (2011) *Virtually perfect: driving innovative and lean products through product lifecycle management.* Florida, U.S.: Space Coast Press.

Grieves, M.W. and Vickers, J.H. (2017) 'Digital twin: mitigating unpredictable, undesirable emergent behaviour in complex systems', in Kahlen, F.J., Flumerfelt, S. and Alves, A. (ed.) *Transdisciplinary perspectives on complex systems.* New York: Springer International Publishing, pp. 85–113.

Gutierrez, A.A. *et al.* (2021) 'Wildfire response to changing daily temperature extremes in California's Sierra Nevada', *Science Advances*, 7(47). doi: https://doi.org/10.1126/sciadv.abe6417

Hall, P.G. (2002) *Cities of tomorrow: an intellectual history of urban planning and design in the twentieth century.* 3rd edn. Hoboken: Blackwell Publishing.

Hamdan, H.A.M., Andersen, P.H., and de Boer, L. (2021) 'Stakeholder collaboration in sustainable neighborhood projects: a review and research agenda', *Sustainable Cities and Society*, 68, p. 102776. doi: https://doi.org/10.1016/j.scs.2021.102776

Henderson, K. (1991) 'Flexible sketches and inflexible data bases: visual communication, conscription devices, and boundary objects in design engineering', *Science, Technology, & Human Values*, 16(4), pp. 448–473. doi: https://doi.org/10.1177/016224399101600402

Hillier, B. (2009) 'Spatial sustainability in cities: organic patterns and sustainable forms', *Proceedings of the 7th International Space Syntax Symposium*, Stockholm, Sweden: Royal Institute of Technology (KTH).

Hongsranagon, P. *et al.* (2011) 'Traffic risk behaviour and perceptions of Thai motorcyclists: a case study', *IATSS research*, 35(1), pp. 30–33. doi: https://doi.org/10.1016/j.iatssr.2011.03.001

Hu, *et al.* (2015) 'Attribute-based access control', *Computer*, 48(2), pp. 85–88. doi: https://doi.org/10.1109/MC.2015.33

Ignatius, M. *et al.* (2019) 'Virtual Singapore integration with energy simulation and canopy modelling for climate assessment', *IOP Conference Series: Earth and Environmental Science*, 294(1). doi: https://doi.org/10.1088/1755-1315/294/1/012018

Intergovernmental Panel on Climate Change (n.d.) *IPCC sixth assessment report, Climate change 2022: impacts, adaptation and vulnerability.* Available at: https://www.ipcc.ch/report/ar6/wg2/

# BIBLIOGRAPHY

International Organization of Motor Vehicle Manufacturers (2023) *International Organization of Motor Vehicle Manufacturers, 2019 production statistics.* Available at: https://www.oica.net/category/production-statistics/2019-statistics/

Jaansoo, A. (2019) *Methodology for stakeholder engagement within the project Inter Ventures.* Available at: https://projects2014-2020.interregeurope.eu/fileadmin/user_upload/tx_tevprojects/library/file_1575537468.pdf

Jamalinia, E. *et al.* (2020) 'Predicting rainfall induced slope stability using random forest regression and synthetic data', *Workshop on World Landslide Forum*, pp. 223–229. doi: https://doi.org/10.1007/978-3-030-60713-5_24

Japan Economic Foundation (2009) 'Japan's cultural economy in a globalising world', *Japan Economic Foundation*, 2, pp. 26–29.

Jasanoff, S. (2004) 'Ordering knowledge, ordering society', in *States of knowledge: the co-production of science and the social order.* 1st edn. London: Routledge, pp. 24–56.

Johnston, P. *et al.* (2007) 'Reclaiming the definition of sustainability', *Environmental Science and Pollution Research – International*, 14(1), pp. 60–66. doi: https://doi.org/10.1065/espr2007.01.375

Joseph, S.A. (2021) *GCC Business News, Qatar's new initiative TASMU platform to enhance the digital economy.* Available at: https://www.gccbusinessnews.com/qatars-new-initiative-tasmu-platform-to-enhance-the-digital-economy/

Kern, L., Dembski, F., and Wössner, U. (2021) 'Digital twins for cities and regions: global challenges, regional initiatives, European approaches', *EU Conference on modelling for policy support*, Brussels, Belgium, 22–26 November, pp. 51–54. Available at: http://193.239.188.150/files2/pdf/2021_EU_CONF_MOD_Booklet_of_abstracts.pdf#page=56

Koetter, F. and Rowe, C. (1979) *Collage city.* Cambridge, MA: MIT Press.

Kruger, K., Human, C., and Basson, A. (2022) 'Towards the integration of digital twins and Service-Oriented Architectures', in Borangiu, T. *et al.* (ed) *Service oriented, holonic and multi-agent manufacturing systems for industry of the future.* New York: Springer International Publishing, pp. 131–143. doi: https://doi.org/10.1007/978-3-030-99108-1_10

Kuhlman and Farrington (2010) 'What is sustainability?', *Sustainability*, 2, pp. 3436–3448. doi: https://doi.org/10.3390/su2113436

Kusters, K. *et al.* (2018) 'Participatory planning, monitoring and evaluation of multi-stakeholder platforms in integrated landscape initiatives', *Environmental Management*, 62(1), pp. 170–181. doi: https://doi.org/10.1007/s00267-017-0847-y.

Latour, B. (2004) 'Why has critique run out of steam? From matters of fact to matters of concern', *Critical Inquiry*, 30(2), pp. 225–248. doi: https://doi.org/10.1086/421123

Lau, N.-C. and Nath, M.J. (2014) 'Model simulation and projection of European heat waves in present-day and future climates', *Journal of Climate*, 27(10), pp. 3713–3730. doi: https://doi.org/10.1175/JCLI-D-13-00284.1

Lehtola, V.V. *et al.* (2022) 'Digital twin of a city: review of technology serving city needs', *International Journal of Applied Earth Observation and Geoinformation*, p. 102915. doi: https://doi.org/10.1016/j.jag.2022.102915

Lexante Law Firm & Advisory (2022) *Lexante Articles & News, New Spatial Planning Act and new Construction Act have passed parliament.* Available at: https://www.lexante.sk/en/post-new-spatial-planning-act-and-new-construction-act-have-passed-parliament.html

# BIBLIOGRAPHY

Li, L. *et al.* (2021) 'Digital twin in aerospace industry: a gentle introduction', *IEEE Access*, 10, pp. 9543–9562. doi: https://doi.org/10.1109/ACCESS.2021.3136458

Loach, K., Rowley, J., and Griffiths, J. (2017) 'Cultural sustainability as a strategy for the survival of museums and libraries', *International Journal of Cultural Policy*, 23(2), pp. 186–198. doi: https://doi.org/10.1080/10286632.2016.1184657

Lombardo, L. *et al.* (2019) 'Environmental monitoring in the cultural heritage field', *The European Physical Journal Plus*, 134(411). doi: https://doi.org/10.1140/epjp/i2019-12800-2

Loukissas, Y.A. (2019) *All data are local: thinking critically in a data-driven society*. Cambridge, MA: MIT press.

Lu, C. *et al.* (2020) 'An overview and case study of the clinical AI model development life cycle for healthcare systems', *arXiv:2003.07678* [Preprint]. doi: https://doi.org/10.48550/arXiv.2003.07678

Lu, Q. *et al.* (2020) 'Developing a digital twin at building and city levels: case study of West Cambridge campus', *Journal of Management in Engineering*, 36(3), p. 05020004. doi: https://doi.org/10.1061/(ASCE)ME.1943-5479.0000763

Marani, M. (2018) 'This digital 3D model of Boston reveals the shadows cast by new construction', *The Architect's Newspaper*, 9 May. Available at: https://www.archpaper.com/2018/05/new-digital-3-d-model-of-boston/

Mark, B. (2012) 'Big data challenges for geoinformatics: an overview', *Geoinformatics & Geostatistics*, 1(1), pp. 1–2.

Maru, Y.T. *et al.* (2018) 'Towards appropriate mainstreaming of "Theory of Change" approaches into agricultural research for development: challenges and opportunities', *Agricultural Systems*, 165, pp. 344–353. doi: https://doi.org/10.1016/j.agsy.2018.04.010

Mavrokapnidis, D. *et al.* (2021) 'A linked-data paradigm for the integration of static and dynamic building data in digital twins', *Proceedings of the 8th ACM International Conference on Systems for Energy-Efficient Buildings, Cities, and Transportation*, pp. 369–372. doi: https://doi.org/10.1145/3486611.3491125

Mawhinney, M. (2002) *Sustainable development: understanding the green debates*. Hoboken: Wiley-Blackwell.

Metropolis Magazine (2006) *Metropolis Magazine, Smart city 2020*. Available at: https://metropolismag.com/programs/smart-city-2020/

Meyers, J. et al. (2020) *Mapping land surface temperatures and heat-health vulnerability in Darwin*. Available at: https://research.csiro.au/darwinlivinglab/wp-content/uploads/sites/278/2020/12/CSIRO_Mapping_LST__Heat_Health_Vulnerability_In_Darwin_Final.pdf

Ministry of Communications and Information Technology (2023) TASMU, *Explore tomorrow's future with Smart Qatar*. Available at: https://tasmu.gov.qa/

Ministry of Land, Infrastructure, Transport, and Tourism (MLIT) website (2023) *PLATEAU, Use case*. Available at: https://www.mlit.go.jp/plateau/use-case/

Moore, J.A. (2015) 'Emerging trends and opportunities in planning and design: integrating GIS, BIM and other technologies', *Real Estate Review*, 44(2), pp. 11–22.

Mott Macdonald (2023) *DTs: better outcomes from connected data*. Available at: https://www.mottmac.com/download/file?id=37140&isPreview=True

Mukherjee, D. and Mitra, S. (2019) 'A comparative study of safe and unsafe signalized intersections from the view point of pedestrian behaviour and perception', *Accident Analysis & Prevention*, 132, p. 105218. doi: https://doi.org/10.1016/j.aap.2019.06.010

# BIBLIOGRAPHY

National Park Board (2022) *Singapore, a city in nature*. Available at: https://www.nparks.gov.sg/about-us/city-in-nature

National Research Foundation (2016) *Uses of Virtual Singapore*. 11 October. Available at: https://www.youtube.com/watch?v=y8cXBSI6o44

National Research Foundation (2021) *Virtual Singapore*. Available at: https://www.nrf.gov.sg/programmes/virtual-singapore

Obi, T. and Iwasaki, N. (2021) 'Smart government using digital twin in Japan', *2021 International Conference on ICT for Smart Society (ICISS)*, Bandung, Indonesia, pp. 1–4. doi: https://doi.org/10.1109/ICISS53185.2021.9533190

Open Geospatial Consortium Inc. (2008) *OpenGIS City Geography Markup Language (CityGML) encoding standard, version 1.0.0*. Available at: https://portal.ogc.org/files/?artifact_id=28802

Oppenheimer, R. (1953) *The Reith Lectures* [Podcast]. 20 Dec. Available at: https://www.bbc.co.uk/programmes/p00hg2d6

Organisation for Economic Co-operation and Development (OECD) (2019) *Measuring the digital transformation: a roadmap for the future*. Paris: OECD Publishig. doi: https://doi.org/10.1787/9789264311992-en

Organisation for Economic Co-operation and Development (OECD) (2021) *Government at a glance 2021*. Paris: OECD Publishing. doi: https://doi-org.vu-nl.idm.oclc.org/10.1787/1c258f55-en

Panofsky, E. (1939) *Studies in iconology*. Oxford: Oxford University Press.

Panofsky, E. (1955) *Meaning in the visual arts*. 1st edn. New York, U.S.: Doubleday Anchor Books, Doubleday & Company, Inc.

Pelenc, J., Ballet, J., and Dedeurwaerdere, T. (2015) *Brief for GSDR United Nations:*

Peta, I. (2018) *Theory of change for development: understanding, usage, and influence*. MA Dissertation. Lund University.

Petrone, J. (2021) *Estonian and Finnish researchers unveil new applications for GreenTwins project*. Available at: https://researchinestonia.eu/2021/12/06/estonian-and-finnish-researchers-unveil-new-applications-for-greentwins-project/

Petrova-Antonova, D. and Ilieva, S. (2018) 'Smart cities evaluation – a survey of performance and sustainability indicators', *2018 44th Euromicro Conference on Software Engineering and Advanced Applications (SEAA)*, Prague, Czech Republic, 29-31 August, pp. 486–493. doi: https://doi.org/10.1109/SEAA.2018.00084

Phanden, R.K., Sharma, P., and Dubey, A. (2021) 'A review on simulation in digital twin for aerospace, manufacturing and robotics', *Materials today: proceedings*, 38, pp. 174–178. doi: https://doi.org/10.1016/j.matpr.2020.06.446.

Pomeroy, J. (2014) *The skycourt and skygarden: greening the urban habitat*. London: Routledge.

Pomeroy, J. (2016) *POG: pod off-grid: explorations into low energy waterborne communities*. Novato, CA: Oro Editions.

Pomeroy, J. (2020a) 'Introduction', in *Cities of opportunities*. 1st Edition. London: Routledge, pp. 2–3. doi: https://doi.org/10.4324/9781003022299

Pomeroy, J. (2020b) 'The rise of the digital economy and its impact on the smart city', in *Cities of opportunities*. 1st Edition. London: Routledge, pp. 190–205. doi: https://doi.org/10.4324/9781003022299

# BIBLIOGRAPHY

Purvis, B., Mao, Y., and Robinson, D. (2019) 'Three pillars of sustainability: in search of conceptual origins', *Sustainability Science*, 14(3), pp. 681–695. doi: https://doi.org/10.1007/s11625-018-0627-5

Pyatkova, K. *et al.* (2019) 'Flood impacts on road transportation using microscopic traffic modelling techniques', in Behrisch, M. and Weber, M. (eds.) *Simulating urban traffic scenarios*. New York: Springer International Publishing, pp. 115–126. doi: https://doi.org/10.1007/978-3-319-33616-9_8

Qi, Q. *et al.* (2021) 'Enabling technologies and tools for digital twin', *Journal of Manufacturing Systems*, 58, pp. 3–21. doi: https://doi.org/10.1016/j.jmsy.2019.10.001

Rasor, R. *et al.* (2021) 'Towards collaborative life cycle specification of digital twins in manufacturing value chains', *28th CIRP Conference on Life Cycle Engineering*, Jaipur, India, 10–12 March, pp. 229–234. doi: https://doi.org/10.1016/j.procir.2021.01.035

Reades, J. *et al.* (2007) 'Cellular census: explorations in urban data collection', *IEEE Pervasive Computing*, 6(3), pp. 30–38. doi: https://doi.org/10.1109/MPRV.2007.53

Reddy, T. and Claridge, D. (1994) 'Using synthetic data to evaluate multiple regression and principal component analyses for statistical modelling of daily building energy consumption', *Energy and Buildings*, 21(1), pp. 35–44. doi: https://doi.org/10.1016/0378-7788(94)90014-0

Ricci, A., Croatti, A. and Montagna, S. (2021) 'Pervasive and connected digital twins: a vision for digital health', *IEEE Internet Computing*. doi: https://doi.org/10.1109/MIC.2021.3052039

Rosen, R. *et al.* (2015) 'About the importance of autonomy and digital twins for the future of manufacturing', *Ifac-Papersonline*, 48(3), pp. 567–572. doi: https://doi.org/10.1016/j.ifacol.2015.06.141

Rowe, P.G. (1999) *Civic realism*. Cambridge, MA: MIT Press.

Sacasas, L.M. (2020) 'The analog city and the digital city', *The New Atlantis*, (61), pp. 3–18. Available at: https://www.thenewatlantis.com/wp-content/uploads/legacy-pdfs/20200306_TNA61Sacasas.pdf

Saracco, R. (2019) 'Digital twins: bridging physical space and cyberspace', *Computer*, 52(12), pp. 58–64. doi: https://doi.org/10.1109/MC.2019.2942803

Sassen, S. (2002) *The global city: New York, London, Tokyo*. Hoboken: Blackwell Publishing.

Sassen, S. (2018) *Cities in a world economy*. California: SAGE Publishing.

Schrotter, G. and Hürzeler, C. (2020) 'The digital twin of the city of Zurich for urban planning', *Journal of Photogrammetry, Remote Sensing and Geoinformation Science*, 88(1), pp. 99–112. doi: https://doi.org/10.1007/s41064-020-00092-2

Schwab, K. (2017) *The fourth Industrial Revolution*. New York: Crown Publishing.

Seebacher, D. *et al.* (2017) 'Visual analytics and similarity search: concepts and challenges for effective retrieval considering users, tasks, and data', *Similarity Search and Applications: 10th International Conference, SISAP 2017*, Munich, Germany, 4–6 October, pp. 324–332. doi: https://doi.org/10.1007/978-3-319-68474-1_23

Segovia, M. and Garcia-Alfaro, J. (2022) 'Design, modelling and implementation of digital twins', *Sensors*, 22(14), p. 5396. doi: https://doi.org/10.3390/s22145396

Sennett, R. (2019) *The craftsman*. London: Penguin.

# BIBLIOGRAPHY

Siemens Healthineer (2019) *Digitalising healthcare: solutions for individual patients.* Available at: https://www.siemens-healthineers.com/perspectives/mso-solutions-for-individual-patients.html

Singh, M. *et al.* (2021) 'Digital twin: origin to future', *Applied System Innovation*, 4(2). doi: https://doi.org/10.3390/asi4020036

Singh, M. *et al.* (2022) 'Applications of digital twin across industries: a review', *Applied Sciences*, 12(11). doi: https://doi.org/10.3390/app12115727

Smart Dublin (2020) *Future planning: 3D data modelling.* Available at: https://smartdublin.ie/future-planning-with-3d-modelling/

Solman, H. *et al.* (2022) 'Digital twinning as an act of governance in the wind energy sector', *Environmental Science & Policy*, 127, pp. 272–279. doi: https://doi.org/10.1016/j.envsci.2021.10.027

Stanford Engineering (2020) *The digital twin for construction.* Available at: https://cife.stanford.edu/digital-twin-construction

Sudjic, D. (2005) *The edifice complex: how the rich and powerful shape the world.* London: Allen Lane.

Tao, F. et al. (2018) 'Digital twin-driven product design, manufacturing and service with big data', *The International Journal of Advanced Manufacturing Technology*, 94(9), pp. 3563–3576. doi: https://doi.org/10.1007/s00170-017-0233-1

Taplin, D.H. et al. (2013) *Theory of change: technical papers: a series of papers to support development of theories of change based on practice in the field.* Available at: https://www.theoryofchange.org/wp-content/uploads/toco_library/pdf/ToC-Tech-Papers.pdf

TASMU Digital Valley (2022) *Qatar Digital Industry metrics.* Available at: https://tasmu.gov.qa/

Tunçer, B. and You, L. (2017) 'Informed Design Platform multi-modal data to support urban design decision making', *35th International Conference on Education and Research in Computer Aided Architecture and Design in Europe (eCAADe)*, Rome, Italy, 20–23 September, pp. 545–552. doi: https://doi.org/10.52842/conf.ecaade.2017.2.545

United Nations (1972) *United Nations Conference on the human environment (Stockholm Conference).* Available at: https://sustainabledevelopment.un.org/milestones/humanenvironment

United Nations (n.d.) *United Nations Environment Programme, The Montreal protocol.* Available at: https://www.unep.org/ozonaction/who-we-are/about-montreal-protocol

Vanlı, T. and Marsap, A. (2018) 'Smart cities, smarter management: developing a smart framework for smart cities management in Europe', *Alshahadeh, T., & Marsap, A. GE-International Journal of Management Research*, 6(9).

Vaughan, L. (2007) 'The spatial syntax of urban segregation', *Progress in Planning*, 67(3), pp. 199–294. doi: https://doi.org/10.1016/j.progress.2007.03.001

Ventegodt, S., Merrick, J., and Andersen, N.J. (2003) 'Measurement of quality of life III. From the IQOL theory to the global, generic SEQOL questionnaire', *The Scientific World Journal*, 3, pp. 972–991. doi: https://doi.org/10.1100/tsw.2003.77

Villegas-Mateos, A. (2023) 'Toward a sustainable entrepreneurial ecosystem in Qatar', *Sustainability*, 15(1), pp. 127–143. doi: https://doi.org/10.3390/su15010127

Wang, X.V. and Wang, L. (2019) 'Digital twin-based WEEE recycling, recovery and remanufacturing in the background of Industry 4.0', *International Journal of Production Research*, 57(12), pp. 3892–3902. doi: https://doi.org/10.1080/00207543.2018.1497819

# BIBLIOGRAPHY

Wataya, E. and Shaw, R. (2019) 'Measuring the value and the role of soft assets in smart city development', *Cities*, 94, pp. 106–115. doi: https://doi.org/10.1016/j.cities.2019.04.019

White, G. *et al.* (2021) 'A digital twin smart city for citizen feedback', *Cities*, 110. doi: https://doi.org/10.1016/j.cities.2020.103064

White, G., Liang, Z., and Clarke, S. (2019) 'A quantified-self framework for exploring and enhancing personal productivity', *2019 International Conference on Content-Based Multimedia Indexing (CBMI)*, Dublin, Ireland, 14–16 September, pp. 1–6. doi: https://doi.org/10.1109/CBMI.2019.8877475

Williams, R., Meharg, S., and Muster, Ti. (2020) *Tracking Darwin – a framework for monitoring, evaluation and learning about change in Darwin and the impact of the Darwin Living Lab*. Available at: https://research.csiro.au/darwinlivinglab/wp-content/uploads/sites/278/2021/06/Tracking-and-Learning-for-Change-In-Darwin-Final-002.pdf

Woodland, R.H. and Hutton, M.S. (2012) 'Evaluating organizational collaborations: suggested entry points and strategies', *American Journal of Evaluation*, 33(3), pp. 366–383. doi: https://doi.org/10.1177/1098214012440028

World Economic Forum (2022) *Digital twin cities: framework and global practices*. Available at: https://www3.weforum.org/docs/WEF_Global_Digital_Twin_Cities_Framework_and_Practice_2022.pdf

Xinhua News Agency (2018) *Hebei Xiong'an New Area planning outline*. Available at: http://www.xiongan.gov.cn/2018-04/21/c_129855813_9.htm

Zou, Y. *et al.* (2021) 'Urban planning as a way to pursue quality-oriented urbanization: anatomy of the urban planning of Xiong'an New Area, China', *Journal of Urban Affairs*, pp. 1–16. Available at: https://doi.org/10.1080/07352166.2021.1974304.

# INDEX

# INDEX

# INDEX

# INDEX

# INDEX

virtual patients 26
virtual population 180–3
Virtual Reality (VR) 93, 176
virtual representation(s) 32, 37, 170
Virtual Singapore (VSg), Singapore 56–61

**W**
waste management 115, 125